CU00794798

Studies in Diplomacy and International Relat

General Editors: **Donna Lee**, Senior Lecture ᵣ
and International Political Economy, Uni̶v̶e̶ɪ̶s̶i̶t̶y̶ ̶o̶ɪ̶ ̶ᴅ̶ɪ̶ɪ̶ɪ̶ɪ̶ɪ̶ɪ̶g̶ɪ̶ɪ̶α̶ɪ̶ɪ̶ɪ̶, ̶ᴜ̶ɪ̶ ̶α̶ɪ̶ɪ̶ᴜ̶
Paul Sharp, Professor of Political Science and Director of the Alworth Institute
for International Studies at the University of Minnesota, Duluth, USA

The series was launched as *Studies in Diplomacy* in 1994 under the general
editorship of G. R. Berridge. Its purpose is to encourage original scholarship on all
aspects of the theory and practice of diplomacy. The new editors assumed their
duties in 2003 with a mandate to maintain this focus while also publishing
research which demonstrates the importance of diplomacy to contemporary
international relations more broadly conceived.

Titles include:

G. R. Berridge (*editor*)
DIPLOMATIC CLASSICS
Selected Texts from Commynes to Vattel

G. R. Berridge, Maurice Keens-Soper and T. G. Otte
DIPLOMATIC THEORY FROM MACHIAVELLI TO KISSINGER

Herman J. Cohen
INTERVENING IN AFRICA
Superpower Peacemaking in a Troubled Continent

Andrew F. Cooper (*editor*)
NICHE DIPLOMACY
Middle Powers after the Cold War

David H. Dunn (*editor*)
DIPLOMACY AT THE HIGHEST LEVEL
The Evolution of International Summitry

Brian Hocking (*editor*)
FOREIGN MINISTRIES
Change and Adaptation

Brian Hocking and David Spence (*editors*)
FOREIGN MINISTRIES IN THE EUROPEAN UNION
Integrating Diplomats

Michael Hughes
DIPLOMACY BEFORE THE RUSSIAN REVOLUTION
Britain, Russia and the Old Diplomacy, 1894–1917

Gaynor Johnson
THE BERLIN EMBASSY OF LORD D'ABERNON, 1920–1926

Christer Jönsson and Martin Hall
ESSENCE OF DIPLOMACY

Donna Lee
MIDDLE POWERS AND COMMERCIAL DIPLOMACY
British Influence at the Kennedy Trade Round

Mario Liverani
INTERNATIONAL RELATIONS IN THE ANCIENT NEAR EAST, 1600–1100 BC

Jan Melissen (*editor*)
INNOVATION IN DIPLOMATIC PRACTICE

THE NEW PUBLIC DIPLOMACY
Soft Power in International Relations

Peter Neville
APPEASING HITLER
The Diplomacy of Sir Nevile Henderson, 1937–39

M. J. Peterson
RECOGNITION OF GOVERNMENTS
Legal Doctrine and State Practice, 1815–1995

Gary D. Rawnsley
RADIO DIPLOMACY AND PROPAGANDA
The BBC and VOA in International Politics, 1956–64

TAIWAN'S INFORMAL DIPLOMACY AND PROPAGANDA

Ronald A. Walker
MULTILATERAL CONFERENCES
Purposeful International Negotiation

A. Nuri Yurdusev (*editor*)
OTTOMAN DIPLOMACY
Conventional or Unconventional?

Studies in Diplomacy and International Relations
Series Standing Order ISBN 0–333–71495–4
(*outside North America only*)

You can receive future titles in this series as they are published by placing a standing order. Please contact your bookseller or, in case of difficulty, write to us at the address below with your name and address, the title of the series and the ISBN quoted above.

Customer Services Department, Macmillan Distribution Ltd, Houndmills, Basingstoke, Hampshire RG21 6XS, England

---

The New Public Diplomacy

Soft Power in International Relations

Edited by

Jan Melissen

Director Clingendael Diplomatic Studies Programme
Netherlands Institute of International Relations, Clingendael

First published 2005 by
PALGRAVE MACMILLAN
Houndmills, Basingstoke, Hampshire RG21 6XS and
175 Fifth Avenue, New York, N.Y. 10010
Companies and representatives throughout the world

PALGRAVE MACMILLAN is the global academic imprint of the Palgrave
Macmillan division of St. Martin's Press, LLC and of Palgrave Macmillan Ltd.
Macmillan® is a registered trademark in the United States, United Kingdom
and other countries. Palgrave is a registered trademark in the European
Union and other countries.

ISBN-13: 978–0–230–53554–1 hardback
ISBN-10: 0–2305–3554–2 hardback

A catalogue record for this book is available from the British Library.

Library of Congress Cataloging-in-Publication Data
The new public diplomacy : soft power in international relations / edited by
    Jan Melissen.
        p. cm.
    Includes bibliographical references and index.
    ISBN 978-0-230-53554-1
    1. International relations.   2. Diplomacy.   I. Melissen, Jan.
JZ1305.N47 2005
    327.1′4—dc22   2005048134

10   9   8   7   6   5   4   3   2   1
14 13 12 11 10 09 08 07 06 05

Transferred to Digital Printing in 2012

For Isabel, Eugenia and Daniel

Contents

Notes on Contributors

Peter van Ham is Director of Global Governance Research at the Netherlands Institute of International Relations 'Clingendael' in The Hague, and Professor at the College of Europe in Bruges. He holds a doctorate in Political Science (International Relations) from the university of Leiden. He was Professor of West European Politics at the George C. Marshall European Center for Security Studies in Garmisch-Partenkirchen (1996–2001); a senior research fellow at the WEU Institute for Security Studies in Paris (1993–96); and has been a visiting scholar at Columbia University (New York), the Royal Institute of International Affairs (London), and the Copenhagen Peace Research Institute (COPRI). His books include: *Mapping European Security after Kosovo* (2002); *European Integration and the Postmodern Condition* (2001); and *A Critical Approach to European Security* (1999). He has published in *Foreign Affairs*, *The National Interest*, *Millennium*, *Security Dialogue* and other academic journals.

John Hemery is the founder and Director of the Centre for Political and Diplomatic Studies. He was educated at Dartmouth College in the United States, and was a postgraduate at both Oxford and Cambridge. After 18 years teaching politics and international relations he developed the UK Foreign and Commonwealth Office's programme of diplomatic training for the new governments of Central and Eastern Europe emerging after 1989. Since then he has designed and directed more than 60 specialist courses for politicians, officials and civil society organizations in 40 countries. These programmes have included one- and two-week courses of training in public diplomacy conducted at Wilton Park in the UK and also abroad. The Centre for Political and Diplomatic Studies is currently developing a new programme of training for public diplomacy that addresses both strategy and professional practice.

Alan K. Henrikson is Director of the Fletcher Roundtable on a New World Order, Fletcher School of Law and Diplomacy, Tufts University. During spring 2003 he was Fulbright/Diplomatic Academy Visiting Professor of International Relations at the *Diplomatische Akademie* in Vienna. At the Weatherhead Center for International Affairs at Harvard University he has been an Associate and Visiting Scholar and has served as Counselor on Canadian Affairs. He received AB, AM, and Ph.D. degrees in History from Harvard University where he was a Harvard National Scholar and a Danforth Graduate Fellow. He also holds BA and MA degrees from the University of Oxford. He has written widely on US foreign policy, US–European Union relations, the security of the Nordic/Arctic area, Canadian–US–Mexican continental integration, and multilateral diplomacy and the UN system. Among his recent publications are: 'The Geography of Diplomacy' in *The Geography of War and Peace* (2005); and 'Good Neighbour Diplomacy Revisited' in *Holding the Line: Borders in a Global World* (2005).

Brian Hocking is Professor of International Relations and Director of the Centre for the Study of Foreign Policy and Diplomacy at Coventry University in the UK. He graduated from the Universities of Bristol and Leicester and received his Ph.D. from the University of London. Before taking up his post in Coventry in 1978, he lectured at the University of Tasmania and was affiliated to the Institute of Commonwealth Studies in London. He is the author of many articles and has written and edited ten books on international relations, trade politics and diplomacy. Among his recent books are: *Trade Politics* (2004, co-editor and contributor with S. M. McGuire); *Integrating Diplomats? Foreign Ministries in the European Union* (2002, editor and contributor with D. Spence); *Trade Politics: Domestic International and Regional Perspectives* (1999, contributor and editor with S. M. McGuire); and *Foreign Ministries: Change and Adaptation* (1999, editor and contributor).

Ingrid d'Hooghe is a research associate with the Clingendael Diplomatic Studies Programme at the Netherlands Institute of International Relations 'Clingendael' in The Hague. She holds an MA degree in Sinology from Leiden University and studied at Fudan University in Shanghai. Her career began at the Netherlands Embassy in Beijing in 1989 and in 1991 she returned to Leiden when she joined the Research and Documentation Centre for Contemporary China at the Sinological Institute. After three years in Geneva (1994–97) she once again joined the Sinological Institute in Leiden, before moving to Clingendael in 2001. She has published on various Chinese domestic and foreign issues, and her current research focuses primarily on China's foreign policy and diplomacy. She has recently written on China's relationship with North Korea, Chinese–ASEM relations, and the effects of '9/11' on China's foreign policy. She co-edited *China's Legal Developments and Their Political Limits* (with Eduard Vermeer 2001).

Jan Melissen is Director of the Clingendael Diplomatic Studies Programme at the Netherlands Institute of International Relations 'Clingendael', The Hague. He is also part-time Professor in the Department of Politics, Antwerp University. He graduated from the University of Amsterdam and received his doctorate at the University of Groningen. Before joining Clingendael in 2001, he worked in British academe and was Director of the Centre for the Study of Diplomacy at the University of Leicester (UK). Jan Melissen is presently working on a project on trends in diplomatic representation. He is co-editor of *The Hague Journal of Diplomacy* and managing editor of the *Discussion Papers in Diplomacy*. He has written many articles in English and in Dutch. His previous books are: *The Struggle for Nuclear Partnership* (1993); *Innovation in Diplomatic Practice* (1999); *Diplomatie: Raderwerk van de internationale politiek* (1999); and *Europese diplomatie* (2000).

Anna Michalski is a Senior Research Fellow at the Netherlands Institute of International Relations 'Clingendael'. She completed her Ph.D. thesis at the London School of Economics and Political Science and held research positions at the Royal Institute of International Affairs and the *Centre d'Etudes et de Recherches Internationales* in Paris. Between 1996 and 2001 she worked at the European Commission's Forward Studies Unit. She was also a leading member of the Forward Studies Group's Scenarios team. At Clingendael Anna Michalski focuses on the role of the European Commission, the European Convention, the future of EU governance and the Lisbon Process. Recent publications include: *The Lisbon Process* (2004); *The Political Dynamics of Constitutional Reform* (2004, editor); *European Convention on the Future of Europe* (2003, with Matthias Heise); *Governing Europe* (2002); *European Futures* (2000, with Gilles Bertrand and Lucio R. Pench).

Wally Olins CBE is a co-founder of Wolff Olins, of which he was Chairman until 1997. He is now Chairman of Saffron Brand Consultants. He was awarded a CBE in 1999, was nominated for the Prince Philip Designers Prize in 1999, received the Royal Society of Arts' Bicentenary Medal for his contribution to design and marketing in 2000, and received the D&AD President's Award in 2003. He has advised many of the world's leading organizations, and he has worked in the public sector and with a number of countries. Wally Olins has written several books including *Corporate Identity*. His publications include *Trading Identities* (1999) and *Wally Olins On Brand* (2003). Wally Olins is one of the world's most experienced practitioners of corporate identity and branding. He has a particular interest in and experience of the branding of regions and nations. He was educated at Oxford and is currently Visiting Fellow at Said Business School in Oxford and at Lancaster University and Copenhagen Business School.

Shaun Riordan was educated at Cambridge, where he received an MA (Hons) in Philosophy. He entered HM Diplomatic Service in 1984. In his early diplomatic career he was posted to the UK's mission to the UN, New York, and the British Embassy in Beijing. At the FCO he worked in the United Nations Department and as Head of the Middle Eastern Section's Security Coordination Department and as Head of the Policy Section of the Eastern Adriatic Unit. In 1995 he became Head of the Political Section at the British Embassy in Madrid. In 2000 he resigned from the Diplomatic Service, and is now Director of ZEIA SL, a Madrid-based consultancy service. In 2002 he was Visiting Research Fellow at the Centre for the Study of Global Governance, London School of Economics. He is author of *The New Diplomacy* (2003), contributed to *Monarchies* (Demos, 2002), and contributes regularly to the Spanish print and electronic media, as well as being a commentator for the BBC on terrorism and Spanish politics.

Cynthia P. Schneider is Director of the Life Science and Society Initiative and Distinguished Professor of Diplomacy at Georgetown University. She was US Ambassador to the Netherlands (1998–2001), and was awarded the Office of the Secretary of Defense's Exceptional Public Service Order, the highest civilian award given by the US Department of Defense. For 2004–06 she has been named Pfizer Medical Humanities Initiative Scholar in Residence. In addition, she is working on a project on 'best practices' in public–private partnerships to bring agricultural biotechnology to the developing world. Ambassador Schneider is a non-resident Fellow at the Brookings Institution and the Institute for the Study of Diplomacy. She is a Supervisory Board member of Royal Ahold, and of the Board of the Institute of Europe at Columbia University, the Institute for Cultural Diplomacy, and of the Anne Frank Foundation American Board. She has published on cultural diplomacy, bioterrorism and biopreparedness, on Rembrandt and seventeenth-century Dutch art.

Paul Sharp is Professor and Head of Political Science at the University of Minnesota, Duluth. He is also founding chair of both the Diplomatic Studies Section and the English School Section of the International

Studies Association (ISA). He is a member of the ISA's Governing Council and Executive Committee. He has recently held visiting fellowships at the University of Malta and the University of Cambridge. His most recent publications include: 'Virtue Unrestrained: Herbert Butterfield and the Problem of American Power', in *International Studies Perspectives* (2004); 'Mullah Zaeef and Taliban Diplomacy', *Review of International Studies* (2003); and 'Herbert Butterfield, the English School, and the Civilizing Virtues of Diplomacy', *International Affairs* (2003). He is currently undertaking research for a book on *Outlaw Diplomacy* and a study of the diplomacy of American Indian tribes in the upper Midwest.

Acknowledgements

Editing collective books takes time and it is a well-known fact that they particularly require patience from conscientious and punctual contributors who hand in their chapter before the editor's (first) deadline. I am particularly grateful to the contributors to this volume whose patience was tested by the inevitable delays that seem to accompany a collaborative scholarly effort.

Editing books is, however, also great fun. The early stages of such a joint venture with colleagues from various countries first of all offer an excellent excuse for a stimulating international conference, and in the process of making a book one often gets to know people with whom it is a pleasure to work. The group of authors contributing to this book has expanded my intellectual horizon and understanding of public diplomacy considerably. Our contacts via email, at the Netherlands Institute of International Relations 'Clingendael' in The Hague, and subsequently at academic gatherings in other places, have resulted in a greater circle of friends and colleagues in diplomatic studies.

I am indebted to numerous diplomats who kindly shared their views and personal experiences with me, and I am also grateful for the support received from colleagues at the Clingendael Institute, where the study of diplomacy is now prioritized alongside diplomatic training for countries from many corners of the world. Time cannot be beaten when making an edited book, but distance is fortunately irrelevant. Rebecca Solheim, who is based in Sweden, went through all of the texts meticulously and from start to finish has turned out to be a fantastic copy editor. I can only hope that we continue to work together on future projects. I am also indebted to Ashvin Gonesh, who compiled the index to this book. Finally, Isabel, Eugenia and Daniel have been enormously supportive. I owe them a lot for putting up with me: the man in the family who was not always there to be a family man.

Introduction

Jan Melissen

The idea to create this book was triggered by the feeling that the debate about public diplomacy after September 2001 had mainly taken place in the press and that the time was ripe for students of diplomacy to look at this phenomenon.

In the early stages of the book it became clear how much confusion still surrounded public diplomacy (that is, the relationship between diplomats and the foreign publics with whom they work) with public debate on the concept being particularly intense in the United States. Between '9/11' and the outbreak of war in Iraq, public diplomacy was beyond any doubt the hottest item in the US foreign policy establishment. Most American think tanks produced advisory reports on public diplomacy, some of them more helpful than others, but so far there has been remarkably little academic literature on post-Cold War public diplomacy. Those interested in it are confronted with an overload of press coverage, comment and analysis as well as instant advice for policy-makers. What is missing, however, is a lack of analysis of deeper trends, and a perspective on how official communication with foreign publics should be seen in the context of wider diplomatic practice.

There are, of course, many ways to look at public diplomacy, and students of diplomacy are fortunately by no means the only academics interested in it. It seems probable that the vantage point of students of global communication, historians of propaganda or international relations' theorists leads to views on public diplomacy that differ from those of students of diplomacy. In this book the practice of diplomacy is the starting point for the majority of the contributions. Most authors believe that public diplomacy can be better understood in the context of broader changes in diplomatic practice and that public diplomacy can at least partly be seen as a symptom of change in the conduct of international relations. In a broader historical perspective it may even be ventured that – for better or for worse – the practice of foreign ministries and embassies in engaging with civil society groups and individuals abroad demonstrates that the evolution of diplomatic representation has reached a new stage. The truth is that foreign publics now matter to practitioners of diplomacy in a way that was unthinkable as little as

25 years ago. In some of the more pioneering countries in this field, one can clearly observe that public diplomacy is gradually moving away from the periphery of diplomatic work. The same has happened to commercial diplomacy – that is, activities by foreign ministries and embassies in support of their country's business and finance sectors – or, at least in Western countries, to consular relations and in particular the effort put into looking after the well-being of a country's own nationals abroad. Many practitioners in the world's diplomatic services may not yet have grasped the significance of communication with foreign publics, but it is a telling sign that in a considerable number of countries it has captured the firm attention of senior management in foreign ministries as well as the political leadership.

It is worth looking at public diplomacy beyond the experiences of the United States or the anglophone world. The debate about the new public diplomacy after 11 September 2001 has become dominated by US public diplomacy, and it has been characterized by a strong emphasis on international security and the relationship between the West and the Islamic world. The US experience should, however, not distract from the observation that many countries became interested in public diplomacy long before '9/11', and for very different reasons. In order to understand public diplomacy properly, it is equally interesting to look at big, medium-sized, small and even micro-states, and also to analyse the way in which non-democratic countries explore this new form of 'outreach' in foreign relations. The strong emphasis in the United States on homeland security, the 'war on terror' and 'winning hearts and minds' in the Islamic world does not mirror the concerns and interests in public diplomacy that are articulated in many other countries. To be sure, September 2001 was an important trigger for the present debate on public diplomacy throughout the global diplomatic community, but for many countries it was not the beginning, nor did the US experience set the terms for thinking on this issue outside North America. This volume is a first attempt to lift the veil on a range of approaches towards public diplomacy. After all, for those who are interested in diplomatic practice, the public diplomacy of the government of Kyrgyzstan is potentially as interesting as the way in which the US State Department is addressing the challenge of communicating with publics overseas.

This book is meant for students of diplomacy and for diplomats. An important driver for some authors is their intellectual curiosity and desire to understand public diplomacy; others tend to blend academic analysis with recommendations for practitioners; and a third category of authors is primarily motivated by the idea that a proper understanding of public diplomacy can contribute to better diplomatic practice and can help to prevent practitioners from misunderstanding its requirements. The book was deliberately conceived as a collective effort by authors from different countries and with varying professional backgrounds. They currently live in the United States, the United Kingdom, the Netherlands or Spain, and are not just academics, but also scholar-diplomats, and consultants or trainers in diplomacy. They are first of all trying to come to grips with public diplomacy from a set of different thematic and national angles, although the book is not designed as a straightforward comparison between different countries. Second, this book looks at public diplomacy as it is practised by different types of countries and by the European Union as an increasingly autonomously operating international organization. Third, the book tries to clarify how practitioners can be more effective as 'public diplomats'. It does not, however, constitute an exercise in school building, nor does it try to force its authors into any form of academic straitjacket. On the contrary, the close reader will not fail to notice that the authors disagree on a number of fundamental points. The book's relatively modest aim is therefore to reflect on public diplomacy today, to assess its importance in the conduct of international relations and, by doing so, to contribute to a wider academic debate on recent trends in diplomacy. The study of public diplomacy is bound to lead to disappointing results if it is dissociated from a broader understanding of diplomatic practice, and students of diplomacy who ignore public diplomacy do little justice to a fundamental aspect of diplomacy's contemporary evolution.

In the first part of this book, Jan Melissen's introductory chapter on the new public diplomacy and Brian Hocking's theoretical reflections on the subject first of all aim at conceptual clarification. They evaluate the new public diplomacy's importance in the present international environment. Both authors consider the new public diplomacy as part of the fabric of world politics, although some of their conclusions on its significance are fundamentally different. Melissen introduces the new public diplomacy as a concept and assesses current developments in this field. His analysis identifies characteristics of good practice and it distinguishes between on the one hand propaganda, nation-branding and cultural relations, and on the other hand public diplomacy. Hocking continues to unpick the various threads of which public diplomacy is composed, re-examines the 'soft power' argument that often surfaces in relation to the discussion on public diplomacy, and contrasts public diplomacy in a hierarchic state-centric image of international relations with a network model.

In the second part of the book, five authors show some of the diversity displayed in the practice of public diplomacy across the world. They look at radically different types of countries and one international organization: the world's leading superpower; two democratic middle powers; an authoritarian great power; revolutionary public diplomacy and communication with foreign audiences by rogue states; as well as the European Union's experiences as a unique international actor. Peter van Ham looks specifically at US public diplomacy and Alan Henrikson's chapter evaluates how the niche diplomacy of Canada and Norway relates to their policies towards the United States. Van Ham's chapter is about US public diplomacy in the context of the debate on 'US Empire'. He examines the normative assumptions on which the dominant discourse of the emerging *Pax Americana* is based, how the US's soft power base has been instrumentalized for the cause of liberal imperialism, as well as the role of public diplomacy in the US's nascent empire. Alan Henrikson's paper compares how Canada and Norway have demonstrated them to be adroit users of public opinion, and how they have succeeded in gaining the respect of other countries as well as public opinion overseas. He discusses the two countries' political strategies in the spheres of power politics and public diplomacy, distinguishing between a confrontational strategy towards the United States, parallel action and an approach aiming at active partnership.

The three remaining chapters in the second section deal with rather exceptional forms of public diplomacy compared to the dominant discourse, which appears to regard public diplomacy as an activity of democratic states or at least states in transition. Ingrid d'Hooghe looks at the characteristics of China's public diplomacy. The Chinese case is particularly interesting because China has a considerable track record in the field of political propaganda and it is a one-party state with a centralist authoritarian regime. D'Hooghe evaluates China's global and bilateral actions in this field, and she points to the public diplomacy asset of China's culture. Paul Sharp's contribution deals with public diplomacy on the periphery of the prevailing international order. His key observation is that a lot of what is called public diplomacy can in fact be traced back to activities practised by revolutionary states such as the Soviet Union, and that it bears striking similarities to communication with foreign audiences by so-called rogue states. Against the background of the 'dark side' of public diplomacy, Sharp's analysis cautions that attempts at counter-revolutionary public diplomacy will undermine the values that public diplomacy purportedly seeks to advance among a wider global audience. The final chapter in this section deals with the European Union as a soft power. Anna Michalski argues that the power of persuasion becomes an existential requirement for the EU's popular legitimacy and credibility, but that in spite of the many actions of the European Commission and the Council Secretariat, the concept of public diplomacy is not employed by many Brussels officials. She discusses how certain values, norms and principles are nevertheless integrated into policies and are instrumentalized in the EU's information and communication strategy.

In the final part of this book, four authors explore public diplomacy's potential. As in Melissen's introductory chapter, they deal with some of the practical aspects of how public diplomacy can be undertaken. Cynthia Schneider argues that cultural diplomacy is a prime example of soft power, but that it is often easily dismissed as too soft and peripheral to the real issues of policy. Her chapter provides an overview of US cultural diplomacy until the end of the Cold War and it examines the reasons behind the decline of US cultural diplomacy from the 1990s. Schneider also identifies good practice and she discusses the strengths and limitations of US cultural diplomacy from a comparative perspective. The contribution by Wally Olins makes a case for nation-branding and stresses that nations have always tried to create and modulate their reputations in order to achieve loyalty at home and influence abroad. He distinguishes a number of areas in which nations are in direct and overt competition with each other and in which he sees nation-branding as an inevitable activity, but he also cautions that it is for the long term, and that the pay-off is slow and not readily measurable. Shaun Riordan states that public diplomacy is part of a newly emerging paradigm of collaborative diplomacy, which requires an approach that is fundamentally dialogue-based. His chapter looks at nation-building and the struggle against international terrorism as two prime examples where such an approach has the potential to contribute to international stability. In this view public diplomacy is increasingly about ideas and values, and involving non-governmental agents is seen as one of the most effective ways of promoting and developing it. In the last chapter in this section, John Hemery looks at variations in training for public diplomacy across the world and discusses what a good course on public diplomacy might look like. He observes that a very limited number of foreign ministries appear to train their diplomats to be players in amorphous transnational networks, and that in many countries public diplomacy training programmes are packages of disparate skills development that fall short of preparing diplomats for operating in the changed architecture of international relations.

Finally, it is self-evident that knowledge of, and a feel for, diplomatic practice is indispensable for a proper understanding of traditional, peer-oriented diplomatic communication. This book's authors, however, believe that students of diplomacy are equally well-placed to make an assessment of diplomacy that takes practitioners out of their protected realm. It is therefore hoped that this book – and indeed diplomatic studies generally – contributes to the debate about public diplomacy, rather than leaving it to others to deal with as mere international communication. Last but not least, this collection of essays indirectly advocates more research on current trends in diplomatic practice. Studies into the history of diplomacy and diplomatic thought have proven to be a boost for the small niche of diplomatic studies in the field of international relations. Confronted with sweeping change, however, it would be appropriate if students of diplomacy also reflect and theorize on current trends and innovations in diplomatic practice, or even turn to scenario studies of what may lie ahead.

Jan Melissen
The Hague, February 2005

Part I
The New Environment

1
The New Public Diplomacy: Between Theory and Practice

Jan Melissen

Introduction

It is tempting to see public diplomacy as old wine in new bottles. Official communication aimed at foreign publics is after all no new phenomenon in international relations. Image cultivation, propaganda and activities that we would now label as public diplomacy are nearly as old as diplomacy itself. Even in ancient times, prestige-conscious princes and their representatives never completely ignored the potential and pitfalls of public opinion in foreign lands. References to the nation and its image go as far back as the Bible, and international relations in ancient Greece and Rome, Byzantium and the Italian Renaissance were familiar with diplomatic activity aimed at foreign publics.

It was not until the invention of the printing press in the fifteenth century that the scale of official communication with foreign publics potentially altered. Towards the end of the Middle Ages, the Venetians had already introduced the systematic dissemination of newsletters inside their own diplomatic service, but it was Gutenberg's invention that cleared the way for true pioneers in international public relations, such as Cardinal Richelieu in early seventeenth-century France. Under the *ancien régime*, the French went to much greater lengths in remoulding their country's image abroad than other European powers, and they put enormous effort into managing their country's reputation, seeing it as one of the principal sources of a nation's power.[1] Identity creation and image projection – nation-branding in today's parlance – reached a peak under Louis XIV.[2] Other countries followed suit, such as Turkey in the aftermath of the Ottoman Empire. Kemal Atatürk was in charge of nothing less than a complete makeover of the face of his country and its identity, without which Turkey's present prospects of integration into Europe would not have been on the EU's political agenda. Less benign twentieth-century versions of identity development and nation-building – such as Fascism and Communism – directly challenged and gave an impetus towards communication with foreign publics by democratic powers. Political leaders' battles for overseas 'hearts and minds' are therefore anything but a recent invention.

The First World War saw the birth of professional image cultivation across national borders, and it was inevitable after the war that the emerging academic study of international politics would wake up to the importance of what is now commonly dubbed as 'soft power'.[3] In the era of growing inter-state conflict between the two world wars, E. H. Carr wrote that 'power over opinion' was 'not less essential for political purposes than military and economic power, and has always been closely associated with them'. In other words, to put it in the terminology recently introduced by Joseph S. Nye, 'hard power' and 'soft power' are inextricably linked.[4] It is now a cliché to state that soft power – the postmodern variant of power over opinion – is increasingly important in the global information age, and that in an environment with multiple transnational linkages the loss of soft power can be costly for hard power. Many practical questions about the power of attraction in international affairs are, however, still unanswered. Political commentators in many countries have become gripped by the notion of soft power and ministries of foreign affairs wonder how to wield it most effectively. As Nye argued, countries that are likely to be more attractive in postmodern international relations are those that help to frame issues, whose culture and ideas are closer to prevailing international norms, and whose credibility abroad is reinforced by their values and policies.[5]

Public diplomacy is one of soft power's key instruments, and this was recognized in diplomatic practice long before the contemporary debate on public diplomacy. The United States, the former Soviet Union and Europe's three major powers invested particularly heavily in their 'communications with the world' during the Cold War. Although conventional diplomatic activity and public diplomacy were mostly pursued on parallel tracks, it became increasingly hard to see how the former could be effective without giving sufficient attention to the latter.[6] In fact, as early as 1917–18, Wilson and Lenin had already challenged one another at the soft power level, long before their countries turned into global superpowers and started colliding in the military and economic fields.[7] The battle of values and ideas that dominated international relations in the second half of the twentieth century evolved into competition in the sphere of hard power, and not vice versa. The world diplomatic community nevertheless woke up late to the fundamental challenges of communication with foreign publics rather than then habitual international dialogue with foreign officials. Diplomatic culture is after all fundamentally peer-orientated, and the dominant realist paradigm in diplomatic circles was a by-product of a long history of viewing international relations in terms of economic and military power. The question today of how foreign ministries can instrumentalize soft power is testing their diplomats' flexibility to the full.

Against this backdrop it may not be surprising to see that most students of diplomacy have given little systematic attention to public diplomacy. The basic distinction between traditional diplomacy and public diplomacy is clear: the former is about relationships between the representatives of states, or other international actors; whereas the latter targets the general public in foreign societies and more specific non-official groups, organizations and individuals. Existing definitions of diplomacy have either stressed its main purpose ('the art of resolving international difficulties peacefully'), its principal agents ('the conduct of relations between sovereign states through the medium of accredited representatives') or its chief function ('the management of international relations by negotiation'). In a sense, such definitions do not take into account the transformation of the environment in which diplomacy is at work. Students of diplomacy saw diplomatic communication in principle as an activity between symmetrical actors. A more inclusive view of diplomacy as 'the mechanism of representation, communication and negotiation through which states and other international actors conduct their business' still suggests a neat international environment consisting of a range of clearly identifiable players.[8]

Diplomacy in a traditionalist view is depicted as a game where the roles and responsibilities of actors in international relations are clearly delineated. This picture no longer resembles the much more fuzzy world of postmodern transnational relations – a world, for that matter, in which most actors are not nearly as much in control as they would like to be. Moreover, the interlocutors of today's foreign service officers are not necessarily their counterparts, but a wide variety of people that are either involved in diplomatic activity or are at the receiving end of international politics. As a result, the requirements of diplomacy have been transformed. As Robert Cooper put it, success in diplomacy 'means openness and transnational cooperation'.[9] Such openness and multi-level cooperation call for the active pursuit of more collaborative diplomatic relations with various types of actors. Public diplomacy is an indispensable ingredient for such a collaborative model of diplomacy.[10]

First of all this chapter introduces and defines public diplomacy as a concept and it assesses current developments in this field. Second, it evaluates the importance of public diplomacy in the changing international environment, and it identifies characteristics of good practice. Third, this chapter distinguishes between on the one hand propaganda, nation-branding and cultural relations, and on the other hand public diplomacy. It concludes that public diplomacy is here to stay, but that its requirements sit rather uneasily with traditional diplomatic culture. Public diplomacy is a challenge for diplomatic services that should not be underestimated. Finally, this analysis indicates that public diplomacy is not a mere technique. It should be considered as part of the fabric of world politics and its rise suggests that the evolution of diplomatic representation has reached a new stage.

Beyond American public diplomacy?

Is it possible to discuss public diplomacy without giving central importance to US public diplomacy and the debates on public diplomacy in the anglophone world? The origins of contemporary public diplomacy, and the current debate on the need for more public diplomacy, are dominated by the US experience. In the mid-1960s the term public diplomacy was allegedly coined by a former American diplomat and Dean of the Fletcher School of Law and Diplomacy, Edmund Gullion, and in the following decades its practice became most closely associated with the United States. Against the backdrop of the Cold War, public campaigns were above all about communicating the American way of life to foreign publics. As becomes clear in Cynthia Schneider's chapter in this book, public diplomacy and promotion of culture were in fact closely connected and served similar purposes. Criticism of public diplomacy as the soft side of foreign relations was silenced by the demands of the Cold War but gained strength after its demise. Budget cuts were one of the main driving forces behind the integration of the United States Information Agency (USIA) into the State Department in the mid-1990s, when the Cato Institute argued that 'public diplomacy is largely irrelevant to the kinds of challenges now facing the United States'.[11] The post-Cold War case against public diplomacy did in fact reinforce ever-present bureaucratic pressures: it has always been difficult to give public diplomacy priority on the State Department's agenda (and few flashy careers were therefore built on diplomatic jobs in the field of information and cultural work). As is well known, the tragedy of 11 September 2001 changed the fortunes of public diplomacy against the backdrop of a troubled relationship between the Islamic world and the West, as well as the 'war on terror' declared by the Bush presidency. Interestingly, when it comes to exercising soft power, the United States possesses unparalleled assets that are accompanied, as it has turned out, by an unrivalled capacity to make a free fall into the abyss of foreign perceptions.

Other countries can learn a great deal from the strengths and weaknesses of present US public diplomacy. This chapter will only point out a limited number of lessons from US public diplomacy, yet the clearest of all is that the aims of public diplomacy cannot be achieved if they are believed to be inconsistent with a country's foreign policy or military actions. US policies towards the Middle East or its military presence in Iraq, for instance, undermine the credibility of public diplomacy. The starting point of this variant of diplomacy is after all at the perceiving end, with the foreign consumers of diplomacy. This may be conventional wisdom among public diplomacy practitioners, but its salience can hardly be overestimated and the age of visual politics is adding a new dimension to this truism. Pictures speak louder than words, and they do so instantaneously and with lasting effect. There is, for instance, little doubt that press coverage of human rights' violations in the Abu Ghraib prison will damage perceptions of the US in the Islamic world for many years. Another lesson from the US experience is that sound policies may be of enormous support to public diplomacy, but that money and muscle are no guarantee for success. The availability of unparalleled financial and media resources does not prevent small non-state actors, even terrorists, from being more successful in their dealings with critical international audiences. To be sure, throwing money at self-advertising campaigns in countries with a sceptical public opinion is based on a gross underestimation of assertive postmodern publics, as was demonstrated by ineffective US television commercials in Indonesia, showing the life of happy Muslims in the US. The rather simplistic practice of selling images and peddling messages to foreign audiences has little chance of paying off.

On the other hand, foreign nations can benefit enormously from the stimulating US debate on public diplomacy and the valuable and free advice produced by foreign policy think tanks and other bodies outside and inside government. There is considerable overlap between the reports and recommendations that were published after September 2001, and not all of the ideas are equally stimulating, but no other country benefits to the same degree from good offices provided by the non-governmental sector.[12]

The US experience also shows the importance of developing a long-term public diplomacy strategy with central coordination of policies. There are evident problems in this area within the US executive branch of government, but it does not take much to see that many other countries have only begun to think about such issues. Coordination and control have always been easier in non-democratic regimes and they are not incompatible with traditional images of public diplomacy. As Ingrid d'Hooghe implies in her chapter, the People's Republic of China excels in central coordination of its public diplomacy activities and can therefore, in a sense, be seen as a leader in public diplomacy. Moreover, US experiences with public diplomacy demonstrate that skills and practices from the corporate sector, in particular from the disciplines of public relations and marketing, can be particularly useful in public diplomacy campaigns. Marketing-oriented thinking was anathema and even a vulgarization to traditional diplomacy, but is slowly but surely entering today's diplomatic services. Finally, US efforts aimed at links with domestic civil society organizations operating overseas and so-called 'citizen diplomacy' confirm the relevance of the hinterland. 'Domestic public diplomacy' can in a way be seen as the successor to public affairs during the Cold War, and its objectives go beyond traditional constituency-building.[13]

After 11 September 2001, which triggered a global debate on public diplomacy, 'PD' has become an issue in foreign ministries from all countries, ranging from Canada to New Zealand and from Argentina to Mongolia. Many ministries of foreign affairs now develop a public diplomacy policy of their own, and few would like to be caught out without at least paying lip-service to the latest fashion in the conduct of international relations. Their association with public diplomacy can be seen as a symptom of the rise of soft power in international relations or, at another level, as the effect of broader processes of change in diplomatic practice, calling for transparency and transnational collaboration. The new public diplomacy is thus much more than a technical instrument of foreign policy. It has in fact become part of the changing fabric of international relations. Both small and large countries, ranging in size from the United States to Belgium or even Liechtenstein, and with either democratic or authoritarian regimes, such as China and Singapore, and including the most affluent, such as Norway, and those that can be counted among the world's poorest nations, for example Ethiopia, have in recent years displayed a great interest in public diplomacy.

It should, however, be stressed that it was not '9/11' that triggered most countries' interest in public diplomacy. Many foreign ministries' motives for prioritizing public diplomacy had relatively little to do with US policy preoccupations such as the 'war on terror' or the relationship with the Islamic world. What is true in a more general sense, however, is that – as in the case of the United States – the rising popularity of public diplomacy was most of the time a direct response to a downturn in foreign perceptions. Most successful public diplomacy initiatives were born out of necessity. They were reactive and not the product of forward-looking foreign services caring about relationships with foreign audiences as a new challenge in diplomatic practice. In Europe, the German variant of public diplomacy – *politische Öffentlichkeitsarbeit* – accompanied the foreign relations of the Federal Republic from the very beginning in 1949, and it was a critical instrument in raising acceptance and approval of Germany in other Western democracies. The external image of postwar France, deeply hurt by the country's humiliation in the Second World War, also relied heavily on its *politique d'influence* and the cultivation of national *grandeur*. Smaller European countries have experiences of their own. Austria's public diplomacy wake-up call, for instance, was the Waldheim affair, discrediting the then UN Secretary-General because of his Nazi past. The Netherlands started seriously professionalizing its *publieksdiplomatie* in the face of foreign opinion that was horrified by ethical issues such as euthanasia legislation and liberal policies on abortion and drugs, and the need for this defensive public diplomacy has by no means abated.

Outside Western Europe, public diplomacy can often be seen to support the most vital interests of nations. Some European countries that were in a sense already part of the West and that have gone through a period of transition, including aspirations of integration into larger multilateral structures, have embraced public diplomacy with particular enthusiasm. This perspective may help us to understand in part the recent success stories of European transition countries such as Spain in the post-Franco era, Finland after the Cold War, or Ireland in the aftermath of a long period of relative isolation from mainland Europe. More recently, Polish public diplomacy was successfully developed in the framework of Poland's strategy for NATO and EU membership (but now leaves that country with a post-accession challenge). Such sharply focused public diplomacy serving strategic foreign policy goals can nowadays be witnessed among EU candidate members such as Bulgaria, Romania, Croatia and Turkey – countries that have invested heavily in persuading supposedly sceptical audiences in Western Europe. These countries' motives in engaging in public diplomacy have everything to do with their desire to integrate into the European and transatlantic world, with all the expected benefits of social stability, security and economic prosperity.

More than nations in transition, Global South countries engaging in public diplomacy have strong economic motives. During the Cold War, public diplomacy was not a major concern in the poverty-stricken part of the world, but more interest could gradually be discerned in how public diplomacy or nation-branding can contribute to development.[14] Apart from the slowly growing interest in the Global South, there are a number of exceptional cases where public diplomacy was triggered by specific events or came into the picture almost naturally. After the 2002 Bali bombing in Indonesia, for instance, public diplomacy was given top priority and received attention at cabinet level. Terrorism caused the Indonesian foreign ministry to prioritize public diplomacy, as it was thought to be instrumental in dealing with the crisis in the tourist sector.

Alternatively, countries that would have gone largely unnoticed outside their own region if geopolitics and security issues had not placed them in the spotlight of world attention have become sharply aware of the power of perceptions in international relations. Pakistan is a case in point. Few diplomats are probably more aware of the effects of foreign views on their country, which is loosely associated with military tensions and skirmishes along the border with India, nuclear proliferation, assistance to the Taliban regime in Afghanistan, and Islamic extremism. So-called 'rogue states' in the Global South, deprived as they are of regular diplomatic networks and structurally handicapped in their diplomatic relations with other states, also see communication with foreign publics as an essential instrument in their diplomatic toolbox. A country like North Korea does not have many alternatives to resorting to the public gallery. Rogue or pariah states, it could be argued, like other small actors in international relations, have even benefited to a disproportionate degree from the decentralization of information power.[15]

But these and other cases of public diplomacy bridging major divides in international relations, such as the well-known practice of communication with foreign publics by socialist powers, are in fact exceptional. As a structural development, public diplomacy above all thrives in highly interdependent regions and between countries that are linked by multiple transnational relationships and therefore a substantial degree of 'interconnectedness' between their civil societies. The emphasis in the present debate on public diplomacy is on the United States and its relationship with the Islamic world, but public diplomacy is widely practised outside North America and much of it in fact antedates the current US preoccupation with 'winning foreign hearts and minds'.

Defining the new public diplomacy

The world in which public diplomacy was considered as one of the leftovers of diplomatic dialogue is rapidly disappearing. So is the world in which public diplomacy can easily be dismissed as an attempt at manipulation of foreign publics. In order to understand the new public diplomacy properly, it is neither helpful to hang on to past images of diplomacy (still prevailing in much diplomatic studies' literature), nor is it advisable to make a forward projection of historical practices into the present international environment (in the case of equalling public diplomacy to traditional propaganda). The new public diplomacy will be an increasingly standard component of overall diplomatic practice and is more than a form of propaganda conducted by diplomats. True, many foreign ministries are still struggling to put the concept into practice in a multi-actor international environment, and some diplomatic services do in fact construct their public diplomacy on a formidable tradition of propaganda-making. But public diplomacy's imperfections should not obscure the fact that it gradually becomes woven into the fabric of mainstream diplomatic activity. In a range of bilateral relationships it has already become the bread and butter of many diplomats' work, as for instance in the US–Canadian relationship, in relations between West European countries, or between some South-East Asian neighbours. As a Canadian ambassador to Washington observed: 'the new diplomacy, as I call it, is, to a large extent, public diplomacy and requires different skills, techniques, and attitudes than those found in traditional diplomacy'.[16] In Europe, public diplomacy has also become a staple commodity in international affairs. A much-quoted 2002 report by the German *Auswärtiges Amt* (foreign ministry) came to a conclusion of historical proportions about the role of EU embassies in other member states: 'in Europe public diplomacy is viewed as the number one priority over the whole spectrum of issues'.[17] Both examples underline a broader point: in regions characterized by a great deal of economic and/or political interdependence as well as a high level of interconnection at the level of civil society, public diplomacy has become essential in diplomatic relations.

Perhaps the most succinct definition of public diplomacy is given by Paul Sharp in his chapter, where he describes it as 'the process by which direct relations with people in a country are pursued to advance the interests and extend the values of those being represented'. Writing 15 years earlier, Hans Tuch defined public diplomacy as 'a government's process of communicating with foreign publics in an attempt to bring about understanding for its nation's ideas and ideals, its institutions and culture, as well as its national goals and policies'.[18] Tuch claimed neither that public diplomacy was something like a new diplomatic paradigm, nor that it in any sense replaced the discreet and confidential relationships between state representatives, which of course it does not. It is indeed important to stress the limits of what is new and not to overstate the importance of public diplomacy.

Tuch's definition is persuasive, but where this analysis differs is first of all that it does not see public diplomacy, or indeed diplomacy in general, as a uniquely stately activity, even though it stresses the practice of states. Large and small non-state actors, and supranational and subnational players develop public diplomacy policies of their own. Under media-minded Kofi Annan, the UN shows supranational public diplomacy in action, and Barroso's European Commission has given top priority to the EU's public communication strategy. Interestingly, however, as John Hemery relates in his chapter, neither of these two organizations is actually giving much attention to public diplomacy training of its internationally operating staff, which seems to be evidence that they are public diplomacy novices. Non-governmental organizations (NGOs) have also demonstrated that they are particularly adept at influencing foreign publics. Definitely not all campaigns by globally operating NGOs such as Greenpeace or Amnesty International have turned out to be equally successful, but their effectiveness has generally drawn the admiration of foreign ministries that are trying to operate in increasingly fluid international networks. What is more, one can observe converging interests among states and NGOs – actors that previously looked at one another with suspicion and as competitors. The 1997 Ottawa Convention (the treaty banning landmines) and establishment of the International Criminal Court are only two prominent examples of a number of global governance initiatives where states, NGOs and the UN have joined forces in mobilizing international public opinion. International companies operating in a global marketplace are now also facing up to their social and ethical responsibilities, and their public diplomacy policies are slowly but surely becoming more sophisticated.[19] Some do better than others: many countries envy the professionalism and public diplomacy muscle of some major multinational corporations. In other words, diplomacy is operative in a network environment rather than the hierarchical state-centric model of international relations, as Brian Hocking argues in the following chapter. What is of interest here is that in the field of public diplomacy different types of actors can learn vital lessons from each other.

Second, public diplomacy is aimed at foreign publics, and strategies for dealing with such publics should be distinguished from the domestic socialization of diplomacy. Nevertheless, separating public affairs (aimed at domestic audiences) from public diplomacy (dealing with overseas target groups) is increasingly at odds with the 'interconnected' realities of global relationships. It is commonly known that information directed at a domestic audience often reaches foreign publics, or the other way round, but the relationship between public affairs and public diplomacy has become more intricate than that. Engaging with one's own domestic constituency with a view to foreign policy development and external identity-building has become part of the public diplomacy strategy of countries as diverse as Canada, Chile and Indonesia.[20] In a domestic context the socialization of diplomacy is a familiar theme for foreign ministries, but it is one that deserves renewed attention as the domestic and foreign dimensions of engagement with 'the public' are more connected than ever before. This is, for instance, the case in the debate on the supposed intercultural divide between the West and the Islamic world, and is illustrated by the fact that the British Foreign Office now talks through Middle Eastern policy with moderate domestic Muslim organizations. Both public diplomacy and public affairs are directly affected by the forces of globalization and the recent revolution in communication technology. In an era in which it has become increasingly important to influence world opinion, domestic and international communication with the public has become an increasingly complex challenge for foreign ministries.

Third, public diplomacy is often portrayed as a one-way information flow, and at best one in two directions, but essentially aimed at relaying positive aspects of a country to foreign publics. In reality, and as is presently emerging in a number of countries, some of the more intelligent initiatives remind us less of the traditional activities of information departments. The main task of press and information departments was, and in many cases unfortunately still is, dissemination of information and coordination of relations with the press. The new public diplomacy moves away from – to put it crudely – peddling information to foreigners and keeping the foreign press at bay, towards engaging with foreign audiences. The innovative 'niche diplomacy' of Norway and Canada – two vanguard countries in the field of public diplomacy that are discussed in the chapter by Alan Henrikson – is a case in point. A learning process is therefore taking place, although not in as many places as one would hope, but it is quite clear that the new public diplomacy is here to stay. International actors accept more and more that they have to engage in dialogue with foreign audiences as a condition of success in foreign policy. To be sure, public diplomacy is no altruistic affair and it is not a 'soft' instrument. It can pursue a wide variety of objectives, such as in the field of political dialogue, trade and foreign investment, the establishment of links with civil society groups beyond the opinion gatekeepers, but also has 'hard power' goals such as alliance management, conflict prevention or military intervention.

As a diplomatic method, public diplomacy is far from uniform and some public campaigns have little to do with international advocacy. As mentioned above, public diplomacy is increasingly prominent in bilateral relations but can also be actively pursued by international organizations.[21] Public diplomacy's national variant is more competitive, whereas multilateral public diplomacy can be seen as a more cooperative form of engagement with foreign publics. Referring to the latter, Mark Leonard rightly suggests that there is little advantage in making, for instance, civil society-building or the promotion of good governance an activity explicitly coming from one single country.[22]

Yet there are other unconventional forms of public diplomacy. A political leader may even engage in public diplomacy in defence of a foreign counterpart's international reputation. This was the case in 2004 when Tony Blair, Gerhard Schröder and other heads of government visited Libyan leader Qaddafi in an ostentatious show of support of this former rogue state leader, who was until recently branded as an international outlaw and exponent of state terrorism. It is not the purpose here to list unusual displays of public diplomacy, but an interesting one deserves mention: the intentional divulging of bad news, such as the deliberate spreading of news about one's own country that is bound to be received abroad as an adverse development. A recent example of 'negative branding' was the Dutch Ministry of Justice's communication in 2004 that 26,000 illegal asylum seekers would eventually be expelled from the Netherlands. This bombshell about the 'expulsion' or 'potential mass deportation' of foreigners by a country with a reputation for liberal immigration policies quickly spread via the worldwide web and did indeed have the intended effect of a subsequent decrease of refugee flows to the Netherlands. Such initiatives have a direct effect on foreign policy and bilateral relations with other countries, which leads our discussion to the more general point of the relationship between public diplomacy and foreign policy.

It is tempting to see public diplomacy as just another instrument of foreign policy, as was mentioned above in relation to the recent debate in the United States. One should caution for too close a nexus between foreign policy and public diplomacy, however, as this may damage a country's credibility in its communications with foreign audiences. The view that public diplomacy activities are essentially aimed at creating a public opinion in a country 'that will enable target-country political leaders to make decisions that are supportive of advocate-country's foreign policy objectives', is too mechanistic and ambitious.[23] What is problematic with the approach of public diplomacy as an immediate foreign policy tool is that it exposes public diplomacy to the contradictions, discontinuities, fads and fancies of foreign policy. If it is too closely tied to foreign policy objectives, it runs the risk of becoming counterproductive and indeed a failure when foreign policy itself is perceived to be a failure. In such circumstances, a foreign ministry's public diplomacy becomes a liability and no longer serves as a diplomatic tool that has the special quality of being able to go where traditional diplomacy cannot. In any case, it should be borne in mind that the influence that government actions can bring about in other societies tends to be limited. US experiences after September 2001 are a case in point. In the first Bush administration's conception of public diplomacy as an instrument in the service of short-term objectives, it appeared hard to steer policy in a direction that dissociated public diplomacy from the 'war on terror' and the 'clash of civilizations'. In these circumstances, and against the background of US policy in the Middle East, target populations in the Islamic world and elsewhere could not be blamed for seeing US public diplomacy under Bush as 'a velvet fist in an iron glove'.[24]

Public diplomacy should of course not be developed regardless of a country's foreign policy, and it should be in tune with medium-term objectives and long-term aims. Public diplomacy builds on trust and credibility, and it often works best with a long horizon. It is, however, realistic to aspire to influencing the milieu factors that constitute the psychological and political environment in which attitudes and policies towards other countries are debated. The milieu aims of public diplomacy should not, however, be confused with those of international lobbying. The latter aims at directly influencing specific policies, and the individuals targeted in lobbying are without exception those who are in the loop of the policy process. In contrast, there is only so much that public diplomacy can achieve, and the case for modest objectives is even stronger where public diplomacy aims at spanning bridges between different cultures. When bilateral relationships are complicated by a cultural divide between the civil societies involved, it will be harder for diplomats to find the right interlocutors and to strike the right tone. It is, for instance, one thing to confess to the necessity of speaking with the

'Arab street', but quite another to get through to youngsters in their formative years in the highly politicized societies of Middle Eastern countries. The next hurdle is to make sure that information is received in the way that it was intended, which is far from easy as people tend to be suspicious of foreign officials' motives. In too many societies, members of the public are unfortunately justified in making fun of anyone who places trust in their own government's representatives. When it comes to dealing with the public, diplomats therefore have to work harder to achieve the credibility that is essential to facilitate foreign relationships. This is true in countries where government is not trusted, but also in stable democracies diplomats know that they may not be the best messengers when it comes to communicating with the public. As Shaun Riordan suggests in his chapter, public diplomacy is made more effective with the help of non-governmental agents of the sending country's own civil society and by employing local networks in target countries.

Public diplomacy and related concepts

Three concepts that deserve brief attention in a discussion on public diplomacy are propaganda, nation-branding and foreign cultural relations. Similar to public diplomacy, propaganda and nation-branding are about the communication of information and ideas to foreign publics with a view to changing their attitudes towards the originating country or reinforcing existing beliefs. Propaganda and nation-branding, however, neither point to the concept of diplomacy, nor do they generally view communication with foreign publics in the context of changes in contemporary diplomacy. The practice of cultural relations has traditionally been close to diplomacy, although it is clearly distinct from it, but recent developments in both fields now reveal considerable overlap between the two concepts.

Separating the new public diplomacy from propaganda

Propaganda has a much longer intellectual pedigree than public diplomacy and in the context of this introductory discussion it is impossible to do justice to the literature on propaganda. Students of propaganda see public diplomacy as an outgrowth of propaganda, a phenomenon with common historical roots and roughly similar characteristics, and there is therefore general agreement that it can be submerged into the pre-existing concept of propaganda. Such an approach is facilitated by a broad and inclusive definition of propaganda. According to Welch, for instance, propaganda is 'the deliberate attempt to influence the opinions of an audience through the transmission of ideas and values for the specific purpose, consciously designed to serve the interest of the propagandists and their political masters, either directly or indirectly'.[25] Definitions such as this are hard to distinguish from some of the definitions of public diplomacy that are given above and are therefore virtually interchangeable. It is then easy to see how public diplomacy can be pictured as a subset of propaganda. In the best case, the former suggests a newly emerging form of interconnection between governments and foreign publics. Traditionalist students of diplomacy's interpretations of public diplomacy approximate this view, albeit from a completely different vantage point.[26] They see public diplomacy as a corrupted form of diplomatic communication that is occasionally useful and therefore not necessarily anti-diplomatic – a view that is shared by some practitioners. As Richard Holbrooke wrote: 'Call it public diplomacy, call it public affairs, psychological warfare, if you really want to be blunt, propaganda'.[27]

Two key features of propaganda are its historical baggage and the popular understanding of it as manipulation and deceit of foreign publics. Propaganda is commonly understood to be a concept with highly negative connotations, reinforced by memories of Nazi and Communist propaganda, Cold War tactics and, more recently, so-called psychological operations in post-Cold War conflicts. But in contemporary diplomatic practice, there are also fundamentally different and less objectionable ways of dealing with foreign publics. Few, for example, would consider public campaigns by West European countries aimed at civil society building, rule of law and the improvement of democracy in Eastern Europe as propaganda. When unwinding the threads of propaganda and public diplomacy, it does not make things easier that in the public campaigns of some countries one can discern a mix of modern public diplomacy and old-style propaganda, although sold as public diplomacy. That should, however, not obscure the emergence of the new public diplomacy as a significant development in contemporary diplomatic practice. A category such as propaganda simply cannot capture the contemporary diversity in relations between diplomatic practitioners and increasingly assertive foreign publics. For instance, it seems hard to equal Dutch diplomats – discussing the Netherlands' integration policy in the context of Germany's debate on the risks of radicalization among Islamic minorities – to propagandists. Neither is a Canadian diplomat discussing environmental issues with US civil society groups necessarily practising propaganda.

For academics there seems to be an easier way out of this conundrum than for practitioners just doing their job. If propaganda is to be a useful concept, as Nick Cull argues, 'it first has to be divested of its pejorative connotations'. In this view, propaganda should be seen a wide-ranging and ethically neutral political activity that is to be distinguished from categories such as information and education. What separates propaganda from education or information (assuming that these two are uncontroversial and straightforward!) is that it 'tries to tell people what to think. Information and education are concerned with broadening the audience's perspectives and opening their minds, but propaganda strives to narrow and preferably close them. The distinction lies in the purpose'.[28] With public diplomacy presented as a variety of propaganda, it would hence also be an activity that has as its conscious or unconscious purpose the narrowing or closing of the minds of targeted publics abroad. At first glance, the record may indeed seem to point in this direction. Governments have tried to fool foreign publics rather too often. Even many of today's official information campaigns aimed at other countries' societies are basically a form of one-way messaging, and a number of countries that pay lip-service to public diplomacy actually have a better track record in the field of manipulating public opinion. It is true that our collective memory of official communication with publics in other countries is contaminated by past examples – more than just occasionally confirmed by present practice – of states practising propaganda in the sense of narrowing people's minds.

Some contemporary authors on public diplomacy hardly seem bothered by such questions and merely assert that today's public diplomacy is different.[29] An early definition of propaganda nevertheless points to a useful indirect differentiation between public diplomacy and propaganda, describing the latter as 'a process that deliberately attempts through persuasion techniques to secure from the propagandee, *before he can deliberate freely*, the responses desired by the propagandist'.[30] The distinction between propaganda and public diplomacy lies in the pattern of communication. Modern public diplomacy is a 'two-way street', even though the diplomat practising it will of course always have his own country's interests and foreign policy goals in mind (which most likely inspired his or her association with the public in the first place). It is persuasion by means of dialogue that is based on a liberal notion of communication with foreign publics. In other words, public diplomacy is similar to propaganda in that it tries to persuade people what to think, but it is fundamentally different from it in the sense that public diplomacy also listens to what people have to say. The new public diplomacy that is gradually developing – and if it is to have any future in modern diplomatic practice – is not one-way messaging. As one senior diplomat said at a British Council conference: 'The world is fed up with hearing us talk: what it actually wants is for us to shut up and listen'.[31] The crux becomes clear in Jay Black's description of propaganda: 'Whereas creative communication accepts pluralism and displays expectations that its receivers should conduct further investigations of its observations, allegations and conclusions, propaganda does not appear to do so'. Black is perfectly right that it is possible to conduct public relations and persuasion campaigns without being unduly propagandistic.[32] Meaningful communication between official agents and foreign publics may have been extremely difficult or even impossible in the past; but it is certainly not too far-fetched in the increasingly complex web of transnational relations that is presently in the making.

Public diplomacy and the challenge of nation-branding

The second concept in relation to this discussion is nation-branding or nation *re*-branding – one of the last frontiers in the marketing discipline. The practice of branding a nation involves a much greater and coordinated effort than public diplomacy. For one, public diplomacy is initiated by practitioners, whereas branding is about the mobilization of all of a nation's forces that can contribute to the promotion of its image abroad. Paradoxically, for the very same reason, nation-branding and public diplomacy are sisters under the skin, and this explains why foreign ministries in a great variety of countries have expressed an interest in branding. In light of the overlap between the two fields, it is in fact surprising that the debates on nation-branding and public diplomacy pass one another like ships in the night. This can partly be accounted for by the fact that students of branding stick to the field of international marketing and have little affinity with the field of diplomacy.[33] Simon Anholt put it perhaps most bluntly, writing that there is 'a lot of confusion about this term "public diplomacy" and what it really means. I myself do not use the term until I really have to'.[34] In this perspective, marketing is seen as the master of all disciplines, and communication with foreign publics is more than anything else a matter of applying its principles to international relations. The contrary view taken here is that it does not serve either nation-branding or public diplomacy if the two discourses are completely separated. They are distinct but not entirely dissimilar responses to the increased salience of countries' identities and also to globalization's effect of international homogenization (next to, of course, a trend towards cultural fragmentation). Modern nations look more and more like one another, and there are few things that officials detest more than their country being confused with others that are seen to be ranking further down the league table of nations. Well known is Slovenia's fear of being taken for Slovakia.

Two conceptual differences between nation-branding and public diplomacy immediately meet the eye. First, branding's level of ambition easily outflanks that of the limited aims and modesty of most public diplomacy campaigns. Put simply, for public diplomats the world is no market and practitioners are constantly reminded of the fact that diplomatic communication is only a flimsy part of the dense and multilayered transnational communication processes. In other words, the strength of public diplomacy lies in the recognition and acceptance of its limitations. Many public diplomacy campaigns are based on the common-sense assumption that they are by no means the decisive factor in determining foreign perceptions. In contrast, the main feature of branding projects is their holistic approach. The language of nation-branders resembles the 'can-do' approach from the practice of marketing and the clarity of strategic vision from the corporate world. It is hard to deny that the idiom of branding is 'cool' and promising, and branding has particularly attracted countries with a weak international image or a reputation that leaves much to be desired. It is looked upon favourably in a number of transition countries and also among the very small and 'invisible' nations. It is perhaps no wonder that the likes of Liechtenstein and Estonia were attracted by the lure of branding, even though it is important to emphasize that to the present day no outside expert has succeeded in re-branding a single country. Experienced consultants know from first-hand experience the immense difficulties of influencing foreign perceptions, as also becomes clear from Wally Olins' chapter. As Anholt writes: 'Brand management is often, as we know, something quite humble: the cautious and slow-moving husbandry of existing perceptions. It is a process as unglamorous as it is unscandalous and, not coincidentally, hard stuff to get journalists excited'.[35]

Second, nation-branding accentuates a country's identity and reflects its aspirations, but it cannot move much beyond existing social realities. The art of branding is often essentially about reshaping a country's self-image and moulding its identity in a way that makes the re-branded nation stand out from the pack. Crucially, it is about the articulation and projection of identity. The new public diplomacy does not at all contradict nation-branding, and there are various reasons to suggest that it prospers particularly well in a country that is also putting an effort into branding. Branding and public diplomacy are in fact largely complementary. Both are principally aimed at foreign publics but have a vitally important domestic dimension, and in contrast to much conventional diplomacy both have foreign rather than one's own perceptions as their starting point. Branding and public diplomacy are also likely to be more successful if they are seen as long-term approaches rather than seen as being dominated by the issues of the day.[36] But instead of aiming at the projection of identity, public diplomacy is fundamentally different from branding in that it is first of all about promoting and maintaining smooth international relationships. In an international environment that is characterized by multiple links between civil societies and the growing influence of non-governmental actors, public diplomacy reinforces the overall diplomatic effort in the sense that it strengthens relationships with non-official target groups abroad.

Interestingly, the modus operandi of the new public diplomacy is not entirely different from the public relations approach. As Benno Signitzer and Timothy Coombs observe in a comparative study, the objectives of both reveal evident similarities: 'Virtually any introductory public relations text will note public relations is used to achieve information exchange, the reduction of misconceptions, the creation of goodwill, and the construction of an image'.[37] To be sure, a lesson that public diplomacy can take on board from the sometimes misunderstood field of PR is that the strength of firm relationships largely determines the receipt and success of individual messages and overall attitudes. Laurie Wilson's conclusion on the creation of strategic cooperative communities also applies to public diplomacy:

> It is important for practitioners to devote some time to identifying and building relationships, or they will forever be caught in the reactive mode of addressing immediate problems with no long-term vision or coordination of strategic efforts. It is like being trapped in a leaky boat: If you spend all your time bailing and none of it rowing, you will never get to shore.[38]

The overlap of cultural relations with the new public diplomacy

Cultural relations are in a way closer to recent trends in the new public diplomacy than propaganda and nation-branding. In cultural relations as much as in the new public diplomacy, the accent is increasingly on engaging with foreign audiences rather than selling messages, on mutuality and the establishment of stable relationships instead of mere policy-driven campaigns, on the 'long haul' rather than short-term needs, and on winning 'hearts and minds' and building trust. Whereas traditional cultural relations are often thought of as a pretty straightfor-ward (and undervalued) adjunct to inter-state relations, they now also include entirely new areas and social responsibilities. To be sure, there are still plenty of reasons for traditional foreign cultural activities, but in the view of many practitioners cultural relations as a wider concept now also include new priorities, such as the promotion of human rights and the spread of democratic values, notions such as good governance, and the role of the media in civil society. As Mette Lending argues, the new emphasis on public diplomacy confirms the fact that the familiar divide between cultural and information activities is being eradicated:

> cultural exchange is not only 'art' and 'culture' but also communi-cating a country's thinking, research, journalism and national debate. In this perspective, the traditional areas of cultural exchange become part of a new type of international communication and the growth of 'public diplomacy' becomes a reaction to the close connec-tion between cultural, press and information activities, as a result of new social, economic and political realities.[39]

Modern cultural relations as a wider concept result in a measure of overlap with the work of diplomats, particularly those practising public diplomacy. This gradual convergence between public diplomacy and cultural relations blurs traditional distinctions and meets opposition. Cultural relations' enthusiasts may fear that the new public diplomacy is encroaching upon their field, whereas traditional public diplomacy practitioners may feel that the practice of influencing foreign publics is being diluted by new practices. Both will have to come to terms with current transformations in diplomatic practice and transnational rela-tions. The new public diplomacy is no longer confined to messaging, promotion campaigns, or even direct governmental contacts with foreign publics serving foreign policy purposes. It is also about building relation-ships with civil society actors in other countries and about facilitating networks between non-governmental parties at home and abroad. Tomorrow's diplomats will become increasingly familiar with this kind of work, and in order to do it much better they will increasingly have to piggyback on non-governmental initiatives, collaborate with non-official agents and benefit from local expertise inside and outside the embassy.

Cultural institutes prefer to keep the term 'cultural relations' for their own activities, serving the national interest indirectly by means of trust-building abroad. Cultural relations are in this view distinct from (public) diplomacy, in the sense that they represent the non-governmental voice in transnational relations. As Martin Rose and Nick Wadham-Smith write, diplomacy is 'not primarily about building trust, but about achieving specific, policy-driven transactional objectives. Trust is often a by-product of diplomacy, but tends to be in the shorter rather than the longer term. Nations don't have permanent friends, as Palmerston put it: they only have permanent interests'. Rose and Wadham-Smith's concern is that if their work becomes indistinguishable from public diplomacy, cultural relations' practitioners will not be trusted: 'they risk being seen as a "front" for political interests. This damages not only our ability to do cultural relations, but also our ability to do public diplomacy'.[40] Arguably, however, diplomacy takes place in an international environment that can no longer be described as exclusively state-centric, and diplomats have a stake in different forms of transnational relations. Tomorrow's public diplomacy practitioners will be operators in complex transnational networks, and trust-building and the facilitation of cross-border civil society links is therefore part of their core business. In his own day Palmerston may have been right in saying that nations did not have permanent friends, but the art of diplomacy now also involves getting other people on one's side. In order to safeguard their interests in a globalized world, countries need 'permanent friends' in other nations. Foreign ministries are therefore unlikely to restrict their public diplomacy to traditional, policy-oriented and increasingly ineffective one-way communication with foreign publics. Whatever the consequences, the overlap between public diplomacy and postmodern cultural relations is bound to grow, unless cultural relations' practitioners return to a more limited conception of their work.

Conclusion: diplomacy and the ordinary individual

Diplomacy is the management of change, and for many centuries the institution of diplomacy has indeed succeeded in adapting to multiple changes in an expanding international society. Diplomatic practice today not only deals with transformations in the relations between states, but progressively it also needs to take into account the changing fabric of transnational relations. For diplomats the host countries' civil society matters in a way that was inconceivable only a generation ago. The ordinary individual is increasingly visible in the practice of diplomacy, particularly in the areas of public diplomacy and consular relations. As to the latter, looking after one's own citizen-consumers abroad has become a major growth sector for foreign ministries, and there is probably no area of diplomatic work that has more potential to affect the foreign ministry's reputation at home. Public diplomacy is another such growth sector and anything but an ephemeral phenomenon. There are, of course, vast areas of diplomatic work and plenty of bilateral relationships where contacts with the public abroad have no priority, but the number of countries exploring public diplomacy's potential will continue to grow. It is probably no exaggeration to suggest that this development is an indication of the fact that the evolution of diplomacy has reached a new stage. Those who see public diplomacy as postmodern propaganda or as lip-service to the latest fashion in the conduct of international relations therefore miss a fundamental point.

People have always mattered to diplomats, but this point has taken on a new meaning. The democratization of access to information has turned citizens into independent observers as well as assertive participants in international politics, and the new agenda of diplomacy has only added to the leverage of loosely organized groups of individuals. Issues at the grass roots of civil society have become the bread and butter of diplomacy at the highest levels. Foreign ministries increasingly take into account the concerns of ordinary people – and they have good reasons for doing so. The explosive growth of non-state actors in the past decade, the growing influence of transnational protest movements and the meteoric rise of the new media have restricted official diplomacy's freedom of manoeuvre. Non-official players have turned out to be extremely agile and capable of mobilizing support at a speed that is daunting for rather more unwieldy foreign policy bureaucracies. The wider public turns out to be an even harder target for diplomats. Foreign publics do not tend to follow agreed rules, nor do they usually have clearly articulated aims. Many diplomats are baffled by the elusiveness and apparent unpredictability of public groups in foreign civil societies, which makes the challenge of public diplomacy a real one.

Working with 'ordinary people' is a formidable challenge for diplomatic practitioners who feel more comfortable operating within their own professional circle. Traditional diplomatic culture is slowly eroding and sits rather uneasily with the demands of public diplomacy. Although there are many success stories that can be told, broadly speaking diplomatic attitudes and habits – steeped in many centuries of tradition – are still more peer-oriented than is desirable for foreign ministries with ambitions in the field of public diplomacy. The dominant perspective in diplomatic services is hardly capable of conceiving of the individual in any other than a passive role. For these and other reasons, the rise of soft power in international relations is testing diplomats' flexibility to the full. Public diplomacy cannot be practised successfully without accepting that the game that nations play has fundamentally changed, and it implies a rather more important role for the twenty-first century ambassador than is sometimes suggested. In recent decades diplomatic services have gone through other difficult transitions, with states adapting to the growing complexity of multilateral decision-making and learning to live with the rise of multiple actors in international affairs, but dealing with foreign publics may prove a harder nut to crack. Engaging with foreign societies requires a totally different mindset. Among other things it supposes the taking of calculated risks, abandoning the illusion of near-complete control over one's own initiatives, and it is based on outreach techniques that were unknown to previous generations of practitioners. Newcomers to the world's diplomatic services therefore deserve good preparation for the changed realities of their profession and students of diplomacy would benefit from new thinking about the conduct of international relations.

Notes

1. Michael Kunczik, 'Transnational Public Relations by Foreign Governments', Sriramesh, Krishnamurthy and Dejan Vercic (eds), *The Global Public Relations Handbook: Theory, Research and Practice* (Mahwah NJ and London: Lawrence Erlbaum Associates, 2003), pp. 399–405. On France and nation-branding, see the chapter in this book by Wally Olins.
2. On nation-branding, see Wally Olins' chapter in this book and *Wally Olins On Brand* (London: Thames & Hudson, 2003).
3. See, for instance, Joseph S. Nye, 'Soft Power', *Foreign Policy*, no. 80, autumn 1990; Joseph S. Nye and William A. Owens, 'America's Information Edge', *Foreign Affairs*, vol. 75, no. 2, March/April 1996; and, for a recent elaboration of this concept, see Joseph S. Nye, *Soft Power: The Means to Success in World Politics* (New York: Public Affairs, 2004).
4. E. H. Carr, *The Twenty Years' Crisis 1919–1939: An Introduction to the Study of International Relations* (Basingstoke: Macmillan, 1983 (first edn 1939)), pp. 132 and 141.
5. Nye, *Soft Power*, pp. 31 and 32.
6. Hans N. Tuch, *Communicating With the World: US Public Diplomacy Overseas* (New York: St Martin's Press 1990); and Wilson P. Dizard, *Inventing Public Diplomacy: The Story of the US Information Agency* (Boulder CO and London: Lynne Rienner, 2004).
7. Arno J. Mayer, *Political Origins of the New Diplomacy 1917–1918* (New York: Vintage Books, 1970).
8. Jan Melissen (ed.), *Innovation in Diplomatic Practice* (Basingstoke: Macmillan, 1999), pp. xvi–xvii.
9. Robert Cooper, *The Breaking of Nations: Order and Chaos in the Twenty-First Century* (London: Atlantic Books, 2003), p. 76.
10. Shaun Riordan, *The New Diplomacy* (London: Polity, 2003), especially ch. 9.

11. *The Cato Handbook for Congress* (Washington DC: The Cato Institute, 1994), p. 308.
12. See, for instance, reports on public diplomacy by the Council on Foreign Relations, the Brookings Institution, the United States Institute of Peace, the Center for Security and International Studies, the Institute for the Study of Diplomacy, and also various US Congressional reports.
13. On US citizen diplomacy, see Sherry Mueller, 'The Power of Citizen Diplomacy', *Foreign Service Journal*, March 2002, pp. 23–9.
14. Simon Anholt, *Brand New Justice: How Branding Places and Products Can Help the Developing World* (Amsterdam: Butterworth Heinemann, 2005).
15. Jamie Frederic Metzl, 'Popular Diplomacy', *Daedalus*, vol. 128, no. 2, spring 1999, pp. 177–9.
16. Allan Gottlieb, *'I'll be with You in a Minute, Mr Ambassador': The Education of a Canadian Diplomat in Washington* (Toronto: Toronto University Press, 1991) p. vii.
17. Ambassador K. T. Paschke, *Report on the Special Inspection of 14 German Embassies in the Countries of the European Union* (Berlin: Auswärtiges Amt, 2002).
18. Hans Tuch, *Communicating With the World: US Public Diplomacy Overseas* (New York: St Martin's Press, 1990), p. 3.
19. On countries and companies 'swapping places', see Wally Olins, *Trading Identities: Why Countries and Companies are Taking on Each Others' Roles* (London: Foreign Policy Centre, 1999).
20. See for instance Evan H. Potter, *Canada and the New Public Diplomacy*, Clingendael Discussion Papers in Diplomacy, no. 81 (The Hague: Netherlands Institute of International Relations 'Clingendael', 2002); and interviews with foreign diplomats.
21. For an interesting case study, see Michael Merlingen and Zenet Mujic, 'Public Diplomacy and the OSCE in the Age of Post-International Politics: The Case of the Field Mission in Croatia', *Security Dialogue*, vol. 34, no. 3, pp. 269–83.
22. On competitive and collaborative diplomacy, see Mark Leonard with Catherine Stead and Conrad Smewing, *Public Diplomacy* (London: Foreign Policy Centre, 2002), pp. 22–30.
23. Michael McClellan, 'Public Diplomacy in the Context of Traditional Diplomacy', in Gerhard Reiweger (ed.), *Public Diplomacy*, Favorita Papers, 01/2004 (Vienna: *Diplomatische Akademie*, 2004), pp. 23 and 24.
24. Mark Leonard, 'Diplomacy by Other Means', *Foreign Policy*, September/October 2002, p. 56.
25. David Welch, 'Powers of Persuasion', *History Today*, 49, August 1999, pp. 24–6.
26. As two lexicographers suggest, public diplomacy is essentially 'a late-twentieth-century form of propaganda conducted by diplomats'; G. R. Berridge and Alan James, *A Dictionary of Diplomacy* (Basingstoke: Palgrave, 2001), p. 197.
27. Richard Holbrooke, 'Get The Message Out', *Washington Post*, 28 October 2001.
28. Nicholas J. Cull, David Culbert and David Welch, *Propaganda and Mass Persuasion: A Historical Encyclopedia, 1500 to the Present* (Oxford and Santa Barbara CA: ABC-Clio, 2003), pp. xv–xxi.

29. Leonard, Stead and Smewing, *Public Diplomacy*, pp. 46–53; Nye, *Soft Power*, p. 107.
30. E. H. Henderson, 'Toward a Definition of Propaganda', *Journal of Social Psychology*, vol. 18, 1943 p. 83, emphasis added.
31. I owe this quotation to Martin Rose from Counterpoint, the cultural relations think tank of the British Council.
32. Jay Black, 'Semantics and Ethics of Propaganda', *Journal of Mass Media Ethics*, vol. 16, nos. 2 and 3, 1986, pp. 133 and 135.
33. Jan Melissen, 'Where is Place Branding Heading', *Place Branding*, vol. 1, no. 1, 2004, pp. 26–7.
34. Simon Anholt, 'Theory and Practice of Place Branding', *Public Diplomacy and the Media: Diplomatic Academy Proceedings*, vol. 6, no. 1 (Zagreb: Diplomatic Academy of the Republic of Croatia, 2004), p. 15.
35. Simon Anholt, 'Introduction', *Journal of Brand Management*, special issue on 'Country as a Brand', vol. 9, nos. 4–5, 2002.
36. Jan Melissen, 'Publieksdiplomatie: een goede tandem met branding', in H. H. Duijvestijn *et al.*, *Branding NL: Nederland als merk* (Den Haag: Stichting Maatschappij en Onderneming, 2004), pp. 48–9.
37. Benno H. Signitzer and Timothy Coombs, 'Public Relations and Public Diplomacy: Conceptual Divergences', *Public Relations Review*, vol. 18, no. 2, summer 1992, pp. 139–40.
38. Laurie J. Wilson, 'Strategic Cooperative Communities: A Synthesis of Strategic, Issue-Management, and Relationship-Building Approaches in Public Relations', in Hugh M. Culbertson and Ni Chen (eds), *International Public Relations: A Comparative Analysis* (Mahwah NJ: Lawrence Erlbaum, 1996), p. 78.
39. Mette Lending, *Change and Renewal: Norwegian Foreign Cultural Policy 2001–2005* (Oslo: Royal Norwegian Ministry of Foreign Affairs, 2000), pp. 13–14.
40. Martin Rose and Nick Wadham-Smith, *Mutuality, Trust and Cultural Relations* (London: The British Council, 2004), pp. 34–5.

2
Rethinking the 'New' Public Diplomacy
Brian Hocking

Introduction

Events since 11 September 2001 have encouraged renewed debate on a dimension of diplomacy that, in varying forms, has a considerable pedigree. But, as with earlier debates concerning what is 'old' and 'new' in the practice of diplomacy, there is a danger here in failing to set the key issues within the framework of broader changes in world politics. More precisely, in the context of the theme of this book, current preoccupations with implementing public diplomacy strategies and developing new mechanisms within foreign ministries for overseeing them lead to the danger of misunderstanding the significance of public diplomacy and confusing its role as a mode of exercising power with the changing environments in which power is projected.

Moreover, this may help to explain the problems that governments confront in utilizing public diplomacy – particularly in environments marked by high levels of intercultural tension and conflict, such as those in which we now find ourselves. This chapter suggests that the current debate about state-based public diplomacy, while by no means unimportant, has to be seen in the context of more profound trends underpinning the changing nature of diplomacy as an activity and the environment of world politics in which it operates. Indeed, public diplomacy may be more important than we realize, but not always in the ways sometimes assumed. Attempting to penetrate the multifaceted nature of public diplomacy requires us first to unpick the threads of which it is composed. Although clearly related, these provide differing perspectives on the goals and assumptions underpinning its deployment. Second, it is suggested that we need to re-examine 'soft power' argumentation with which much of the public diplomacy debate has become entwined. Finally, the place of public diplomacy in two contrasting models of diplomacy will be distinguished: on the one hand, a state-centred, hierarchical model in which renewed emphasis is given to public diplomacy within the traditional image of intergovernmental relations; and, on the other, a 'network' model of diplomacy. The suggestion here is that there may be tension between the assumptions on which the more traditional approaches to public diplomacy are constructed and the requirements of reconstituted public diplomacy strategies that a network approach demands.

Unpicking the threads of public diplomacy

One of the problems in evaluating the place of public diplomacy within the changing frameworks of world politics is that it subsumes a number of themes that often suggest differing – if not conflicting – aims and objectives. Recognizing this helps to explain both the roots of public diplomacy strategies and why the expectations of their practitioners may well be frustrated. The proposition that there is – or should be – a link between the public and the practice of diplomacy embraces distinctive elements. On the one hand, there is the thread of democratic accountability, which Harold Nicholson identified as one of the elements of the changing international environment following the Great War, and which he feared would compromise the exercise of effective diplomacy.[1] However, a normative belief in 'open diplomacy', whose precise definition was generally obscure, certainly did not imply an active role on the part of the 'public', however that might be defined. Veteran practitioners such as Canning – who recognized the potency of what he referred to as 'the fatal artillery of public excitation' – Metternich and Talleyrand were only too aware of the power of public opinion in the maelstrom of European politics in the wake of the French Revolution and sought to manipulate foreign opinion through use of the press.[2] A century and a half later, the impulse towards democratic accountability had evolved into belief in the possibility of, or necessity for, direct public involvement in diplomacy, as represented by advocates of 'citizenship summitry' in what was to prove the closing phases of the Cold War. According to one proponent of this approach, governments as complex entities respond to many impulses but are most likely to respond to perceptions of external threats, whereas the main source of peaceful initiatives are 'ordinary citizens and voluntary associations'.[3]

The second thread is much more recent and weaves together some of the assumptions underpinning the legacy of open diplomacy with those associated with globalization argumentation: the intensification of social networks that transcend traditional boundaries, both geographical and those separating foreign and domestic policy agendas; the expansion of social relations from those represented by financial markets to those of terrorist groups; the compression of time and space and the impact that each of these processes has on the way in which people view their place in local and global environments.

These are linked together with a third thread, often subsumed within the globalization debate but of particular significance in the evolution of diplomacy, namely the technological developments implicit in such terms as 'cyber-diplomacy', linking the impact of innovations in communications and information technology (CIT) to foreign policy and diplomacy.[4] Potter argues that the primary force underpinning globalization processes is the proliferation of linkages that developments in fibre optics, cable and satellite communications affords and that these carry with them profound questions for the future of diplomacy that are essentially 'about how states exchange, seek and target information'.[5]

All of these developments offer opportunity for the redefinition of public diplomacy in terms of an active role for publics rather than as passive objects of government foreign policy strategies. The growth of civil society and global social movements is changing the character of multilateral diplomacy, as its intergovernmental credentials are redefined in the light of growing participation by non-governmental organizations.[6] Utilization of new technologies – particularly the internet – by NGOs in contexts such as the 1999 World Trade Organization (WTO) summit in Seattle and the failed negotiations on the Multilateral Agreement on Investment appear to offer groups and individuals a scope for direct action in international affairs that was not hitherto available.

The impact of the media, despite its close association with developments in CIT, has come to assume a very significant fourth thread in the public diplomacy debate that deserves separate treatment. The proposition that electronic media is no longer a tool of governments' public diplomacy strategies but is now itself capable of determining foreign policy, especially in situations of dramatic humanitarian crisis, is enshrined in the much-debated 'CNN effect'. This is regarded as impacting on the policy-maker–public link by generating pressure on the former to respond to crisis events, and to do so in an often unplanned and incoherent fashion.[7] In fact, as a number of studies have argued, the reality is much more complex. Whereas the media is able to act both as agenda-setter in international politics and also gatekeeper, determining and regulating flows of information to publics, in practice it plays a variety of roles, some of which may well be supportive of the goals of official diplomacy. Moreover, technological developments such as the miniaturization of IT equipment are producing what Livingston has termed a 'post-CNN' effect, as an unprecedented degree of global transparency in public affairs, enabling individuals and groups to acquire information directly, makes the quest for diplomatic confidentiality during negotiations ever harder to maintain.[8]

A fifth thread in the public diplomacy tapestry has become the subject of increasing debate since the mid-1990s, that is the preoccupation with image in international politics and the possibility of states 'rebranding' themselves in the global marketplace. Of course, the significance of image is not a new phenomenon in international politics. Just as Louis XIV was aware of the significance of Versailles in an era when prestige was an essential component of power, so Napoleon was conscious of the impact of the portraits of him painted by his favourite artist, Jean-Louis David. Image, in this sense, has a place on the realist agenda, as John Hertz noted in the early 1980s when he suggested that half of power politics consists of image-making.[9] However, the concern with image and branding has moved on to reflect newer preoccupations, reflecting the fact that the direction of image management has shifted from policy elites to a broader, mass market. Hence Mark Leonard's observation that 'public diplomacy is based on the premise that the image and reputation of a country are public goods which can create either an enabling or a disabling environment for individual transactions'.[10] This has come about, it is argued, because of fundamental changes in the nature of international politics as power politics are reconfigured in an era of globalization.[11] On the one hand, in a situation where economic power has enhanced significance, and the concepts of the 'trading state'[12] and the 'competition state'[13] replace that based on the primacy of military security, image determines the capacity to promote exports, attract foreign investment and promote a country as a desirable tourist destination.[14]

Looked at another way, concerns with a country's image might be interpreted as a defensive reaction to globalization whereby governments, pressured by internal and external forces, seek to redefine their identity and role in an environment that challenges both.[15] In terms of goals, image management aims to fulfil a range of objectives, from simply making target audiences more familiar with a country (and the particular brand being peddled) to influencing the actions of others – potential foreign investors, for example. But unlike one of the original functions of commercial branding, namely a guarantee of product quality, country branding reflects the belief that a flood of global communications is making it harder for national communities to maintain a voice and identity amid a welter of competing messages.

Taken together, these pieces in the public diplomacy jigsaw produce a more intricate picture than is apparent at first sight – and certainly one more complex than the assumptions on which some governments' official public diplomacy efforts appear to rest. Ideas now underpinning contemporary analyses of public diplomacy rest on differing perceptions of what constitutes the 'public' and where it fits in diplomatic practice. Thus one approach defines the public as a target of influence generating pressures on foreign governments through their own domestic constituencies, or even acting as an indirect tool in influencing opinion at home. A variant on this perspective portrays the public as a mode of influence on foreign policy-makers generated by media manipulation of public opinion.

In contrast, public diplomacy is increasingly defined as diplomacy *by* rather than *of* publics. Here, individuals and groups, empowered by the resources provided by the CIT revolution – and particularly the internet – are direct participants in the shaping of international policy and, through an emergent global civil society, may operate through or independently of national governments.

A further variant sees the public as neither a target nor a generator of diplomatic activity but as a *consumer* of diplomacy, a reflection of global mobility and the twin forces of tourism and terrorism. The growth of mass tourism has vastly increased the extent to which people now come face to face with diplomats and has enhanced the significance of consular services, for long regarded as inferior elements in the panoply of diplomatic representation. How governments deal with their citizens abroad has become a sensitive issue, not least in the popular press. A recent report on the Finnish Foreign Service makes the point that the dramatic growth of overseas travel is making many more Finns 'potential customers for the services of the MFA' and that consular matters dealt with by the Finnish Embassy in London have doubled in recent years.[16] Taking this point outside the realm of diplomacy by states, Bruter suggests that the EU Commission's delegations have begun to carve out a diplomatic niche for themselves in developing a consumer-oriented diplomatic strategy that is distinctive from that of the EU member state missions.[17]

More dramatically, terrorism has tested these same qualities, sometimes to breaking point. As citizens find themselves caught up in acts of terrorist violence or taken hostage in the promotion of some political objective, so the demands placed by them on foreign ministries and their diplomatic networks grows. The reaction of the UK diplomatic service to criticisms of its handling of events in the wake of the Bali bombings in 2002 is a case in point, stinging the Foreign and Commonwealth Office into a major review of its capacity to respond to the demands of such incidents.

Public diplomacy and power: hard, soft and sticky

In the light of these distinctive yet interlinked facets of public diplomacy, it is not surprising that we are confronted with apparently contradictory interpretations of its significance and the techniques deemed appropriate to the implementation of public diplomacy strategies. At root, these reflect the complexities of contemporary statecraft ('actorcraft' is a more appropriate term for a mixed actor milieu) and the modalities of power relevant to the pursuit of policy goals. Few analysts have done more to tease apart these complexities – albeit from a US perspective – than Nye.[18] Indeed, his contrast between the utility of hard and soft power has become a key principle in the current debate on the significance of public diplomacy. Arguments relating to the limitations of hard, or military, power and the advantages that can accrue from the use of 'attractive' power rooted in factors such as culture, ideals and values, which, it is argued, encourages others to want what you want, are basic assumptions among advocates of an enhanced role for public diplomacy. Added to these, argues Mead, is what he terms 'sticky' power or the power of economic attraction, which once imbibed becomes addictive and hard to escape from.[19] Over time, both Britain and the US have been able to deploy this variant of power play. After 1945, the US built its sticky power on the pillars of free trade and the Bretton Woods institutions, together with the reality that the economic well-being of other countries was linked to that of the US.

Several related issues flow from these dimensions of power that help us to appreciate better some of the problems that surround both the concept and the deployment of public diplomacy. First is the linkage between the three modalities. As was observed during an Aspen Institute round table, 'soft power supports the exercise of military and hard economic powers, and arrogant or unjust use of hard power can erode soft power'.[20] Moreover, it should come as no surprise to policy-makers that the emphasis on 'homeland' security in the post-11 September security agenda should result in policies diametrically opposed to the projection of soft power. The US has discovered this in, for example, the sudden and significant decline in the numbers of overseas students enrolling in its universities in the wake of increasingly restrictive visa policies.[21] The relationship between soft power and Mead's variant of sticky power is clearly evident. Economic power is partly configured from the appeal and exportability of economic principles, exemplified in the doctrine termed the 'Washington Consensus' that was developed in the early 1990s as a model for developing countries. But the attractiveness of this model is being challenged by another: the 'Beijing Consensus', which appears to be more relevant to their needs, 'attracting adherents at almost the same speed the US model is repelling them.[22] This, it is argued, is enabling China to become a far more successful deployer of soft power than the US, as other countries seek to embrace it as a political partner.[23]

Second, contrary to the impression that some recent writings have given, public diplomacy does not in itself constitute a new paradigm of international politics, in the sense that it replaces earlier and older patterns. More specifically, it is not the case that public diplomacy is itself uniquely the expression of soft power. Rather, there is a public diplomacy of hard, sticky as well as soft power and this helps us to recognize why it is that application of public diplomacy techniques is often frustrated. Not least, it goes a long way towards explaining why soft power itself is the cause of misunderstanding as to how the dynamics of world politics operate. As Niall Ferguson has pointed out, one problem with soft power is that it is soft![24] Despite (or perhaps because of) the cacophony of messages surrounding them, people are able on the one hand to relate the actions of governments and other actors to the messages that public diplomacy strategies seek to project, while on the other hand dissociating these messages from their own actions. Thus they may be happy to carry anti-Starbucks placards in one hand and a Coke bottle in the other. But of greater significance to US foreign policy managers, they may adopt aspects of American culture while resisting global policies emanating from Washington. This phenomenon, suggests Ferguson, is rooted in historical precedent: '...it was precisely from the most Anglicized parts of the British Empire that nationalist movements sprang'.[25] While still arguing the significance of soft power, Nye in his later writings has acknowledged this as a problem for the United States. There is a link between the successful deployment of hard or coercive power and soft power, and if the present US addiction to unilateralism is pursued in an overbearing and insensitive fashion, then soft power will not be much help to it.[26] Realization of this has stimulated concern among American business leaders that anti-US sentiment following events in Iraq is threatening their interests. Hence the creation of Business for Diplomatic Action, a non-profit, private-sector organization whose aim is to promote the recognition among business leaders of the dangers that anti-Americanism presents and to devise strategies to counter it.[27]

All this helps to illuminate one of the logical inconsistencies in soft power/public diplomacy argumentation: namely, why public diplomacy should be such a major preoccupation if the underlying rationale of the 'politics of attraction' really works. If people want to do what you want them to do through cultural affinity, why expend so much energy on public diplomacy? The answer lies partly, of course, in the fact that few actors possess soft power in the form presented by Nye in the US context. Indeed, it is precisely the lack of soft power of hegemonic proportions that energizes the public diplomacy strategies of many governments.

But additionally, there are a range of public diplomacies in circulation, some state-centred and reflecting the desire of governments to project and 'sell' their policies together with the fact that states are no more unitary actors in this dimension of their activities than in others. However, a potential multiplicity of government-generated messages is reinforced by the activities of non-state actors for whom, as suggested later, public diplomacy strategies are central to their identities and a major component of their capacity as actors.

Public diplomacy: hierarchies and networks

This latter point greatly reinforces the dilemmas confronting governmental policy-makers who are increasingly faced with skilled public diplomacy practitioners outside the domain of the state and its agencies. The reality is that there are in a sense 'two worlds' of public diplomacy that intersect, overlap, collide and cooperate in a variety of contexts. On the one hand we have a traditional, 'hierarchical' image of diplomatic systems, and, on the other, what has come to be termed a 'network' model. As indicated above, both rest to a considerable degree on arguments about the significance of soft power. But the two models appear to carry with them very different implications for understanding soft power and its relationship to public diplomacy.

Looking at the first (the hierarchical) model, we are presented with an image of diplomacy that stresses the centrality of intergovernmental relations, in which the foreign ministry and the national diplomatic system over which it presides act as gatekeepers, monitoring interactions between domestic and international policy environments and funnelling information between them. To be sure, this national diplomatic system has been required to adapt to pressures from within states and society – so, for example, the conduct of diplomacy is diffused more widely throughout bureaucratic systems – and from a rapidly changing external environment. But the emphasis tends to be on top-down processes and this is reflected in approaches to public diplomacy, particularly those reflected in post-11 September 2001 writings, especially those coming out of the United States.

Paying homage to the growing significance of soft power, the advocates of enhanced public diplomacy view it in terms of top-down information flows. Having been accused of ignoring its significance by several reports on US diplomacy, such as that produced by the Center for Strategic and International Studies (CSIS) in the late 1990s, this is suddenly forced to the centre of the diplomatic agenda.[28] However, it embraces a much more refined approach, which accords closely to what has been termed by Manheim as 'strategic public diplomacy' founded on theories of strategic political communication.[29] Claiming to be an 'applied transnational science of human behavior', this is much more sophisticated than simple images of influencing publics suggest – whether in the domestic or foreign arenas. Ultimately, it implies a high level of awareness of the varying attributes of human behaviour determined by culture and patterns of media usage as well as a deep knowledge of overseas news organizations and political systems. In other words, it demands the kind of holistic approach to building a 'public diplomacy chain' identified by Leonard and Alakeson.[30]

As already noted, this approach colours much of the post-11 September preoccupations with public diplomacy. In the US context and elsewhere, the central emphasis is now on the allocation of more resources to public diplomacy and better coordination – as exampled by the transfer of the US public diplomacy effort at reimaging the US from the State Department to the White House.[31] Beyond this, the agenda includes enhanced programmes of foreign exchanges, better public–private collaboration, the ability to respond to crisis situations flexibly and rapidly – the concept of 'surge capacity', being the soft power equivalent of the military 'rapid reaction force' – and more subtle programmes of influence that engage with, rather than target, foreign publics.[32] But despite its apparent sophistication and nods in the direction of changing patterns in world politics, all of this rests on established realist models of public diplomacy as propaganda, which is precisely the point that Manheim himself makes about strategic public diplomacy: 'It is, within the limits of available knowledge, the practice of propaganda in the earliest sense of the term, but enlightened by half a century of empirical research into human motivation and behaviour'.[33] Thus public diplomacy remains a technique for achieving policy objectives; it is not in itself a description of a new environment for world politics. As Hill has pointed out, the rationale of the soft power paradigm is that people are *targets* of foreign policy.[34]

While not denying the significance of these developments in official diplomatic strategies, the network model provides a fundamentally different picture of how diplomacy works in the twenty-first century and, thereby, the significance of its public (as well as its private) dimension. Underpinning the various definitions of networks is the proposition that they are now indispensable in managing increasingly complex policy environments through the promotion of communication and trust. In this sense, a policy network can be defined as 'a set of relatively stable relationships which are of a non-hierarchical and interdependent nature linking a variety of actors, who share common interests with regard to a policy and who exchange resources to pursue these shared interests acknowledging that cooperation is the best way to achieve common goals'.[35] This is the fundamental principle on which Reinecke's concept of global public policy networks rests.[36] Starting from the premise that globalization has highlighted the deficiencies of governments, both acting alone or in concert, in terms of their scope of activity, speed of response to global issues and range of contacts, he identifies the significance of the emergence of networks incorporating both public and private sector actors. It is not, he suggests, that multigovernmental institutions are irrelevant but that the more diverse membership and non-hierarchical qualities of public policy networks promote collaboration and learning and speed up the acquisition and processing of knowledge.[37] Furthermore, as the Aspen Institute report referred to earlier argues, centralized decision-makers are at a disadvantage when confronted by decentralized networks, in that the latter face fewer transactional barriers and are able to direct relevant information speedily to where it will have greatest effect.[38]

In contrast to assumptions of control exercised by the agents of government over international policy, the emphasis here is on the limitations confronted by all of the actors – both state and non-state – in achieving their policy objectives. Challenged by evermore complex, multifaceted agendas, there is a necessity to establish policy networks of varying scope and composition, which may, for example, bring together governmental actors, civil society organizations (CSOs) and business.

This has been described elsewhere as 'catalytic' diplomacy, a form of communication that acknowledges that a range of actors has the capacity to contribute resources to the management of complex problems, whether these assume the form of knowledge and financial resources or, less tangibly, the conferment of legitimacy on processes.[39] There are numerous examples of these network processes in a variety of areas. The example of the Ottawa Process relating to landmines is one of the most oft-cited examples. More recently, the establishment of the Kimberley Process dealing with the problem of the sale of illicit 'conflict' or 'blood' diamonds is a good example where an NGO – Global Witness – acted as a catalyst to a process in which national diplomats, especially British and American, and the EU Commission together with journalists and De Beers, the global diamond firm, each contributed to the establishment of a diamond regime.

In such situations, hierarchical flows of information are replaced by highly fissile, multidirectional flows. 'Secret' diplomacy is, of course, still in the frame, but the point is that it is both harder to maintain secrecy and less relevant to the management of many pressing issues. Frequently, the real challenge is managing 'openness' constructively. Nevertheless, there is an obvious tension between the concept of strategic public diplomacy as presented above and the realities implicit in the network image where the appropriate mode of public diplomacy goes way beyond traditional prescriptions, however much they are being modified to suit the needs of security in an era increasingly defined in terms of global terrorism. Not insignificantly, policy-makers and diplomats stand in increasing danger of getting their messages mixed. It is not merely a problem of coordinating the public diplomacy effort as the handbooks adjure, but one of recognizing that it is increasingly hard to segment the target audience when delivering the message. One oft-cited example is that of President Bush's 'axis of evil' speech, devised for domestic consumption but absorbed by foreign policy elites and publics. In short, public diplomacy may be needed increasingly, but it is much harder to deliver in a coherent and effective fashion.

Reflecting the permeable nature of public diplomacy in the networked diplomatic environment in which transnational coalitions range alongside governments in the quest for policy influence, this apparently quintessential manifestation of soft power is, in fact, becoming hard power – obviously not in the sense that it is *military* power, but because it is often used coercively in the pursuit of policy objectives. Moreover it is a resource that civil society is becoming extremely effective in deploying – not least because it is one of the few at its disposal. Nye notes this development as one of the several challenges that threatens to undermine American power. On the one hand, NGOs and other actors have the capacity to play the 'attractive power' game and to use the results to coerce governments.[40] Indeed, NGOs have become central players in the image stakes because their own 'brand' as forces for good, unencumbered by the trappings of sovereignty and untainted by realpolitik, appears to give them a moral edge over governments and big business. Manipulating the images of other actors, creating what might be termed 'image dissonance', based on the exploitation of differences between images that countries project of themselves and those that other actors can be persuaded to regard as more accurate, has indeed become a new 'great game'. The essence of the game lies not in the strength but in the vulnerabilities of soft power as manifested in the fragility and porosity of image. In other words, this is the diplomacy of the sovereignty-free actor. Two recent examples illustrate the point.

The first was the well-orchestrated campaign engineered by environmental NGOs and directed towards Canadian forest industry companies regarding their forest management practices. The manipulation of Canada's cherished reputation as a good international citizen and the substitution of the badge 'Brazil of the North' was telling and effective. The second was the campaign waged by a variety of groups against Swiss Banks concerning their dealings with Nazi Germany before and after the Second World War and their subsequent treatment of Holocaust victims and their descendants. Again, a considerable part of the success of this campaign turned on the deftly deployed strategy of questioning the image of probity enjoyed by the banks and the reputation for neutrality that is a key element in the Swiss self-image.

But as critics of the image of a beneficent global civil society have pointed out, the centrality of public diplomacy in world politics and the importance of establishing a voice in the marketplace of messages poses as many dilemmas for NGOs and other non-state actors as it does for states. One recent analysis of the relative success of local protest movements in finding a voice in this marketplace points to the importance of NGOs as key gatekeepers. Only those movements able to sell their cause to influential NGOs stand a chance of penetrating the global information flows.[41] And for NGOs, the centrality of image to their survival as organizations is a factor in determining who they choose to support.

Public diplomacy and diplomats

A central aspect of the public diplomacy debate turns on the impact that it is having on national diplomatic systems. This, of course, is subsumed within the broader debate regarding the present status and future role of professional diplomats and the environments in which they operate. Nevertheless, the two images of public diplomacy set out above suggest somewhat different pictures of its implications for the diplomat. As we have seen, the hierarchical image of public diplomacy creates new tasks. Current reports and foreign ministry working papers are replete with acknowledgements of the need to expand, refine and better coordinate the public diplomacy effort. But much of this rests on the demands that this places on the diplomatic infrastructure and is often used as a rationale for justifying the central role of the foreign ministry. This is linked to the well-recognized point that diplomats, by the nature of their work, lack effective domestic constituencies. Enhancing the public diplomacy role may help to lessen this problem, inasmuch as it stresses the services that diplomatic services can provide for people as distinct from policy elites. Thus the Paschke Report on Germany's bilateral representation within the European Union concludes that the most critical function of the diplomat in this context is that of public diplomacy.[42] And this is used as a key rationale for maintaining bilateral missions in the EU, countering arguments that question the relevance of bilateralism in a complex, multilayered policy environment.

The second – network – image of diplomacy does not deny the significance of the 'outreach' functions that are now deemed central to any self-respecting diplomat's duties, but takes them much further and in a direction that places new demands on diplomats but which also affirms their significance in the world of image management.[43] In part these result from the proliferation of information flows, which adherents of the CNN-effect arguments have taken to imply a diminishing role for professional diplomacy. Livingston, however, in arguing that the CNN effect is overstated, argues that the proliferation of global information places a premium on the capacity to sift valuable information from 'white noise'.[44] He concludes that ' . . . if the diplomatic community can maintain a reputation for unflinching honesty at a time when publics everywhere are inundated by yet more undigested data, the diplomatic community will actually improve its position', and warns of the dangers of being suborned by the lure of image management, which is likely to make the foreign ministry simply another voice in the global wilderness.[45] In short, this is a reaffirmation of the classic function of diplomacy adjusted to the demands of globalization. Cohen makes a not dissimilar point when arguing that diplomacy has an 'old-new' role in the contemporary global environment, namely to 'work on the boundary between cultures as an interpretive and conjunctive mechanism; to act as an agent of comprehension'.[46] However, rather than acting as gatekeepers, claiming to control linkages with public constituencies, the imperatives of diplomacy are defined increasingly as the capacity to contribute to policy networks. Consequently, the role of the diplomat in this context is redefined as that of facilitator in the creation and management of these networks.

Conclusion

In the current preoccupation with public diplomacy, stimulated by the post-11 September security environment, there is a real danger of confusing its varying manifestations. To a degree, this confusion reflects a misunderstanding of what soft power is – and how it relates to other modes of power. Public diplomacy in its state-based 'strategic' guise is a more sophisticated variant of a well-established idea – namely that 'publics' matter to governments as tools of national foreign policy. In this sense, public diplomacy is hardly a new paradigm of international politics but a strategy located within a hierarchical image of how those politics are configured and the information flows underpinning them. At the same time, however, governments are reworking their public diplomacy strategies in a changing milieu of world politics, within which access to modes of communication with publics around the world have become of prime importance to all categories of international actor. This is redrawing the environment in which much contemporary diplomacy is now conducted, bringing the diplomat's traditional skills to the management of complex policy networks. In short, public diplomacy is now part of the fabric of world politics wherein NGOs and other non-state actors seek to project their message in the pursuit of policy goals. Image creation and management is a key resource and one where non-state actors may have an advantage, helping to explain why the more traditional, hierarchical concept of strategic public diplomacy often fails to achieve its goals.

Notes

1. H. Nicolson, *The Evolution of Diplomatic Method* (London: Thornton Butterworth, 1939), p. 90.
2. K. Hamilton and R. Langhorne, *The Practice of Diplomacy: Its Evolution, Theory and Administration* (London: Routledge, 1995), pp. 124–7.
3. D. Carlson and D. Comstock, *Citizen Summitry: Keeping the Peace when it Matters Too Much to be Left to Politicians* (Los Angeles CA: Tarcher, 1986), p. 13.
4. E. Potter (ed.), *Cyber-Diplomacy: Managing Foreign Policy in the Twenty-First Century* (Montreal and Kingston: McGill-Queen's University Press, 2002).

5. Potter, *Cyber-Diplomacy*, p. 7.
6. See, for example, R. A. O'Brien, M. Goetz, J. A. Scholte and M. Williams, *Contesting Global Governance: Multilateral Economic Institutions and Global Social Movements* (Cambridge: Cambridge University Press, 2000).
7. E. Gilboa, 'Real-Time Diplomacy: Myth and Reality', in Potter, *Cyber-Diplomacy*, p. 85.
8. S. Livingston, 'The New Media and Transparency: What are the Consequences for Diplomacy?', in Potter, *Cyber-Diplomacy*, pp. 110–27.
9. J. Hertz, 'Political Realism Revisited, *International Studies Quarterly*, vol. 25, no. 2, June 1981, pp. 182–97.
10. M. Leonard, *Public Diplomacy* (London: Foreign Policy Centre, 2002), p. 9.
11. P. van Ham, 'Branding Territory: Inside the Wonderful Worlds of PR and IR Theory', *Millennium*, vol. 31, no. 2, 2002, pp. 249–69.
12. R. Rosecrance, *The Rise of the Trading State: Commerce and Conquest in the Modern World* (New York: Basic Books, 1986).
13. P. Cerny, 'Paradoxes of the Competition State: The Dynamics of Political Globalization' *Government and Opposition*, spring 1997, pp. 251–74.
14. W. Olins, *Trading Identities: Why Countries and Companies are Taking On Each Other's Roles* (London: Foreign Policy Centre, 1999), pp. 1–3.
15. C. Hill, 'Introduction', *The Image, the State and International Relations*, EPU Working Papers, no. 2001/2, London School of Economics and Political Science, p. 9.
16. Finnish Ministry for Foreign Affairs, *Challenges for the Finnish Foreign Service in the Twenty-First Century* (Helsinki: Ministry for Foreign Affairs, 2001), pp. 6 and 21.
17. M. Bruter, 'Diplomacy without a State: The External Delegations of the European Commission', *Journal of European Public Policy*, vol. 6, no. 2, 1999, pp. 183–205.
18. See J. Nye, *Bound to Lead: The Changing Nature of American Power* (New York: Basic Books, 1990); and J. Nye, *Soft Power: The Means to Success in World Politics* (New York: Perseus, 2004).
19. W. R. Mead, 'America's Sticky Power', *Foreign Policy*, March/April 2004, p. 48.
20. Comment made by Waring Partridge, in D. Bollier, *The Rise of Netpolitik: How the Internet is Changing International Politics and Diplomacy*, a report of the eleventh annual Aspen Institute round table on Information Technology (Washington DC: Aspen Institute, 2003), p. 17.
21. C. Grimes, 'US Universities Failed by Visa Process', *Financial Times*, 12 May 2004.
22. J. C. Cooper, 'China has Discovered its Own Economic Consensus', *Financial Times*, 8 May 2004.
23. R. McGregor, 'China's Success Inspires Envy and Awe', *Financial Times*, 28 May 2004.
24. N. Ferguson, 'Power', *Foreign Policy*, January/February, 2003, p. 21.
25. Ferguson, 'Power'.
26. J. Nye, 'America's Power: The New Rome Meets the New Barbarians', *The Economist*, 23 March 2002, p. 24; J. Nye, *The Paradox of American Power: Why the World's Only Superpower Can't Go It Alone* (Oxford: Oxford University Press, 2002).
27. K. Reinhard and T. Miller, 'A Business Problem', *International Herald Tribune*, 27 May 2004.

28. Center for Strategic and International Studies, *Reinventing Diplomacy in the Information Age* (Washington, DC: CSIS, 1998).
29. J. Manheim, *Strategic Public Diplomacy and American Foreign Policy: The Evolution of Influence* (New York and Oxford: Oxford University Press, 1994).
30. M. Leonard and V. Alakeson, *Going Public: Diplomacy for the Information Society* (London: Foreign Policy Centre, 2000), pp. 86–98.
31. M. Woollacott, '"Soft Power" Can Win the Battle for Hearts and Minds', *The Guardian*, 2 August 2002.
32. See C. Ross, 'Public Diplomacy Comes of Age', *Washington Quarterly*, vol. 5, no. 2, spring 2002; D. Hoffman, 'Beyond Public Diplomacy', *Foreign Affairs*, vol. 81, no. 2, March/April 2002; Council on Foreign Relations, *Finding America's Voice: A Strategy for Reinvigorating US Public Diplomacy*, report of an independent Task Force (New York: Council on Foreign Relations, 2003).
33. Manheim, *Strategic Public Diplomacy and American Foreign Policy*, p. 7.
34. C. Hill, *The Changing Politics of Foreign Policy* (Houndmills: Palgrave Macmillan, 2003), p. 279.
35. D. Stone, Networks, *Second-Track Diplomacy and Regional Cooperation: The Role of Southeast Asian Think Tanks*, paper presented to the 38th International Studies Convention, Toronto, March 1997.
36. W. Reinecke, *Global Public Policy: Governing without Government?* (Washington DC: Brookings, 1998); W. Reinecke, 'The Other World Wide Web: Global Public Policy Networks', *Foreign Policy*, vol. 117, 2000, pp. 44–57.
37. In a recent book, Anne-Marie Slaughter argues the case for a network approach to diplomacy but does so in the context of exclusively governmental networks. See A-M. Slaughter, *A New World Order* (Princeton NJ: Princeton University Press, 2004).
38. Bollier, *The Rise of Netpolitik*, p. 9.
39. B. Hocking, 'Catalytic Diplomacy: Beyond "Newness" and "Decline"', in J. Melissen (ed.), *Innovation in Diplomatic Practice* (London: Macmillan, 1999), pp. 21–42.
40. Nye, 'America's Power'.
41. C. Bob, 'Merchants of Morality', *Foreign Policy*, March/April 2002, pp. 36–45.
42. *Paschke Report: Report on the Special Inspection of 14 German Embassies in the Countries of the European Union*, Berlin, German Federal Foreign Ministry, September 2000.
43. Many diplomats have noted how the 'outreach' function has dramatically expanded. See, for example, K. Rana, *Inside Diplomacy* (New Delhi: Manas Publications, 2000).
44. Livingston, 'The New Media and Transparency', p. 122.
45. Livingston, 'The New Media and Transparency'.
46. R. Cohen, 'Reflections on the New Global Diplomacy', in J. Melissen (ed.), *Innovation in Diplomatic Practice* (Houndmills: Macmillan, 1999), p. 16.

Part II
Shifting Perspectives

3
Power, Public Diplomacy, and the *Pax Americana*

Peter van Ham

> The empire, one might say,
> is an engine that tows societies
> stalled in the past into contemporary
> time and history.[1]

Introduction: an American Empire by default?

An idea is roaming the world, the idea of an American Empire. Like Marx's spectre of revolution, the possibility of a *Pax Americana* is either welcomed, or looked at with great concern. Some states support the United States because they consider it a particularly benign, liberal power, whose values and policies they share. Others resent the US's power predominance, often violently. These states accuse the US of playing 'Globocop', engaged in a dangerous and risky game of global social engineering. The argument about the role of the United States in the world has seldom been more controversial than today, both within the US and outside. Since the US is the *primus inter pares* within the international community, and also considers itself more equal than others, the idea of 'empire' has again emerged as a metaphor and model. 'Empire' has quickly turned into the infamous 'e-word' of US foreign policy: hotly debated, but also often misread.

The US invasion of Iraq and the toppling of Saddam Hussein's regime in March 2003 have reinforced the image of US unilateralism driven by realpolitik and based on military superiority. Washington seems to follow Machiavelli's dictum that it is far better to be feared than to be loved, and better to compel than to attract. However, as history may indicate, empires are not based solely – or perhaps even mainly – on the exercise of military power. On the contrary, empires have relied on a broad range of tools, incentives, and policies to establish and maintain dominance, ranging from political persuasion and cultural influence, to coercion and force.[2] Most empires have sought domination rather than direct and full control within their territories and dependencies. And although military ('hard') power has often been instrumental in empire-building, the 'soft' power of legitimacy, credibility, cultural superiority, and related normative dominance has been essential in maintaining that rule. Arguably, both the British and the Soviet Empires fell into decline because they lost legitimacy among their own people. Within the British Empire, the idea of 'white superiority' was no longer deemed credible (as Mahatma Gandhi demonstrated), and the erosion of communist ideology led to its ultimate decay under Mikhail Gorbachev, who realized that no number of tanks could maintain Soviet control over the central European 'satellites'.

Imperial power is therefore based on a blend of military domination and the legitimacy offered by ideology, or religion. The US's emerging 'empire' follows a similar pattern. Especially today, policy-makers in Washington sell the idea of US leadership-cum-hegemony as a godsend and a guarantee for democracy, liberty and prosperity, not just for the US but also for the world as a whole. US President George W. Bush argued in November 2003 that '[l]iberty is both the plan of Heaven for humanity, and the best hope for progress here on Earth ... It is no accident that the rise of so many democracies took place in a time when the world's most influential nation was itself a democracy'.[3] This would imply that US 'imperialism' is not just to be considered altruistic, but also inevitable. The United States's 'empire' is not a quest for oil, but for freedom, and those who oppose US foreign policy are either 'evil' or misinformed, since they try to halt time's unidirectional arrow of progress.

This chapter examines two issues. First, what are the normative assumptions on which the dominant discourse of the emerging *Pax Americana* is based? What constitutes the normative (or ideological) basis of US imperialist heritage? It also asks how the US's soft power has been instrumentalized for the cause of liberal imperialism since the strategic revolution of '9/11.'

Second, this chapter examines the role of public diplomacy in the debate about the US's nascent empire. Public diplomacy is widely seen as an essential tool to win over the 'hearts and minds' of foreign audiences, and to convince them that their values, goals and desires are similar to those of the US. Since '9/11', the Bush administration has therefore initiated a flurry of initiatives to rebrand the US from a 'global bully' to a 'compassionate hegemon'. In an effort to touch ordinary citizens of Muslim countries (and especially the so-called 'Arab street'), public diplomacy is considered crucial to exercise the US's ample soft power assets. The argument is that 'millions of ordinary people...have greatly distorted, but carefully cultivated images of [the US] – images so negative, so weird, so hostile that a young generation of terrorists is being created'.[4] US policy towards the Muslim world is based on the assumption that these negative ideas should be neutralized, and, in the end, changed, by a focused effort of public diplomacy. This approach has quickly become a central plank of the United States's 'war on terror'. Washington now realizes that you cannot kill ideas with bombs, however precision-guided they may be.

But how can soft power be exercised as public diplomacy? And how important is public diplomacy to establish, or maintain, the liberal empire, which is also known as *Pax Americana*?

Soft power, hard power, and the 'indispensable nation'

Empire is obviously a complex phenomenon informed by power, economic interests, as well as cultural and religious ideas. The imperative of 'progress' has been especially forceful. Rudyard Kipling's famous poem about what he called 'the white man's burden', illustrates this *mission civilisatrice*. In his poem, Kipling referred to the responsibilities of empire, directing them at the United States's decision to go to war with Spain in 1898.[5] Although the US has been instrumental in reducing the British, Dutch, and other imperial systems to the modest size that they are today, Washington has always justified its own foreign interventions in the classical imperial way, namely as a force for good. As Max Boot writes in *The Savage Wars of Peace*, the United States has been involved in the internal affairs of other countries since 1805 (so well before Kipling's famed warning). This multitude of often small interventions – which began with Jefferson's expedition against the Barbary Pirates, and was followed by small, imperial wars from the Philippines to Russia – have played an essential role in establishing the United States as a world power.[6]

Ideologically, these many wars have (among others) been justified by the so-called 'Roosevelt Corollary' to the US's Monroe Doctrine, which stated that 'chronic wrongdoing, or an impotence which results in a general loosening of the ties of civilized society, may...ultimately require intervention by some civilized nation'.[7] This is the historical backdrop of the 'Bush doctrine' of pre-emptive (military) action, which was put forward in the US National Security Strategy of 2002. It illustrates that the US invasion-cum-liberation of Iraq has a long pedigree.

Today, however, no US policy-maker would go on record arguing that Washington has explicit imperial ambitions. In January 2004, Vice-President Dick Cheney claimed that the US is no empire, since '[i]f we were an empire, we would currently preside over a much greater piece of the Earth's surface than we do. That's not the way we operate'.[8] But as mentioned earlier, US history obviously has more imperialist overtones than the United States's self-image would like to accept. The US's role in Europe during the Cold War has also been hotly debated: in the 1980s Geir Lundestad labelled the US-controlled 'West' an 'empire by invitation';[9] whereas Paul Kennedy saw the US in decline due to 'imperial overstretch'.[10] One could therefore call the US an 'empire in denial', or (for want of a better name) a 'liberal empire'.

Clearly, the age of formal empire is dead. Direct physical control of territories outside one's own, except as a temporary expedient in response to crisis (as in Afghanistan and Iraq), is nearly always a burden, rather than an asset. It might therefore be possible to recognize the US and its sphere of influence as an empire, but deny that it is imperialist. Nevertheless, the naked facts must be recognized: the US is the only nation policing the world through five global military commands; maintains more than one million men and women under arms on four continents; deploys carrier battle groups on watch in every ocean; guarantees the survival of several countries, from Israel to South Korea; drives the wheels of global trade and commerce; and fills the hearts and minds of an entire planet with its dreams and desires. On top at that, Washington sets the global economic, political and security agenda. If not a formal empire, this certainly resembles a *Pax Americana*.

This implies that the contemporary international system is changing from an anarchical to a hierarchical structure, with the US firmly in charge. But like imperial powers of the past, this new US-led hierarchy is not only based on military power, but also by a new narrative structure. The key question is therefore which normative assumptions are at the basis of the discourse of an emerging *Pax Americana*? The US follows a dual-track policy, using both performative and discursive means. The performative side concerns the US's behaviour, more particularly the long tradition of interventionism that gives it the reputation and aura of *machismo* based on a 'can-do' mentality. By assuming responsibility as the global policeman, the US establishes itself as *primus inter pares*, as 'more equal than others', and as the *de facto* 'leader of the free world'. Moreover, the US tradition of (military) intervention sets it apart from its Western allies (such as the European Union).

But as the 'Roosevelt Corollary' indicates, US leaders in general consider these US interventions morally justified, and far from frivolous or self-interested. The accepted discourse on US intervention focuses on their legitimacy, derived from the understanding that US (military) actions guarantee international order. The US considers itself the 'lender of last resort' of law and order within the international system, providing the public good of security for all, even for critical free-riders. Former US Secretary of State Madeleine Albright therefore called the US the 'indispensable nation', the only state that has both the military might and political will to play the role of benign hegemon, offering stability, predictability and transparency. US military interventions and wars – be they fought in Korea in the 1950s, Vietnam in the 1970s or Iraq in the 1990s – are often put forward to confirm this critical role.

The United States's current 'war on terror' offers Washington maximum leeway for an invigorated campaign of liberal imperialism. President Bush has indicated that terrorists are everywhere and nowhere. Hence, the US's 'war on terror' 'will not end until every terrorist group of global reach has been found, stopped and defeated...From this day forward, any nation that continues to harbour or support terrorism will be regarded by the United States as a hostile regime'.[11] As the war against Iraq indicates, this is not only a discursive process, but also a performative one. By embarking upon this 'war on terror', the US has taken advantage of '9/11' to widen the scope of its hegemonic reach, using the justifiable cause of combating international terrorism to garner support and legitimacy.

Using war to strengthen, or even alter, a state's identity is not new. As Erik Ringmar argues (taking Sweden's interventions during the Thirty Years War as a case study), states can fight wars mainly to get recognition for a different identity, to be taken 'seriously' as a Great Power, rather than for objective, rational, realist reasons of pre-established national interests.[12] War – won, lost, or merely endured – often confronts states with a new political reality, making a commensurate identity shift appear reasonable, almost natural. European examples are the change in Germany's national identity after the Second World War, the United Kingdom's post-colonial identity after the dissolution of its Empire, as well as, more recently, Russia's shift towards a post-imperial identity after the end of the Cold War and the demise of the USSR. War is a critical juncture, making it both necessary and easier for elites to promote different ideas about political order and the role of their own state in a novel power constellation.

The post-'9/11' wars in Afghanistan and Iraq are confirming the US's role of global hegemon. US foreign policy works on the assumption that its military might and the guts to actually *use* it offer it the status and credibility that constitutes the very basis for the US's ample soft power. This understanding that imperial interventionism is an essential basis for US soft power, rather than undercutting its cultural and ideological appeal, may well be considered counter-intuitive. Much of global anti-Americanism feeds on the image of the US as a trigger-happy capitalist crusader. It is frequently argued that hard and soft power are juxta-posed, as if hardnosedness detracts from attractiveness. Indeed, soft power can be defined as the ability to achieve the policy outcomes one wants by attraction and persuasion, rather than by force and coercion.[13]

However, in the case of the *Pax Americana* one could well argue that the US's hard and soft power are dialectically related: US interven-tionism requires the cloak of legitimacy (morally or under international law), and without it, coercion would provoke too much resistance and be both too costly and ultimately untenable; vice versa, soft power requires the necessary resources and commitment to put words into actions. Without hard power, attractiveness turns into shadow-boxing, and, at worst, political bimboism. In today's world, loose lips no longer sink ships. Instead, when we read President Bush's lips, we are well aware of the immense military machine backing up his words. Arguably, US liberal imperialism requires both hard *and* soft power. Current US foreign policy is therefore based on the assumption that without the US's hard power and its status as 'the world's only remaining superpower', its soft power would shrink promptly.

In today's Washington, this is considered not just as an ideological hypothesis, but instead is often framed as a 'historical lesson' of recent US experiences in global politics. Two examples stand out. First, US prestige in central Europe is closely related to the general consensus that US military superiority, steadfastness, and moral clarity has 'won the Cold War'. This is put in start contrast with Europe's wishy-washy Ostpolitik. This was again illustrated by the depiction of the US's Cold War President Ronald Reagan in the obituaries after his death in June 2004 as 'the man who beat communism'. Here, again, it is argued that only hard power begets soft power. Second, it is claimed that the US may be hated in the Middle East, but that it is also most certainly respected. This, again, stands in sharp contrast with the marginal influence of Europe (and the European Union in particular), which remains reluc-tant to bring together *der Wille zur Macht*, which comes so naturally to the US. This is not to say that hard power suffices to reach political results, and certainly not in the longer term. But it is important to recognize that the use of coercion and force, even through military intervention, may pay off in soft power by increasing a country's credibility and reputation. The challenge for all imperial powers is to turn hard power into soft power, to turn fear into respect, and to turn terror into legitimacy.

Obviously, this challenge is a difficult one. One may be reminded here of the famous dialogue from *The Life of Brian* from the Monty Python crew,[14] where a number of 'revolutionaries' debate the merits of the Roman Empire:

REG:
> They've bled us white, the bastards. They've taken everything we had, and not just from us, from our fathers, and from our fathers' fathers.

LORETTA:
> And from our fathers' fathers' fathers.

REG:
> Yeah.

LORETTA:
> And from our fathers' fathers' fathers' fathers.

REG:
> Yeah. All right, Stan. Don't labour the point. And what have they ever given us in return?!

XERXES:
> The aqueduct?

REG:
> What?

XERXES:
> The aqueduct.

REG:
> Oh. Yeah, yeah. They did give us that. Uh, that's true. Yeah.

COMMANDO #3:
> And the sanitation.

LORETTA:
> Oh, yeah, the sanitation, Reg. Remember what the city used to be like?

REG:

>Yeah. All right. I'll grant you the aqueduct and the sanitation are two things that the Romans have done.

MATTHIAS:

>And the roads.

REG:

>Well, yeah. Obviously the roads. I mean, the roads go without saying, don't they? But apart from the sanitation, the aqueduct, and the roads –

COMMANDO #1:

>Irrigation.

XERXES:

>Medicine.

COMMANDOS:

>Huh? Heh? Huh...

COMMANDO #2:

>Education.

COMMANDOS:

>Oh...

REG:

>Yeah, yeah. All right. Fair enough.

COMMANDO #1:

>And the wine.

COMMANDOS:

>Oh, yes. Yeah...

FRANCIS:

>Yeah. Yeah, that's something we'd really miss, Reg, if the Romans left. Huh.

COMMANDO #1:

>Public baths.

LORETTA:

>And it's safe to walk in the streets at night now, Reg.

FRANCIS:

>Yeah, they certainly know how to keep order. Let's face it. They're the only ones who could in a place like this.

COMMANDOS:
> Heh, heh. Heh heh heh heh heh heh heh.

REG:
> All right, but apart from the sanitation, the medicine, educa-tion, wine, public order, irrigation, roads, a fresh water system, and public health, what have the Romans ever done for us?

XERXES:
> Brought peace.

REG:
> Oh. Peace? Shut up!

This love-hate relationship is closely related to what Josef Joffe labelled the 'HHMMS' – the 'Harvard and Hollywood, McDonald's and Microsoft Syndrome'. Today, the US offers both 'Harvard' (which stands for intellectual power) and 'Hollywood' (superiority in popular culture), both 'McDonald's' (US dominance in popular food chains), and 'Microsoft' (technological supremacy).[15] As Joffe indicates, this is a very powerful and seductive concoction of power-tools. Yet, he claims, 'seduction is worse than imposition. It makes you feel weak, and so you hate the soft-pawed corrupter as well as yourself'.[16] The argument that especially Arab anti-Americanism is rooted in feelings of powerlessness and humiliation is a strong one. It also touches upon the complex psychology behind the practice of public diplomacy.[17]

The United States now faces a unique challenge. Its hard (economic and military) power is unparalleled and its soft power rules an 'empire' on which the sun truly never sets. But, as both history and political psychology indicate, this supremacy may well spawn counter-power, like a boomerang that may take some time to hit the US, but whose arrival seems inevitable. Some may see the events of '9/11' as a perverse version of that boomerang, originating from Islamic frustration and anger *vis-à-vis* the United States's steamrolling culture. In this context, Isaiah Berlin once argued that 'to be the object of contempt or patron-izing tolerance . . . is one of the most traumatic experiences that individ-uals or societies can suffer'. They will respond, Berlin suggests, 'like the bent twig of poet Schiller's theory lashing back and refusing to accept their alleged inferiority'.[18]

The trend of mounting anti-Americanism within Europe, Asia, and other parts of the world is an element of that same process.[19] Opinion polls conducted by the German Marshall Fund and the Pew Charitable

Trusts[20] indicate that the US's image has declined precipitously in most European countries because of Washington's foreign policy conduct since '9/11'. For example, less than half of the population of Germany (45 per cent), France (43 per cent) and Spain (38 per cent) have a favourable attitude towards the US. And, as the Pew report points out,

> the bottom has fallen out of support for the US in the Muslim world. Negative views of the US in the Muslim world – which had been largely confined to the Middle East – are now echoed by Muslim populations in Indonesia and Nigeria . . . [F]avorable ratings for the US have fallen from 61 per cent to 15 per cent in Indonesia and from 71 per cent to 38 per cent among Muslims in Nigeria.

Furthermore, a CSIS report of May 2003 indicates that Latin American attitudes follow a similar pattern of distrust and criticism towards the US and its foreign policies.[21]

Media research in the 1990s made much of the rise of public opinion and the media and their potential to influence key decisions of global politics. Terms such as the 'CNN effect' and 'Gallup democracy' testify to these optimistic expectations.[22] However, in the emerging hierarchical international order it is even less clear than before what impact external public pressure may have on US foreign policy. But if US hard *and* soft power create resentment, how can the US ever be successful in winning the 'hearts and minds' of its foes and rivals and keep the allegiance of its allies? This is the serious challenge with which US public diplomacy is confronted today.

Public diplomacy: wielding soft power

In this context, one could argue that the terrorist attacks of '9/11' have challenged – even provoked – the US's identity as a superpower. Many Americans were shocked to be confronted with such a violent hatred against their country and everything it stands for: its foreign policies as well as its values. Could anyone dislike the land that offers Harvard *and* Hollywood, McDonald's *and* Microsoft? 'Why do people hate us so much?' soon became a key question, not only for ordinary Americans, but for policy-makers in Washington as well.

Several advisory committees, task forces and hearings have spurred the debate about public diplomacy and its uses.[23] Elaborate public opinion research 'showed an Arab world that fears the United States as a threat to its way of life, a Europe that largely does not trust the

United States and wants to pull further away, and a dwindling support for the US-led war on terror'.[24] The Bush administration has since embarked upon a 'war of ideas', a 'war' in which public diplomacy plays a central role. It was acknowledged that anti-Americanism endangers US national security and compromises the effectiveness of its diplomacy. Most reports argued that this anti-Americanism could not be 'managed' by a quick and easy fix. Instead, Washington should take the views, politics, and cultural (as well as religious) beliefs of others into account while formulating and communicating its own policies in order to make US actions better understood, accepted, and hence more effective.

By its very nature, public diplomacy is an essentially contested concept. A general consensus is emerging that it involves activities in the fields of information, education and culture aimed at influencing a foreign government through influencing its citizens. It also aims to clarify (in our case: US) foreign policies by explaining why they are beneficial to other nations and peoples. Public diplomacy is widely considered an essential post-modern tool of statecraft, which generates legitimacy and acknowledges that in our globalized world the state has lost its monopoly on the processing and diffusion of information. It recognizes that new communication technologies offer new (and arguably unprecedented) opportunities to interact with a wider public by adopting a network approach and making the most of an increasingly multicentric global, interdependent system.

From the onset, the Bush administration has said to recognize the importance of public diplomacy to win its 'war on terror'. In the short term, public diplomacy was considered an essential (and long-underrated) tool to influence opinions and mobilize foreign publics in direct support of US interests and policies. Initially, public diplomacy focused on 'selling' the war against Iraq, claiming that this was not just a war but a 'just war' that could not be avoided. Almost inevitably, some of the 'selling' of the upcoming war against Iraq could also easily be labelled propaganda, information warfare, and most certainly perception management.[25] It was used to put pressure on foreign governments to toe the US-line and accept its concept of preventive war. In the mid-term, the focus of public diplomacy was more far-reaching and fundamental, namely to build an open dialogue with key foreign publics, to open up closed societies in the understanding and expectation that this would strengthen support for shared ideas and values. With the stabilization effort in Iraq facing serious problems, Washington now puts more emphasis on the opportunities for a renewed and intensified democratic dialogue between the US and the Muslim world. However, as the current situation in Iraq testifies, both aspects of US public diplomacy seem to be failing dramatically.

To some extent, this debacle is surprising. US policy-makers could have learned from their experiences in Yugoslavia and the Gulf Wars of the 1990s that a political mandate from the 'international community' (preferably the UN Security Council) comes with the handy permission to use foreign bases, allied troops, financial means to fund the operation, and – most importantly – the credibility and status of legitimacy. If anything, 'Iraq' indicates the limits of hard power and the value of soft power. It recognizes that the old Thespian cliché that 'acting is easy, comedy is hard' also applies here: military invasion is simple, but changing 'hearts and minds' is rather more difficult.

US foreign policy-makers have worked on the mistaken assumption that Saddam Hussein's regime change and the democratization of Iraq (and the rest of the Middle East) will sway doubters and silence critics. Under the optimistic motto that 'nothing succeeds like success', the soft power factor of legitimacy was ignored, expecting that the 'smoking gun' of Iraqi WMD capabilities and facilities would compensate for this afterwards. Moreover, the (then) dominant neo-conservative mood in Washington gladly ignored words of advice and caution. What is more, neo-conservatives seemed to imply that the very lack of a UN mandate signalled the dawn of a new era of US supremacy, officially constituting the *Pax Americana* for which they had been longing. This approach assumes that the US 'is strong enough to do as it wishes with or without the world's approval and should simply accept that others will envy and resent it'.[26]

However, the lack of legitimacy has turned into one of the main obstacles for the US (and its coalition partners) to stabilize Iraq. The vast majority of European and Arab public opinion already seriously questioned the rationale for a 'preventive war' on Iraq in the first place. But now that no Iraqi WMD programme has been found, the argument for intervention has become all the more flimsy and unconvincing. After the speedy collapse of Saddam Hussein's regime, the quest therefore became to gain international support and legitimacy by making a democratic Iraq a showcase of reform in the Middle East. President Bush made it clear that 'Iraqi freedom will succeed, and that success will send forth the news, from Damascus to Tehran, that freedom can be the future of every nation...America has put its power at the service of principle. We believe that liberty is the design of nature; we believe that liberty is the direction of history'.[27] Or, as US Secretary of State Colin Powell defined the United States's mission in the Middle East: 'We're selling a product. That product we are selling is democracy'.[28] This policy has now been labelled a 'forward strategy of freedom in the Middle East'. It is part of a US strategy to build an 'empire by invitation', where Washington intends to make offers that other states cannot refuse.

The limits of PR and spindoctoring

Selling the idea of a *Pax Americana* has thereby changed from a left-wing allegation to a right-wing (or neo-conservative) prerogative, perhaps even responsibility. As Charles Krauthammer argued (a few weeks before '9/11'), 'after a decade of Prometheus playing pygmy', the US has to reinstate itself as an empire.[29] Proponents of US ascendancy argue that '9/11' has proven the risks of passivity and meekness: 'Weakness is provocative' is one of US Secretary of Defense Donald Rumsfeld's famous rules. They conclude that the US should protect and enlarge the community of free and democratic states, building a *de facto* 'empire of liberty'.[30] This new imperialism does not desire to rule permanently over foreign countries, but only aspires to indirect and informal empire. It may threaten, coerce and at times even invade, but it does so with the claim to improve (that is, democratize) states and then leave.[31]

In this strategy of liberal imperialism, both hard and soft power play crucial roles. It can be claimed that preventive wars and interventions (namely Iraq) liberate authoritarian regimes and create the very preconditions for freedom and democracy to take root and flourish. Nevertheless, the central question remains of what role public diplomacy plays in establishing this 'liberal empire' throughout the 'Greater' Middle East, as well as towards much less hostile European territory? How valid is the claim that the (successful) use of military (hard) power generates the requisite (soft) power of legitimacy? Looking at today's Iraq and the dismal standing of the US in public opinion polls across the Middle East, the opposite argument seems much more likely, namely that ostentatious (hard) power play simply eclipses low-profile public diplomacy. With the disclosure in June 2004 of images of abuse and torture by US soldiers of Iraqi detainees at Abu Ghraib prison, the already tainted US image reached its nadir.[32] Only one conclusion can therefore be drawn, namely that (as national-branding consultant Simon Anholt has argued): 'You can't smash them with your left hand and caress them with your right. It you're going to war you should suspend diplomacy, because if you're attacking a nation that's all there is to it'.[33]

Staunch proponents of US liberal imperialism David Frum and Richard Perle have been much more confident and sanguine, arguing in their book *An End to Evil* that a residue of opposition and even guerrilla warfare is only to be expected after a US-led 'liberation'. Referring to post-Second World War experiences in Europe and Japan, they expect this resistance to subside after the benefits of freedom and the effects of public diplomacy hit home.[34] This process – following the above-mentioned 'what have the Romans ever done for us?' cycle – was expected to be a key element in the strategy to 'win the peace', in order subsequently to 'win the hearts and minds' of people across the Middle East. Clearly, and in retrospect recklessly, the Bush administration has followed this 'neo-con' course. But with every new suicide bomb killing US soldiers, Washington's blue-eyed faith in the inevitability of a happy Iraqi ending slowly dissipates.

This one-dimensional and overly optimistic approach to US policy *vis-à-vis* Iraq and the Middle East stands in sharp contrast to the bulk of sophisticated and nuanced reports warning Washington of the complexity, pitfalls, and risks of any attempt to modernize this region. Given that public diplomacy is still predominantly an American discipline, with the post-'9/11' Middle East as the most obvious case study, it is remarkable how little impact scholarly research has had on the implementation of US foreign policy.

The most important failure has been that the practice of US public diplomacy has gone little beyond the goal of 'getting the American message out'. The assumption has been that the United States's image problems are either because of envy of US power and prosperity, or simply a basic misinterpretation of US foreign policy goals. Washington's post-'9/11' public diplomacy initiatives reflect this approach. These efforts included setting up American Corners (with libraries and information) across Muslim-majority countries, the production of documentary material, and the launching of Persian and Arab-language radio stations (like Radio Farda and Radio Sawa), and an Arab-language satellite TV station (Alhurra) that seeks to compete with the popular, but rather anti-American Aljazeera. Most proposals to adjust the course of US public diplomacy aim to make the American machinery to communicate with the Arab and Muslim world more effective.[35] For example, a new Arab youth initiative was started in 2004, together with a so-called Partnership for Learning (P4L) encompassing a US high school exchange programme with the Arab and Muslim world. Policy suggestions have further included strengthening the coordination of public diplomacy with the executive branch and stronger Presidential leadership, recognizing that a 'one size fits all' approach is bound to fail (since the public in Egypt, Indonesia and Senegal obviously differ markedly), and increasing the active support of Arab and Muslim communities in a real dialogue with the US (and the West in general).

The key problem with this approach to public diplomacy, however, is that it does not fully take into account a simple, basic rule of marketing: 'It's not what you *say*, but what others *hear*, that is important!' Whereas US policy-makers say 'freedom, justice, and opportunity', the general Arab population seems to hear 'domination, chaos, and cynicism'. When Washington says 'liberation', a majority of Arabs and European see 'occupation'. Obviously, the proof of the pudding is in the eating, and for many Arabs US foreign policy just does not taste good. The problem is that Arabs and Muslims will not attach credibility to US public diplomacy as long as US policies in the Middle East and beyond remain unchanged. Especially as long as US support to autocratic Arab regimes and Israel continues unabated, Washington's rhetoric about freedom and democracy carries little conviction.[36] As long as US policy and rhetoric are considered worlds apart for most Arabs, public diplomacy is unlikely to create a better image for the US, either in the Arab and Muslim world, or across Europe. Most official US public diplomacy activities try to communicate the United States's basic goodness (the 'HHMMS'), but fail to clarify effectively what is so good about US foreign policy per se.

The United States's current practice of public diplomacy further underestimates the central role of (extremist) Islam, which underpins both anti-Americanism and offers a cultural filter that distorts the US's communications with the region. US public diplomacy seems to take for granted that Muslim culture accepts the constituent elements of modernity, and that all Muslims have an innate, be it repressed, desire to support both liberal democracy and capitalism. This implies that despite the obvious political differences between the US and (at least some) Muslim countries, American and Muslim cultures do not 'clash' but are in agreement. It further assumes that although ordinary Muslims may be opposed to US policies in the Middle East, they continue to be drawn to 'American values' such as individual choice and freedom. This distinction between hostile, extremist Islamic governments and political groupings and the 'silent majority' of a wider and larger Muslim community around the world is a central tenet of US public diplomacy. It is also highly dubious, since it reduces a complex set of political concerns and often confronting interests and values to mere problems of poor communication and cleverer branding. It also allows for the doubtful claim that 'the peoples of the world, especially those ruled by unelected regimes, comprise our true allies. We are allies because we share common aspirations – freedom, security, prosperity – and because we often face common enemies, namely the regimes that rule over them'.[37]

Academic criticism of current US public diplomacy towards the Arab and Muslim world has been harsh, at times even fierce. But the main point of critique and disapproval is that the 'Bush administration needs to recognize that the elite Arab public can speak for itself. It deeply resents being condescended to and ignored. Only by treating Arabs and Muslims as equals, listening carefully and identifying points of convergence without minimizing points of disagreement, will a positive message get through'.[38] True dialogue, rather than mere one-way communication, is therefore seen as the essential starting point to fix the US's serious – but probably not yet fatal – image problem around the world. With the United States having *de facto* responsibility for the economic and political transformation of Iraq, public diplomacy may only be effective when the basic rules of marketing are followed, in particular that the 'product matches up to the promise'.

While a true dialogue is a good start, Washington should also pursue a more even-handed policy towards the Israeli–Palestinian conflict, and understand that only credibility, responsibility and reliability may restore a constructive relationship with the Arab and Muslim world. The bottom line for US public diplomacy is that all PR and branding efforts are only as good as the 'product' being sold. This means that the jury is still out on the prospects for US public diplomacy winning the 'hearts and minds' of the global Muslim population. Since this is a long-term effort, the prevailing reports about the death on arrival of US public diplomacy still remain premature. However, without more successful and forceful efforts to convince a sceptical Muslim populace of the merits of US policies and the United States's underlying good intentions, the military battle may be won, but the real 'war' will most certainly be lost.

This also seems to form the basis of the crisis of confidence that still troubles the transatlantic relationship. In February 2003, US Secretary of State Colin Powell expressed his fear that NATO was 'breaking up', and Henry Kissinger concluded that the war over Iraq 'produced the gravest crisis in the Atlantic Alliance since its creation five decades ago'.[39] For the *Pax Americana* to build up and expand, the US requires loyal allies and a wide circle of supporters around the globe, but especially in Europe. But since many European states and their respective populations feel that they have been treated with contempt by Washington during the Iraqi war, there is little sense of 'ownership' over the ongoing crisis in Iraq. Europeans obviously follow the Pottery Barn rule of international politics: 'If you break it, you own it!'[40] However, because most Europeans consider the United States as the clumsy elephant in the porcelain shop that remains deaf to Allied words of caution and calm, the emerging civil war in Iraq is now considered mainly a US problem (although unfortunately therefore also *ipso facto* a European problem . . .).

Conclusion: a tough sell for liberal imperialism

Marketing experience teaches that it is more important to *show*, than to *tell*. For US public diplomacy, this implies that the United States's performance on the global stage will speak louder than any smooth words that it may voice simultaneously. The war in Iraq and its aftermath reveal the limits of US power in general, both in its hard and soft variety. They indicate that the scope of social engineering is limited, both domestically and on the global scene. How influential was the US when on 15 February 2003 over eight million people marched on the streets of five continents against a war that had not even started yet? This could be seen as one of the largest, most global, popular mobilizations against the US and its policies.[41] Against this popular anti-American (or is it anti-Bush?) revolt, no public diplomacy effort can hold its own.

The failure to stabilize Iraq and turn it into a model for the region, and the massive popular disapproval of the US and its foreign policies, are the obvious indicators of the impracticality and unfeasibility of establishing a *bona fide* 'liberal empire'. The global 'public' has obviously become sufficiently sophisticated to differentiate between the upbeat message and fancy packaging of US rhetoric and the less fancy reality of its foreign policies. US public diplomacy may only marginally affect global opinion, and is unlikely to accomplish a swing vote in its favour. This implies that the impact of soft power and public diplomacy are real, without being decisive. Luckily, *Wag the Dog* is only a movie. Clearly, 'liberal imperialism' is theoretically tilted towards liberalism, whereas in practice it still feels like undiluted and conventional imperialism. US public diplomacy today sets the very notion in a negative light. Anholt was most likely right in claiming that no country can effectively conduct a military offensive and a charm-offensive at the very same time. No amount of soft power can sell a war to a reluctant body of global political 'consumers'.

For the United States as a political 'brand', the damage may well be far-reaching and consequential. Because of clear policy failures in Iraq, the Abu Ghraib prison scandal, and the doubtful legality of the imprisonment of Muslim detainees at Guantanamo Bay (just to mention the most controversial issues), the United States's moral authority has eroded. In its 'war on terror', the US hardly leads by example. Quite the contrary, human rights' workers now argue that in some countries (mainly in Asia and Africa), the United States has become a different kind of model, since non-democratic governments now refer to the US Patriot Act or the Guantanamo prison to justify their own judicial crackdowns or extrajudicial detentions.[42]

These dilemmas and the inherent problems of establishing and maintaining a post-modern empire demonstrate the futility of the very idea of a *Pax Americana*. If anything, they show that the soft power that can be derived from legitimacy, authority, and perceived altruism is a precondition for the effective use of military power. Neo-conservatives within the Bush administration have wilfully ignored this to prove to themselves (and the world) that US hard power can go it alone and *post hoc* generate the legitimacy that comes with success. In this they have failed miserably. However, one must also fear that they have set a trend of new militarism that builds on power without authority, eventually followed by chaos and disaster.[43]

The *Pax Americana* may only have a future as (what Martin Walker has called) a 'virtual empire'.[44] Walker's idea of empire is that of a system led by a hegemon that is itself 'open to argument and persuasion', but also willing and able to offer valued public goods such as international law and order. This Janus-faced empire – offering both openness and resolve – is probably too good to be true. It is beyond doubt that the hard power of military force remains important, perhaps even essential, for any hegemon to do its job properly. But the wheels of hard power can only function smoothly with the lubricant of soft power, of which public diplomacy is a key element. As Iraq testifies, there is probably not enough soft power around to compensate for the friction of war. Perhaps this is an often-overlooked reason why all empires eventually decline. It may also explain why the *Pax Americana* may not even be properly established in the first place.

Notes

1. Uday Singh Mehta, *Liberalism and Empire: A Study in Nineteenth-Century British Liberal Thought* (Chicago and London: University of Chicago Press, 1999), p. 82.
2. Dimitri K. Simes, 'America's Imperial Dilemma', *Foreign Affairs*, vol. 82, no. 6, November/December 2003.

3. *Remarks by the President at the 20th Anniversary of the National Endowment for Democracy*, United States Chamber of Commerce, Washington DC, 6 November 2003, at http://www.whitehouse.gov/news/releases/2003/11/20031106–2.html, 30 March 2004.
4. Charlotte L. Beers, *Prepared Testimony Before the Committee on Foreign Relations of the United States Senate on 'American Public Diplomacy and Islam'*, 27 February 2003.
5. *Monthly Review editors*, 'Kipling, the "White Man's Burden", and US Imperialism', *Monthly Review*, vol. 55, no. 6, November 2003.
6. Max Boot, *The Savage Wars of Peace: Small Wars and the Rise of American Power* (New York: Basic Books, 2003).
7. See http://www.state.gov/r/pa/ho/time/gp/17660.htm. For the full text, see http://www.uiowa.edu/~c030162/Common/Handouts/POTUS/TRoos.html of 28 July 2004.
8. 'Cheney Exhorts Europe to Promote Diplomacy', *Los Angeles Times*, 25 January 2004.
9. Geir Lundestad, *The United States and Western Europe Since 1945: From 'Empire' by Invitation to Transatlantic Drift* (Oxford: Oxford University Press, new edition 2003).
10. Paul Kennedy, *The Rise and Fall of the Great Powers* (New York: Random House, 1987).
11. President George W. Bush, *Address to a Joint Session of Congress and the American People*, Washington DC, 20 September 2001.
12. Erik Ringmar, *Identity, Interest and Action: A Cultural Explanation of Sweden's Intervention in the Thirty Years War* (Cambridge: Cambridge University Press, 1996).
13. Joseph S. Nye, *Soft Power: The Means to Success in World Politics* (New York: PublicAffairs, 2004).
14. For the full script, see http://www.geocities.com/pythoninsanity/Lifeof-Brian.html of 27 July 2004.
15. Josef Joffe, 'Who's Afraid of Mr. Big?', *The National Interest*, no. 64, summer 2001, p. 45.
16. Joffe, 'Who's Afraid of Mr. Big?', p. 46.
17. For this argument, see Shibley Telhami, 'History and Humiliation', *Washington Post*, 28 March 2003.
18. Isaiah Berlin, 'The Bent Twig: A Note on Nationalism', *Foreign Affairs*, vol. 51, no. 1, October 1972, pp. 17–18.
19. Pew Global Attitudes Project, *A Year After Iraq: A Nine-Country Survey* (Washington DC: The Pew Charitable Trusts, March 2004).
20. GMF Transatlantic Trends 2003 and the Pew Global Attitudes Project, http://www.transatlantictrends.org/ and http://www.pewtrusts.com/index.cfm of 27 July 2004.
21. See Sidney Weintraub, 'US–Latin American Attitudes: Mistrust and Indifference', *CSIS Issues in International Political Economy*, no. 41, May 2003, http://www.csis.org/simonchair/issues200305.pdf of 27 July 2004.
22. Timothy Luke and Gearoid Ó Tuathail, 'On videocameralism: The Geopolitics of Failed States, the CNN International and (UN)Governmentality', *Review of International Political Economy*, vol. 4, no. 4.
23. An Independent Task Force on Public Diplomacy was set up by the Council on Foreign Relations; the US Advisory Commission on Public Diplomacy is a

long-standing bipartisan panel created by Congress and appointed by the President; and hearings were conducted by the Committee on International Relations in the House of Representatives in November 2001.
24. *Finding America's Voice: A Strategy for Reinvigorating US Public Diplomacy*, report of an Independent Task Force sponsored by the Council on Foreign Relations, 2003, p. v.
25. Sheldon Rampton and John Stauber, *Weapons of Mass Deception: The Uses of Propaganda in Bush's War on Iraq* (London: Constable & Robinson, 2003).
26. Joseph S. Nye, 'The Decline of America's Soft Power', *Foreign Affairs*, vol. 83, no. 3, May/June 2004, p. 16.
27. *President Bush Discusses Freedom in Iraq and Middle East*, National Endowment for Democracy, Washington DC, 6 November 2003.
28. See 'Brand USA', *Foreign Policy*, no. 127, 2001, p. 19.
29. Charles Krauthammer, 'The New Unilateralism', *Washington Post*, 8 June 2001.
30. Sebastian Mallaby, 'The Reluctant Imperialist: Terrorism, Failed States, and the Case for American Empire', *Foreign Affairs*, vol. 82, no. 2, March/April 2002; and Boot, *The Savage Wars of Peace*, ch. 15.
31. Michael Mann, *Incoherent Empire* (London and New York: Verso, 2003), p. 13.
32. Jeremy Grant, 'Middle America Meets the Middle East in a Battle for Hearts and Minds', *Financial Times*, 20 July 2004.
33. Quoted in Elen Lewis, 'Branding War and Peace', *Brand Strategy*, no. 167, 2003, p. 28.
34. David Frum and Richard Perle, *An End to Evil: How to Win the War on Terror* (New York: Random House, 2003), pp. 12–13, and ch. 6.
35. *Testimony of Under Secretary for Public Diplomacy and Public Affairs Margaret Tutwiler to the Committee on Foreign Relations of the United States Senate*, 26 February 2004, http://foreign.senate.gov/testimony/2004/TutwilerTestimony040226.pdf, of 4 May 2004.
36. Derk Kinnane, 'Winning Over the Muslim Mind', *The National Interest*, spring 2004.
37. Henry J. Hyde, *The Message is America: Rethinking US Public Diplomacy*, hearing before the Committee on International Relations, United States House of Representatives, 14 November 2002, serial no. 107–54, p. 2.
38. Marc Lynch, 'America is Losing the Battle For Arab Opinion', *International Herald Tribune*, 23–24 August 2003.
39. Quoted in Ivo H. Daalder, 'The End of Atlanticism', *Survival*, vol. 45, no. 2, summer 2003, p. 147.
40. This 'rule' was put forward by Bob Woodward in his book *Plan of Attack* (New York: Simon & Schuster, 2004). However, the firm of Pottery Barn actually denies that such signs exist in their shops. They claim that they just write off any broken merchandise as a 'loss'. Unfortunately, such an option is not open to the world community.
41. Tariq Ali, *Bush in Babylon: The Recolonization of Iraq* (London and New York: Verso, 2003), especially ch. 6.
42. Thomas Fuller and Brian Knowlton, 'US is seen Losing its Moral Authority', *International Herald Tribune*, 5 July 2004.
43. Mann, *Incoherent Empire*, p. 252.
44. Martin Walker, 'America's Virtual Empire', *World Policy Journal*, vol. 19, no. 2, summer 2002.

4
Niche Diplomacy in the World Public Arena: the Global 'Corners' of Canada and Norway

Alan K. Henrikson

Introduction

Niche diplomacy, although often associated with very small countries, has in fact been more fully developed by countries that have sufficient size and capacity to play notable roles on the international stage but that are not strong enough to impose their positions or solutions. They can sometimes exercise persuasive influence, but rarely deciding force. Even if not considered 'middle powers' in terms of military or other basic strength or in terms of international rank, they can sometimes play significant roles as intermediaries, as key providers of assistance, or in other precise ways. Very large powers too, it should be noted, may develop niche diplomatic and other particular capabilities. The difference is that great powers, unlike small or middle-sized countries, lack either the necessity or the incentive to do so. They can usually exert influence, as well as exercise power, across the board. Sometimes, however, even they fail, and have to defer to others – with less strength but, perhaps, even more favourable vantages.

It was Gareth Evans, when serving as foreign minister of 'middle-power' Australia, who gave 'niche diplomacy' its name. For Evans, the term essentially meant specialization. It suggested 'concentrating resources in specific areas best able to generate returns worth having, rather than trying to cover the field'.[1] Evans's concept of niche diplomacy, although probably for the most part political in inspiration, relied on the logic and language of economics, and more particularly of business. The ability of a nation's diplomacy to 'generate returns', primarily for the country itself, depends on very careful selection of the policy-product lines to be developed and also on an accurate reading of global political-market conditions. According to this calculus, there is no point in adopting policy positions that will not 'sell' – either at home to the domestic public (the sphere of 'public affairs'); or abroad to foreign publics (the sphere of 'public diplomacy').

There is something else, less conspicuous in Evans's brief definition, that merits attention: this is his further phrase, 'worth having', which implies not just ordinary 'returns', but truly meaningful ones. To pursue objectives 'worth having' suggests a different and higher criterion than usually applied even in the formal realm of foreign policy. If a country carries out measures for the international good, even what might be deemed the 'global public good', then it is seeking something that is 'universalizable', extending well beyond national self-interest.[2] It is sometimes possible for a country to do very well by doing good. To support 'good' works, to perform 'good' deeds, to use 'good' words, and to project 'good' images can pay off in terms of international prestige, and in even more practical expressions of others' appreciation. A country can become known, admired, and also rewarded for its 'goodness' – which becomes a kind of niche in itself.

Two countries that have, remarkably and also consequentially, often acted in this 'altruistic' way, for genuinely noble purposes as well as for self-advancing, are Canada and Norway. Canada was once described by former US Secretary of State Dean Acheson in Wordsworth's phrase (from 'Ode to Duty') as the 'Stern Daughter of the Voice of God'. Indeed, it has become a model of good international citizenship. Owing partly to its dual English and French heritage, it is an active member of many international organizations, including the Commonwealth and *la Francophonie*. Perhaps most notably, it has pioneered in the field of peacekeeping. Canada has also been a major contributor of assistance to developing countries, including the poorest. It is also known for leading the international effort to ban anti-personnel landmines – the 'Ottawa process'. Meanwhile, Norway, which is long known for the Nobel Prize for Peace, is also a generous aid donor to poor countries. Its giving level, as a percentage of national income, is the highest in the world. Even more remarkable in the realm of diplomacy is its work in peace facilitation, its most famous effort being focused on the Middle East – the 'Oslo process'.

Canada and Norway, although on different continents and disparate in size, make a pair. They have frequently collaborated in international undertakings, both bilaterally and in formal and informal multilateral settings. They are among the 'like-minded' in their common approaches to global and regional issues. Canada and Norway, together with four

Nordic neighbours (Iceland, Denmark, Sweden and Finland), vote the same way in the United Nations 90 per cent of the time. Both are active in the UN system and are also long-time allies in the North Atlantic Treaty Organization (NATO), of which they were founding members. Having a common interest in northern environmental and socio-economic as well as geostrategic issues, they have recently joined to help form the new Arctic Council. They even share a northern artistic perspective.[3]

For Canada, Norway is probably the most intimately 'allied' of all the northern countries. It is its largest trading partner in the Nordic region. Their officials often meet.[4] Not surprisingly, their diplomacies as well as their foreign policies are very similar. In the field of public diplomacy, however, there is a marked difference, of which both Canadian and Norwegian officials are aware. A senior Canadian official indicated increasing internal dissatisfaction within his ministry, and perhaps Canada generally, with Canada 'trying to be all things to all people'.[5] The Canadians observe that Norway does not attempt such broad appeal, and appears to be succeeding. Norwegian officials are aware of the Canadians' interest in their experiences with more concentrated approaches. They perceive other differences too. One is that the instruments of Canadian foreign policy seem much less 'integrated' than are the Norwegian, and also less flexible in their use. The Canadian government cannot so easily deploy or adjust its aid programme, for example, as an incentive and a support for peace negotiations in which it may take an interest. Norway can act more quickly, and with sizeable funds, in part because both the minister of foreign affairs and the minister of development cooperation are together in the foreign ministry. Another difference is that the Canadian government seems to feel a greater political need to 'take credit' at home for its foreign policy and diplomacy. It is this mutual awareness of the two countries' official communities that makes a comparison of their public diplomacies especially interesting.

The power of 'the better argument'

Both Canada and Norway have been adroit users of public opinion, for they have had to rely on the goodwill of others, far as well as near, rather than on their own physical might, to maintain their national independence and wider influence. Goodwill is, of course, something that has to be cultivated over time. Canada's and Norway's public diplomacy, in which both countries invest heavily, appears to be exemplary, for both have long enjoyed high international regard. The sources of their favourable reputations are many. Michael Ignatieff explains the standing, and the sway, of his own country, Canada, as follows: 'The idea of influence derives from three assets: moral authority as a good citizen, which we have got some of; military capacity which we have got a lot less of; and international assistance capability'. With regard to Canada's neighbour, the United States, he observes, probably with Canada's UN and other multilateral relationships in mind: 'We have something they want. They need legitimacy'.[6] Norway, being a smaller country and with nothing so grand as legitimacy to offer, thinks of itself more modestly as offering, basically, utility. A smaller country is not in a position 'to impose its views on others', acknowledges Norway's foreign minister, Jan Petersen. 'However, smaller countries can sometimes offer useful advice and contribute to creative solutions where multilateral efforts have not produced results or others have failed.'[7] Usefulness – of the kind that Norway, in its independent way, wishes to provide – is one of the keys to its present high international standing, which in the area of 'peace mediation and reconciliation' is perhaps second to none.

While much of the diplomacy involved in Canada's and Norway's work over the years was and remains hidden, or at least out of the international limelight, important elements of very publicly oriented diplomacy have been involved. For both the Canadian and Norwegian governments, diplomatic success has involved close collaboration with non-governmental organizations (NGOs) and direct engagement with civil society. Canadian and Norwegian officials and diplomats are master networkers, and they have used their contacts to considerable advantage. Canada's own NGOs, anglophone and francophone, have been very active in foreign fields, receiving support from the Canadian International Development Agency (CIDA). So, too, the government of Norway has partnered NGOs, often assisted by the Norwegian Agency for Development Cooperation (NORAD). 'Norwegian NGOs have over several decades gained wide international experience', attests Foreign Minister Petersen. 'As a result, we have a number of contact points with non-governmental actors in many countries.'[8]

Networking is a quiet, methodical business. To have a 'niche' – or privileged or protected corner – in diplomacy, as in business or any other activity, requires wide recognition as well as a secured position. Creating and maintaining a niche in a globalizing competitive world of attention-seeking entities requires publicity. Some of a nation's publicity effort must be straightforward and forthright. The indirect shaping of the political environment through international public relations may not be sufficient. Outright advocacy by officials and diplomats themselves may be required. Vigorous argumentation is sometimes called for, and controversy may be the result.

Public diplomacy should therefore be thought of as a form of engagement – intellectual engagement, as well as political and social engagement. Minds, as well as hearts, must be won. The 'power of the better argument' should thus be considered integral to the concept of public diplomacy. It is not just, or even mainly, a matter of imagery, or positive branding. Diplomatic argumentation should be a matter of conviction, resulting from and resulting in the transference of genuine belief grounded in understanding of the issues and knowledge of the facts. A certain fundamental level of honesty and consistency is expected. When a leader, government or country takes actions or adopts positions that are manifestly incompatible with previous acts or stances, especially high-minded or 'altruistic' ones, credibility can easily be lost. Those who live by public diplomacy can die by public diplomacy.

'Niche diplomacy' in the public arena

Much of Canada's and Norway's success lies in the high regard in which they are held by other countries, including interested segments of these countries' populations. The diplomacy of a nation, no matter how energetic, cannot be separated from the international community's expectations. In the cases of Canada and Norway, how have these expectations been created? What methods of diplomacy have helped to generate them? Is 'niche diplomacy' a key factor?

A primary implication of the 'niche' term is that the advantage, or 'corner', that a country may have by virtue of its favoured situation, special competence or unique product is more or less permanent. Such an advantage might be considered as being *locational*, *traditional* or *consensual* – or some combination thereof. It may be locational because it is based on geographical realities – such as Canada having the world's second largest land area, with all its natural resources, and also because it shares with the United States, a friendly superpower, the globe's longest 'unguarded' (although currently highly sensitive) border. Canada's relationship with the United States is, in the words of one Canadian diplomat, 'the envy of the world'.[9] A country's niche advantage may alternatively be traditional, because it is inherited from past commitments and is reconfirmed by years of faithful observance, as with Norway's administration and awarding of the Nobel Prize for Peace. 'Although other similar prizes are given by other institutions all over the world', a Norwegian government publication points out, 'the Nobel prizes have maintained a unique position since the first one was awarded in 1901'.[10] A country's niche advantage may also be consensual, because it is reflective of deep social interest and responsive to the prevailing public sentiment of a country, irrespective of political partisanship – so much so that its very identity becomes involved. Canada's and also Norway's long support for and active involvement in international peacekeeping is illustrative. The welcome that Canadian and Norwegian peacekeepers have generally received around the world reinforced both countries' self-identification with peacekeeping.

To maintain a distinct national niche over a long period is becoming more and more difficult, especially in the present circumstances of a changing post-Cold War political structure and the dynamic flux of globalization. As in Darwin's evolutionary world, old niches disappear and new ones appear. Organisms must constantly adapt – or perish. Circumstantial forces, however, are not the only determinant. 'Niches' today are not just given externally, or decided by factors beyond national control. They are also deliberate *constructs*. Some international roles are written by their authors – political leaders and policy planners – and by those who perform them – a country's officials and diplomats, including public diplomats. So might public diplomacy, imaginatively conceived and cleverly conducted, actually transform the very environment within which a nation's foreign policy is carried out?

There are obviously limits to the extent at which promulgation of a national self-image, brand idea or mission statement can alter the fundamental political circumstances or even the ephemeral climate of opinion within which a national government conducts its affairs. Even when carried out by the government of a well-to-do middle power such as Canada or wealthy smaller country such as Norway, a state's foreign policy is unlikely to prosper without very close attention to the current pattern of, and particularly the shifts in, the wider geopolitical equilibrium – especially the international military balance at local, regional, and global levels. This is the multi-tiered 'public arena' – a kind of Roman Colosseum for public-diplomatic performance – within which foreign policy today must be conducted. Realists may still consider it to be the dominant world in which we live. Even the militarily-oriented analyst, however, must also recognize the 'hard power' of massed, organized public opinion. The new 'Roman' gallery that watches diplomacy can be fickle, and can even turn vicious – as some of the violent protests against Group of Eight (G8) and other advanced-country summit meetings have demonstrated. Henry Kissinger fears that 'attacks on globalization could evolve into a new ideological radicalism, particularly in countries where the governing elite is small and the gap between rich and poor is vast and growing'. In the last analysis, Kissinger, despite being a traditional realist, recognizes that 'world order requires consensus'.[11]

Soft power and political strategies

The currently fashionable notion of 'soft power', as explained by Joseph S. Nye, overemphasizes the pervasiveness of the phenomenon of power and also makes much too simple a distinction between forms of power, as well as the resources that underlie it – those that involve coercion in contrast with those that rely instead on attraction, or 'co-optation', as he calls it. Nye himself writes: 'Hard and soft power are related because they are both aspects of the ability to achieve one's purpose by affecting the behavior of others. The distinction between them is one of degree, both in the nature of the behavior and in the tangibility of the resources'.[12] Nonetheless he is certainly correct to emphasize the importance of non-military expressions and the subtler uses of power, for it is these that are usually manifested in diplomacy – which, however, also embodies and expresses much more than power. 'Political leaders', he writes, 'have long understood the power that comes from attraction'.[13] It should be stressed that what comes first is the attraction. This can be generated and also expressed in completely non-power-related ways.

To assimilate *publicly*-conducted diplomacy in particular to 'soft power' would be a conceptual mistake, and far too reductionist, because a diplomacy that is expected to have public appeal and to win favour for a country must rely on the moral, political and intellectual assent of the populations addressed by it. Most publics cannot be entirely won over – either coerced or co-opted – by intimations of power, however subliminal or politely veiled. 'Power' is a misnomer in diplomacy. A country's foreign policy goals are in any case rarely stated today in such terms – those of power-seeking or other kind of aggrandizement. This is very certainly true of Canada and Norway, whose declared purposes tend to be either quite specific, concrete and internally motivated (to bring benefits home) or more general, abstract and externally intended (to bring benefit to the world). To be sure, their policy goals can be stated in ways that blur the difference. Citing Canada and Norway as examples, Joseph Nye observes: 'Sometimes countries enjoy political clout that is greater than their military and economic weight would suggest because they define their national interest to include attractive causes such as economic aid or peacemaking'.[14]

The sphere of power politics and the sphere of public diplomacy are not, of course, completely separate. They do overlap. What may be perceived by the United States or other large countries as a geostrategic or other power imperative – such as winning the current 'War on Terror' – can fill the American and also wider international public space. This can have the effect of driving the various protagonists and practitioners of 'niche diplomacy' back into their corners, forcing them to reconsider both their outlook upon the world and the outreach that their countries can or should wish to have within it. Canada, because of its physical adjacency to the United States, and to a lesser extent Norway, because of its desire to remain close as a NATO ally, have both felt the inhibiting effects of the present militancy of the world's sole surviving superpower. The security arena tends today to be the central or main world arena, especially in the international circumstances following the terrorist attacks of 11 September 2001.

Here is where smart political strategies can come into play. The role of diplomacy, as conducted by non-great-power but nonetheless resourceful and influential nations in such circumstances, could be one of the following: (1) to try to shift the terms of international debate away from realism, if necessary through direct and open ideological *confrontation* with the superpower and cooperating countries; (2) to attempt gently to foster a more 'enlightened' version of realism through *parallel action* alongside the superpower and its coalition partners; or (3) to engage in active *partnership* with the dominant power, perhaps with some differentiation of roles, or specialization, on a realistic footing.

Canada, through its Ottawa process and other initiatives in which it has participated (such as the movement to establish an International Criminal Court and the promotion of 'human security'), has at times attempted the first, or confrontational, strategy. Norway, with its Oslo process and other peace-facilitation efforts in the Philippines, the Balkans, Colombia, Guatemala and Sri Lanka, has often favoured the second, or parallel action, strategy. Both Canada and Norway have also long practised partnership – the third strategy – with the United States and their European allies within NATO. In the post-11 September international situation, the theme of partnership has increased saliency in official thinking in Ottawa and Oslo, as well as in many other capitals.

By 'going public' with their foreign-policy preferences, the Canadian and Norwegian governments can to some degree escape the constraints of US and European Union power, which could exert a kind of gravitational control over them. Public diplomacy is to an extent an equalizer – even a negator – of power. Without subscribing fully to the thesis of 'the death of realism', one can nonetheless accept the observation of the French political scientist Bertrand Badie that in today's global conditions major states are required 'to compromise with ordinary actors their powers and their private strategies in the international arena'. Strong states as well as weak states, argues Badie, are 'increasingly under scrutiny in an "international public space" constituted by a large number of non-state actors'.[15] In this more highly populated international public space, how best can middle-sized and smaller countries act to secure themselves and their interests, both within their national 'niches' and throughout the global arena?

From the Canadian and Norwegian experiences, it would seem that the most effective overall public-diplomatic approach, whichever particular political strategy is chosen, is to present national policy as serving the 'global good' – that is, benefiting humanity as a whole – even if prompted by a country's self-interest or reflecting its self-concept. To the extent that such national identification with international betterment is widely accepted abroad as well as at home, well-focused diplomatic efforts can then proceed with a reasonable chance of success, if supported with sufficient funding and enough personnel. The United States and other large powers may find in dismay that whatever reservations they may have about initiatives taken by Canada or Norway are *politically inexpressible*. Their actual or potential opposition may effectively be neutralized by the endorsement that Canadian or Norwegian moves receive from world public opinion – the international community. By the same token, if the battle for control of 'international public space' is not won by non-great countries – that is, middle or rich and small – through the aggressive exercise of diplomacy, including open advocacy as well as public relations activities, then their ambitions beyond mere national survival may well fail.

Canada: risks and rewards of open confrontation

The beginning of Canada 'going public' in its ordinary diplomacy occurred not in the wider international arena but within the more limited, continental public forum of the Canadian–US relationship. The precipitant was acid rain, but the deeper cause was the systemic influence of US domestic processes in general – political as well as economic – on Canada. The country had to defend itself. Rather than restricting its representations to the US State Department or other departments of the US administration, by the early 1980s the Canadian embassy in Washington also began addressing members of Congress, which without its old seniority system was less susceptible to executive-branch leadership and was becoming more and more decentralized and media-oriented. The Canadian embassy also engaged in PR activities using private firms and collaborated with environmentalist and other like-minded NGOs throughout the United States. The primary reason for the Canadians' resort to 'public diplomacy', as Canadian officials frankly called it, was that US domestic legislation and administrative regulations were adversely affecting so many of Canada's interests that 'classical diplomacy' had to be supplemented with a new approach.

If 'American foreign policy toward Canada is largely an aggregation of domestic economic thrusts', reasoned Canadian Ambassador Allan Gotlieb, the result is that 'Canadian foreign policy is the obverse side of American domestic policy affecting Canada'. Although the US federal administration – which would remain 'our principal interlocutors' – would not be left 'off the hook', Gotlieb stressed that Canadians must 'recognize, realistically, that a great deal of work has to be done ourselves'. That meant dealing directly with the American public, and not relying on the US federal government to do so for Canada. Gotlieb stated the logic of the new, tough Canadian strategy: 'public diplomacy, which is the only possible antidote, is meant to impress the constituents of legislators of the wisdom in not taking action against Canadian interests. Not because such action is not nice, but because it hurts specific American interests'.[16]

By 1995, in a Canadian government foreign policy review, public diplomacy was recognized as a 'third pillar' of Canadian foreign policy on the global level.[17] The formal rubric was 'Projecting Canadian Values and Culture'.[18] One of these values – preservation of natural resources and the environment – carried differences between Canada and the United States to the world, over the head of the US government, so to speak. It is the landmine issue, however, that has most clearly brought the Canadian government into confrontation with US officials. The lines were drawn by the Convention on the Prohibition of the Use, Stockpiling, Production and Transfer of Anti-Personnel Mines and on Their Destruction, signed in Ottawa on 3–4 December 1997, with more than 120 countries participating. The Convention was the result of a coalition of like-minded non-governmental organizations and activist individuals (the NGO elements being mostly coordinated by the International Campaign to Ban Landmines) as well as national governments – particularly Austria and Norway, both of which had provided venues for some of the negotiations, and also other members of a 'core group' (including Belgium, Germany, Ireland, Mexico, the Philippines,

South Africa and Switzerland). But Canada was the leader. This was an autonomous diplomatic development, arranged entirely outside any international organization. It was driven by a humanitarian sense of urgency and by ferocious publicity – a non-bureaucratic communications effort that relied innovatively on fax messages and then electronic mail.[19] The Ottawa Convention – the 'most rapidly ratified' such international treaty ever – came into force on 1 March 1999. The US government, mainly for reasons relating to the military status quo on the Korean peninsula, did not join in the ratification.

The Ottawa process, as it came to be called, was accompanied by a high justifying (and 'good' internationalist) idea: Foreign Affairs Minister Lloyd Axworthy's somewhat dogmatic, but very well articulated, 'human security' concept. Out of it an extensive Human Security Network (HSN) has developed of some 12 well-placed smaller countries around the world.[20] Axworthy's concept was radical in its implications, for it placed the safety of the individual rather than the security of the state ('national security') at the centre of concern. 'It's not a position that makes me very popular with the striped pants crowd', admitted Axworthy, 'but I think it has resonance with the public.' A *New York Times* reporter agreed: 'The striped pants crowd of traditional diplomats, backed by academics and conservative columnists, indeed has trouble swallowing Mr Axworthy's brand of pulpit diplomacy'.[21]

The destruction of the World Trade Center and damage inflicted on the Pentagon on 11 September 2001 changed the entire situation of Canadian diplomacy. Unconfirmed reports in the US press that the perpetrators had come – or could have come – through Canada were alarming to Ottawa, as to all of Canada. Corrective advocacy as well as precautionary measures were called for. The Canadian Department of Foreign Affairs and International Trade (DFAIT) realized that it was on the front line: 'The September 11 terrorist attacks had a significant effect on all international operations of the Department, and on the Public Diplomacy program in particular', a DFAIT assessment stated. The department's focus quickly shifted to 'new national security priorities': Afghanistan; the Canadian–US border; and anti-terrorism planning. The Bush administration's declaration of its 'war on terror' was filling the international public space, displacing Canada's messages. 'Promoting Canada externally was increasingly demanding in the face of intense image promotion by other countries and some adverse foreign media coverage of Canadian security capacity', DFAIT recognized. Different, more continentally focused messages were needed. It was obviously necessary, by means of targeted communications and outreach activities, 'to promote Canada as a good neighbor and reliable partner of the United States'.[22]

DFAIT officials did not wish, however, to give up their longer-term efforts to 'strengthen Canadian identity and social cohesion' by continuing to represent Canada abroad as a culturally diverse, technologically advanced, federally balanced democracy 'with extensive links to the rest of the world' – in short, to show that Canada was still a global player, in its own eyes as well as in the eyes of others. 'Long-term strategies aimed at projecting Canadian values' through arts promotion and academic relations had continued to produce 'good returns', the department pointed out, without specifying the 'returns' however, except to note that demand for Canadian 'educational and cultural goods and services exports' had grown.[23] Being the Department of Foreign Affairs *and* International Trade (whereas until 1982 it had been the Department of External Affairs alone) meant that the economic 'returns' as well as the political rewards of DFAIT's work, such as the Ottawa Convention, could comprehensively be taken into account.

On 12 December 2003 – in order 'to better serve Canadians' – DFAIT was somewhat abruptly divided into two departments: Foreign Affairs Canada, which 'promotes peace, prosperity and Canadian values around the world'; and International Trade Canada, which 'works to position Canada as a business leader for the twenty-first century'.[24] The logic behind the move was not entirely clear from the outside. This formal separation of the foreign political and trade functions of the Canadian government was plainly associated, however, with the replacement of Prime Minister Jean Chrétien by his long-time Liberal Party rival, Paul Martin – an internationally experienced former finance minister with a different style, and his own ideas of how to provide good government.

A consequence of the change in leadership – and the increased need for the prime minister to provide coordination – was a higher reliance on public diplomacy. During an early trip to Washington, Prime Minister Martin announced the establishment of a new public advocacy and legislative secretariat in the Canadian embassy building in Washington – a monumental structure of modern design prominently situated on Pennsylvania Avenue near the Capitol. This unprecedented step would, he said, improve the 'management and coherence' of Canada's relations with the United States, adding that Canadians are best served by 'a more sophisticated approach' that recognizes and respects 'the valuable role of legislators and representatives from various levels of government'.[25] Further innovative steps would be the joint location of provincial and territorial representatives at the embassy and the extension of assistance to Canadian parliamentarians visiting the US capital and other US cities. These non-diplomats could also be advocates and defenders of Canadian interests. 'The new secretariat', which would be headed by Colin Robertson who had been serving as Canada's Consul General in Los Angeles, 'will enhance Canada's overall advocacy in the United States, while supporting a single Canadian voice', Prime Minister Martin said.[26]

Norway: a parallel and still independent course

'Norway' is an unusually mobile presence in the world. The reputation of its shipping fleet – one of the world's largest – for efficiency, safety and cleanliness enhances the generally positive image of the Atlantic-oriented Scandinavian country. There are negatives to be sure, one being Norway's continued involvement in whaling, which poses a small but serious problem for the Norwegian government in its public diplomacy, because of the apparent incompatibility of Norway's whaling tradition with its modern, deeply ecological commitment to the preservation of natural life. The Brundtland Commission on Sustainable Development – a major new 'good' idea – contributed what is still the dominant comprehensive rationale for adjusting economic growth to the laws of nature and to human requirements for resources.

Norway's international peace work, which is the particular focus here, is legendary. Some of its present peace activities originated long ago in the Lutheran Church's missionary work overseas in Africa and elsewhere around the world. As Norway's ambassador in the United States, former foreign minister and chairman-in-office of the Organization for Security and Cooperation in Europe, Knut Vollebaek, has pointed out by way of historical explanation, Norway was the country in Europe with 'the highest number of missionaries per capita'. Returning missionaries brought home 'a global, social awareness'.[27] This mentality provides consensual ground for the already-noted Nobel Prize for Peace, which has been awarded in Oslo since 1901. The Swedish industrialist Nobel's gift has enabled Norway to construct a powerful instrument of peace advocacy, implicit as well as explicit. It is a very active and incomparable 'niche'.

The aforementioned Oslo peace process – Norway's effort at peace mediation between the Israelis and Palestinians expressed in the Oslo Accord of 1993 – is perhaps Norway's most distinctive national diplomatic effort.[28] It developed partly outside the official sphere. Norwegian politicians, particularly from the labour movement and also from Christian circles, had long maintained close and friendly relations with their Israeli colleagues. These links, and others involving academic researchers, resulted in the opening of the so-called highly secret Oslo channel. Confidentiality was assured, almost physically, by the geographical remoteness of the Norwegian 'niche' in Europe's northern periphery. The Oslo Accord, which was publicly announced at the end of August 1993, laid down basic principles for the gradual establishment of peace between Israel and the Palestinians. 'When the negotiations became known', recalls one participant, Marianne Heiberg, wife of then foreign minister Johan Jørgen Holst, 'there was a collective Norwegian pride'.[29] Norway had demonstrated an international influence that seemed in power terms quite incongruous – a feeling that was captured in the book title of another participant, Jan Egeland: *Impotent Superpower – Potent Small State*.[30]

The 'Oslo process' touched off, as *New York Times* correspondent Frank Bruni records in a vivid account that includes many of the elements of Norway's present international image, 'a frenzy of Norwegian peacemaking, or at least peacetrying, that has put peace somewhere alongside oil and timber as one of this country's signature exports'. He writes: 'Over the last decade, Norwegians have had a hand in peace talks between Communist rebels and the Philippine government; Croatia and Yugoslavia; and Colombia's government and the FARC rebel movement. Norwegians have ventured into Cyprus and Somalia and Sudan'. Most notably, Norwegian negotiators were able in February 2002, their quiet efforts going back to 1998, to broker a power-sharing agreement, albeit tenuous, between the government of Sri Lanka and the Tamil Tigers. Norway's claim to global fame through peacemaking, Bruni comments, is 'rarer' than its 'tenacious winter', its 'awful lot of herring', or anything else about it, including its economic assets, vacation attractions, or culinary skills. 'Now, more than ever, Norway seems to be the international capital of peace.'[31]

This somewhat caricatured portrait inevitably conceals as well as reveals. It does, however, suggest what might be further publicized. Mark Leonard and Andrew Small in their commissioned study, *Norwegian Public Diplomacy*, have observed that Norway's problem is not so much one of 'rebranding' as it is of 'invisibility'. One of the unheard national 'stories' that the Norwegian government could and should tell is that of Norway as a *'humanitarian superpower'*, they propose. 'Norway might be only 115th in the world in terms of its size, but it is leading the world as a humanitarian power, outperforming all other countries in terms of its contributions to aid, its role in peacekeeping and peace processes and its commitment to developing new kinds of global governance. This commitment goes far beyond the activities of the Norwegian state – infusing every aspect of Norwegian society from NGOs and business to ordinary citizens.'[32]

Are there structural factors at work to support the role of Norway in such a 'humanitarian superpower' niche? Phrasing the question differently, Bruni asks 'what makes Norway such a welcome interloper and lulling force?' Norwegian deputy foreign minister Vidar Helgesen has given a partial answer: 'We're small, we're way up here and we have no colonial past'. Because Norway does not have and really cannot have any grand designs to impose on others, this reasoning goes that it will not engender suspicion. Moreover, being separated (unlike Canada) from the United States by several thousand miles, and being detached from the main body of integrated Europe too, 'Norway is not perceived to be doing the bidding of larger, more muscular and more meddlesome nations', Bruni writes. 'While it belongs to NATO, it does not belong to the European Union. It has alliances, but wears them lightly.' But, being disconnected, Norway can also be disregarded.

'To gain influence, we have to be noticed', then Norwegian state secretary Thorhild Widvey said at Images of Norway: A Conference on Public Diplomacy, held in Oslo in March 2003. 'We need partnerships', she declared frankly.[33] Partnerships result from dialogue, which is a more effective way to build relationships than logo manipulation or branding, which do not involve real reciprocity. Partnerships, which for Norway tend to be specialized rather than general and mass-market-oriented, do not have to be only with other governments. They could also be with companies and civil society. And they could be formed with people all around the world. In an address in Canada to the Norwegian-American Chamber of Commerce, Widvey emphasized the point that 'visibility and image-building through dialogue is important to a nation, for political and ethical as well as economic reasons'.[34]

A key to Norway's success in forming useful as well as durable relationships has been that it has something to offer, and that it can offer it quickly, quietly, and, if in financial or material form, unconditionally and in significant quantity. It is also able to coordinate with others. The Utstein Group partnership that Norway's minister for development cooperation Hilde Frafjord Johnson formed with her counterparts from Germany, the Netherlands and the United Kingdom, with Sweden and now Canada joining, is an example.[35] By these means and methods, Norway is able to be 'an interesting and reliable partner'.[36] 'We gain some access', Petersen explains, by being at so many negotiating tables. Norway's niche knowledge of many of the world's crisis areas elevates its relevance – utility – for the larger countries with which it trades. Thus there can be advantageous political and other by-products of Norway's idealistically motivated mediatory and humanitarian diplomacy. According to Petersen, Norway got the ears of European countries to which it exports seafood because it had privileged insight into elections in Africa that those countries wanted to monitor. 'You can put it this way', he said, 'we talked about Zimbabwe and fish.'[37]

These are, however, not Norway's only stocks in trade. The country's main asset is not its 'brand' but its reputation. Thorhild Widvey acknowledges that Norway is sometimes portrayed in the press as 'a rich, self-centred and rather self-sufficient country', and is also seen by the world as 'a tradition-bound country of mountains, fjords, Vikings and the midnight sun'.[38] It is also recognized, however, as an honest broker, a generous giver and a reliable partner.

Conclusion: lessons from northern corners?

Can other countries, particularly medium-sized and smaller, profit from the examples of Canada's and Norway's experiences in projecting themselves, and their values and images, abroad? In both cases, it has been seen that geography – that is, location and resources – has been a defining precondition. Canada and Norway good-naturedly compete for the top spot in the United Nations Development Programme's annual ranking of 'the best countries in which to live'.[39] Their somewhat isolated, northern-peripheral situations, combined with their considerable natural endowments and skill in exploiting them, including petroleum reserves, have permitted but also required extensive diplomatic outreach. Although militarily weak, they are global players. It has been said that each 'punches above its weight' in the world public arena. Whether hard or soft, impact is not the issue. It is the Canadians' and Norwegians' influence, not power, that is so remarkable.

How have they done it? In both the Canadian and Norwegian cases, there has been an overarching ideology: 'good' ideas, such as well-articulated concepts of 'sustainable development'; more recently 'human security'; and now also 'the responsibility to protect'.[40] These notions were conceived as being for the global public good as well as for the benefit of the sponsoring countries. And this has been recognized.

Both countries have very effectively used public diplomacy, including the 'power of the better argument'. Canada has done so by lobbying, as well as through open advocacy, sometimes confrontational in style. Norway has concentrated on performing high-profile acts in faraway places, rather than using high-profile words close by. Its verbal expressions, although characteristically straightforward, have been much quieter. It has tended to move in parallel with power, rather than to oppose proposals and policies that it does not like. Its greater physical distance from the United States has given it much more freedom of international manoeuvre, although its growing closeness to the enlarged and constituted European Union may increasingly require vociferous defences of its domestic and international interests (and not only relating to fisheries).

Both Canada and Norway have used networks to great advantage, for themselves and for others. The multilateral context of the United Nations, NATO and the OSCE, and for Canada the Commonwealth and *la francophonie*, and for Norway the Council of Europe (which it chaired in late 2004), have given the two countries organizational scope for forming friendships (Norway's non-membership of the EU is, however, a disadvantage). Their NGO, civil society and corporate relationships also keep them in close working partnership with the world. Although some of Canada's and Norway's affiliations derive from who and where they are (for example, the Canadian humanitarian involvement in Haiti), such networking methods are not peculiar or exclusive to themselves. They can be replicated by almost any country in any part of the world. Some of their closest allies in the diplomatic world are from the 'South'. The largesse that both Canada and Norway can bestow, however, is a privilege – as well as a responsibility – that arises from their nations' wealth, including their own peoples' energy and inventiveness.

In Gareth Evans' and Bruce Grant's formulation of the 'niche diplomacy' idea, both countries, but more especially Norway, have also concentrated resources 'in specific areas best able to generate returns worth having, rather than trying to cover the field'.[41] The crucial 'worth having' standard consists not just of external criteria, including universal moral principles, but also of serious political requirements. Some of these are internal. In the case of Canada, as Evan Potter has pointed out, 'a considerable number of activities identified as "public diplomacy" in official DFAIT documents are, in fact, communications and consultation programmes directed at domestic audiences'.[42] A unifying foreign policy helps to produce a united nation, and even to define a national identity. Canada's prime 'niche' activity – peacekeeping – has long served exactly this role, within as well as outside Canada. Embarrassing setbacks, however, not to mention entry into the peacekeeping sphere of many new countries, have put into question this traditional

Canadian identifier. Bangladesh now contributes more personnel to peacekeeping than does Canada.

Norway's particular emphasis on peace mediation and reconciliation, as demonstrated in Sri Lanka, has also generated resistance, with the Norwegian peace facilitators being called 'salmon-eating busybodies' by a Sri Lankan political critic.[43] As Thorhild Widvey observes, 'a national image must satisfy three requirements. It must be genuine and trustworthy, it must be internally anchored, and it must be perceived as attractive in those markets we wish to target'.[44] Especially given the distance and the differences between countries like Norway and Sri Lanka, these are very difficult criteria to meet.

To be known for one thing or a single 'niche' role, even if practised over a long period of time and in many places, is very risky in diplomacy – as it is in nature. 'For small countries like Norway, which people in most countries have no idea of at all, it is a special challenge to avoid being stereotyped', said Widvey.[45] It is too easy for a country to be discredited, and soon forgotten about, even though its efforts are inherently worthwhile and are made for the best of motives. For this same reason, national 'branding' is an especially dangerous idea. It creates rigidities. Instead, countries that choose to specialize, as most smaller countries must now do to some degree in a globalizing economy with so many competitors active, should maintain maximum possible flexibility and the highest possible economic and political 'market' awareness.

For smaller countries that are situated geographically in the very middle of regions – a military–strategic centre, an industrial–financial core, or a transportation–communications crossroads – omni-directional thinking may come more easily than for Canada and Norway. If the centrally located country – Belgium or the Netherlands, for instance – has a similarly high level of competence and wealth on which to draw, it may be able to play an active intermediary role, taking part simultaneously and constantly in many games that are political as well as economic. As hypothesized, this would come largely by virtue of location. In other regions of the world too, certain centrally placed smaller countries – one thinks of Singapore, Jordan or Costa Rica – can play important intermediary roles, with their fingers in many pies. The more distinctive and specialized 'niche' functions seem to be reserved, however, for the world's corners, although not exclusively. It may be easier to concentrate resources if located on the periphery – as in Ottawa or Oslo. Yet in an age of globalization, the diplomacy that accompanies 'niche' specialization need not, as the examples of Canada and Norway demonstrate, be confined to any margin. It can cross, if not fill, the world public arena.

Notes

1. Gareth Evans and Bruce Grant, *Australia's Foreign Relations in the World of the 1990s* (Melbourne: Melbourne University Press, 1991), p. 323. For applications of the idea to the foreign policy behaviour of other middle-sized countries, see Andrew F. Cooper (ed.), *Niche Diplomacy: Middle Powers after the Cold War* (London: Macmillan, 1997).
2. For an explanation of the concept of 'global public goods' in various fields, see Inge Kaul, Pedro Conceição, Katell Le Goulven and Ronald U. Mendoza (eds), *Providing Global Public Goods: Managing Globalization* (New York: Oxford University Press, published for the United Nations Development Programme, 2003).
3. Roald Nasgaard, *The Mystic North: Symbolist Landscape Painting in Northern Europe and North America* (Toronto: University of Toronto Press, 1984).
4. During the 16 months prior to July 2004, for example, all four of the state secretaries of Norway's Ministry of Foreign Affairs visited Canada, some of them twice.
5. In conversation with Alan Henrikson, Cambridge MA, 13 April 2004.
6. Michael Ignatieff, 'Canada in the Age of Terror: Multilateralism Meets a Moment of Truth', *Policy Options*, February 2003, pp. 16 and 17, quoted in Joseph S. Nye, *Soft Power: The Means to Success in World Politics* (New York: PublicAffairs, 2004), p. 10.
7. Jan Petersen, 'Peace Mediation and Reconciliation', joint Belgian-Norwegian seminar on the occasion of the Norwegian state visit to Brussels, 21 May 2003, *Utenriksdepartementet*, odin.dep.no/ud/engelsk/aktuelt/taler/statsraad_a/032171-090127/dok-bn-html.
8. Petersen, 'Peace Mediation and Reconciliation'.
9. 'Welcome Message from Colin Robertson, Consul General', Canadian Consulate General, Los Angeles CA, www.dfait-maeci.gc.ca/can-am/menu-en.asp?mid = 9.
10. 'Editorial – The Accidental Peace Awarder', *News of Norway*, November 2001. The Peace Prize is given by the Norwegian Nobel Committee, an independent body whose members are appointed by the *Storting* (Norwegian parliament) on the basis of the relative strengths of the political parties in the *Storting*. Members of the government or parliament do not serve on the Norwegian Nobel Committee, however.
11. Henry Kissinger, *Does America Need a Foreign Policy? Toward a Diplomacy for the Twenty-First Century* (New York: Simon and Schuster, 2001), pp. 227 and 230.
12. Nye, *Soft Power*, p. 7.
13. Nye, *Soft Power*, p. 6.
14. Nye, *Soft Power*, p. 9.
15. Bertrand Badie, 'Realism under Praise, or a Requiem? The Paradigmatic Debate in International Relations', *International Political Science Review/Revue internationale de science politique*, vol. 22, no. 3, July 2001, p. 258.
16. Allan E. Gotlieb, 'Canada–US Relations: Some Thoughts about Public Diplomacy', address to The Empire Club of Canada, 10 November 1983, *The Empire Club of Canada Speeches 1983–1984* (Toronto: The Empire Club Foundation, 1984), pp. 101–15, www.empireclubfoundation.com/details.asp?SpeechID = 2120&FT = yes. Allan Gotlieb, *'I'll Be with You in a Minute, Mr*

Ambassador': *The Education of a Canadian Diplomat in Washington* (Toronto: University of Toronto Press, 1991), colourfully describes the Canadian shift towards new influence channels and the use of public diplomacy.

17. Evan H. Potter, 'Canada and the New Public Diplomacy', *International Journal*, vol. 58, no. 1, winter 2002–03, p. 51. See also Evan H. Potter, *Canada and the New Public Diplomacy*, Clingendael Discussion Papers in Diplomacy, no. 81 (The Hague: Netherlands Institute of International Relations 'Clingendael', 2002).

18. *Canada and the World: Canadian Foreign Policy Review 1995*, www.dfait-maeci. gc.ca/foreign_policy/cnd-world/menu-en.asp.

19. Partly as an outgrowth of the landmines' ban communication experience, Canadian foreign minister Lloyd Axworthy launched a comprehensive national public diplomacy plan: the Canadian International Information Strategy (CIIS). This was based on a Task Force report, *Connecting with the World: Priorities for Canadian Internationalism in the Twenty First Century* (November 1996). The ambitious CIIS scheme never made it to the table of the Canadian Cabinet for full discussion and government decision. It did, however, encourage a vanguard of Canadian officials to bring public diplomacy into the institutional mainstream. The multilingual Government of Canada 'Canada International' website is, in effect, a derivative of the CIIS.

20. Human Security Network, www.humansecuritynetwork.org. The first ministerial meeting of the HSN took place at Lysøen in Norway on 20 May 1999, with South Africa, a somewhat larger country, participating as an observer.

21. Anthony DePalma, 'A Canadian Routs Diplomacy (and Ruffles the US)', *New York Times*, 10 January 1999. The 'pulpit diplomacy' characterization is from two Canadian scholars, Fen O. Hampson and Dean F. Oliver. See their 'Pulpit Diplomacy: A Critical Assessment of the Axworthy Doctrine', *International Journal*, vol. 53, no. 3, summer 1998, pp. 379–406.

22. *Departmental Performance: Public Diplomacy*, 7 February 2003, Department of Foreign Affairs and International Trade, Canada, www.dfait-maeci.gc.ca/ department/performance/section21-en.asp.

23. *Departmental Performance: Public Diplomacy*.

24. *Foreign Affairs Canada*, 14 June 2004, www.fac-aec.gc.ca/menu-en.asp; and *Information about the Changes*, 1 April 2004, www.dfait-maeci.gc.ca/department/ focus/dfait_changes-en.asp.

25. Larry Luxner, 'Canadian Embassy Planning Legislative Secretariat in Washington', *The Washington Diplomat*, August 2004, p. A-18.

26. Luxner, 'Canadian Embassy Planning Legislative Secretariat in Washington', p. A-18.

27. 'Peace Prize for Norway', *News of Norway*, February 2004. Ambassador Vollebaek was presented with the Peacemaker/Peacebuilder Award by the National Peace Foundation in Washington on 30 January 2004.

28. 'Norway's Involvement in the Middle Eastern Peace Process', *News of Norway*, November–December 1999.

29. Andy Altman-Ohr, 'In Oslo, Home of the '93 Accords, Collective Frustration Pervades', *Jewish Bulletin of Northern California*, 27 October 2000, www.jewishsf. com/bk001027/imidnorway.shtml.

30. Jan Egeland, *Impotent Superpower – Potent Small State: Potentials and Limitations of Human Rights Objectives in the Foreign Policies of the United States and Norway* (Oslo: Norwegian University Press, 1988, distributed by Oxford University Press).
31. Frank Bruni, 'A Nation That Exports Oil, Herring and Peace', *New York Times*, 21 December 2002.
32. Mark Leonard and Andrew Small, *Norwegian Public Diplomacy* (London: Foreign Policy Centre, 2003), pp. 1 and 3. The other 'stories' that Leonard and Small suggest stressing are 'living with nature', 'equality', and 'internationality/spirit of adventure' (pp. 3–4).
33. Thorhild Widvey, 'Opening Speech', Images of Norway: A Conference on Public Diplomacy, Oslo, 7 March 2003, odin.dep.no/ud/engelsk/aktuelt/taler/p10001532/bn.html. She has subsequently been appointed minister of petroleum and energy.
34. Thorhild Widvey, 'Public Diplomacy', address to Norwegian-American Chamber of Commerce, Ottawa, 7 November 2003, odin.dep.no/ud/norsk/aktuelt/taler/taler_politisk_ledelse/032171-090183/dok.bn.html.
35. For more on the Utstein Group partnership, see www.u4.no/about/u4partnership.cfm.
36. Norwegian foreign minister Jan Petersen, 'Norwegian Public Diplomacy', address at the Nordic Heritage Museum, Seattle, 12 April 2004, odin.dep.no/ud/norsk/aktuelt/taler/statsraad_a/032171-090220/dok-bn.html.
37. Bruni, 'A Nation that Exports Oil, Herring and Peace'.
38. Widvey, 'Opening Speech' at Images of Norway conference.
39. 'Norway Heads Quality of Life Index; Canada Miffed', Reuters, 8 July 2003.
40. *The Responsibility to Protect: A Report of the International Commission on Intervention and State Sovereignty* (Ottawa: International Development Research Centre, 2001). The ICISS joint chairs were Gareth Evans (Australia) and Mohamed Sahnoun (Algeria). The chairman of the Advisory Board was Canada's Lloyd Axworthy.
41. Evans and Grant, *Australia's Foreign Relations in the World of the 1990s*, p. 323.
42. Potter, 'Canada and the New Public Diplomacy', p. 47.
43. 'Norway Suspends Peace Role in Sri Lanka', *Financial Times*, 14 November 2003.
44. Widvey, 'Public Diplomacy'.
45. Widvey, 'Opening Speech' at Images of Norway conference.

5
Public Diplomacy in the People's Republic of China
Ingrid d'Hooghe

Introduction

Public diplomacy may not be a current term in China, yet China has certainly developed a remarkable array of activities that together form a consistent and quite effective public diplomacy policy. Perceptions and the behaviour of both China's domestic and international publics are having a growing impact on China's foreign policy. Rising to play a more substantial role in world politics and economics, and often feeling misjudged by the international community, the Chinese leadership is increasingly making effective use of public diplomacy tools to project an image of China that in their view does more justice to reality: China as a trustworthy, cooperative, peace-loving, developing country that takes good care of its enormous population. Examples of this are China's role as honest broker and responsible world power in the North Korean nuclear crisis, China's campaign to win the 2008 Olympic Games, and its policy to convince neighbouring countries that they do not have to fear a rising China.

This chapter looks at how China has discovered and developed its public diplomacy. It gives an overview of China's actions in this field, on a large-scale global level as well as on a small-scale bilateral level. It also addresses a dimension to which the regime does not pay a great deal of attention, but which has enormous potential from a public diplomacy perspective: China's culture. Cinema, painting and calligraphy, literature (the Nobel Prize), traditional medicine, acupuncture, martial arts and Chinese cuisine have conquered the world without deliberate action by the Chinese government, but are powerful assets in creating a positive image abroad.

Two factors make China's public diplomacy especially interesting: the fact that China is a one-party state with a centralist authoritarian regime that has far-reaching control over public diplomacy instruments; and the fact that China can build on a tradition of political propaganda. These characteristics explain both China's strengths and weaknesses with regard to its public diplomacy. As illustrated later, China's leaders understand and address the importance of both domestic and foreign audiences, but the focus of their foreign policy strategy is solely on formal intergovernmental contacts. This makes the Chinese case an outstanding example of what Hocking calls the 'state-centred, hierarchical model of diplomacy' and Manheim terms 'strategic public diplomacy': when the government of one country uses strategic political communication to influence opinion in another.[1] Playing an active role in a global policy network with public and private actors is something for a distant future, as China's civil society is only cautiously developing and China's leaders do not allow independent actors to engage in foreign policy.

China's foreign policy and diplomacy

The development of China's public diplomacy cannot be detached from the rapid development of China's diplomacy as a whole during the last decade, which, in its turn, cannot be detached from the enormous economic and political changes that have taken place and that are still taking place in China. Today's China is a booming economic power with a pragmatic outlook on the world. It is the world's sixth largest economy and the fourth largest trading nation. China is a country in rapid transition, halfway on the road from a poor, backward and isolated country with a centrally planned economy to a rapidly developing, outward-looking country with a (socialist) market economy, integrating into the world economy and largely working within the international system of multilateral organizations. At the same time it is a growing political power, deploying an ever more proactive, assertive and effective diplomacy to achieve its goals. Over the last few years China has become an important player in world affairs, and its diplomacy has moved from the back to front stage. Deng Xiaoping's adage of the early 1990s – 'keep a low profile and never take the lead' – in world affairs has largely been abandoned. While former Chinese leaders hardly ventured abroad, President Hu Jintao, Premier Wen Jiabao and Minister of Foreign Affairs Li Zhaoxing make innumerable visits to all continents. In 2002 China knocked on NATO's door and in June 2003 President Hu Jintao attended an informal Enlarged Dialogue meeting between G8 leaders and heads of eleven developing countries, whereas in the past China had always kept its distance from what it used to call the 'rich man's club'.

China's foreign policy, however, is subordinate to the country's primary aim: attaining rapid domestic growth and modernization. China's leaders realize that their regime is legitimized by China's economic growth. At the sixteenth Chinese Communist Party Congress in 2002, a blueprint for China's long-term national goal was presented: to transform the current Chinese society by 2020 into a 'little prosperity' (*xiaokang*) society where people enjoy a comfortable life. To reach that goal China's gross domestic product would have to quadruple by 2020. A stable international environment is necessary for China's economic growth and in practice this means that China will do its best to avoid conflicts or dependency on one country or region. China's New Security Concept, launched in the late 1990s but firmly established in 2002, promotes the idea that in the post-Cold War period, nations are able to increase their security through diplomatic and economic interaction instead of through competing and antagonistic blocs. Beijing now actively seeks to boost its influence in the region, but at the same time aims for a 'full strategic partnership' with the European Union in areas including trade, culture, technology, defence and space exploration, as well as a stable relationship with the United States. It is against this background of further opening up and stepping into global politics that China has become more active in the field of public diplomacy.

China's political and economic successes on the international stage are evident and spark applause as well as fears. In the United States the 'China Threat' debate[2] flares up regularly and in many Asian capitals policy-makers are concerned that China's economic strength will sooner or later encourage it to dominate the region or even to assert its power militarily. To succeed in sustaining its economic growth and convince other countries that China only seeks peaceful development, mutual prosperity and no hegemony, Beijing has looked at how it could improve its diplomacy and image abroad and has developed an answer to the American 'China Threat' debate and Asian worries. In doing so, it has come up with the concept of 'China's Peaceful Rise' (*Zhongguo de heping jueqi*). Wherever and whenever Chinese leaders get the chance, they stress to regional audiences that China envisages a mutually beneficial growth leading to co-prosperity. The concept of 'China's Peaceful Rise' – or 'Peaceful Development of China' as it has recently been named by some to avoid the threatening connotation of the word 'rise' – is now a cornerstone of China's public diplomacy.

Before further exploring China's current public diplomacy, a brief overview of China's past handling of international perceptions will be described, as it illustrates that reaching out to foreign audiences has always been on China's Communist Party's agenda.

Targeting foreign audiences from 1949 onwards

China is deeply sensitive to foreign perceptions of China and its policies abroad. Both foreign appraisals of China's diplomatic perform-ance and negative perceptions of China's domestic situation are often mentioned and quoted in articles in the Chinese press. Chinese govern-ment officials hold the Western media responsible for creating a negative image of China. Minister Zhao Qizheng of the State Council Information Office, while on a visit to Moscow in August 2003, lashed out at Western media coverage of China. He complained that the Western media not only controls public opinion but also damages China's image in the world: 'Using their media dominance, they are stressing the negatives in China without pointing out recent positive developments'.[3]

Understanding the importance of creating a positive image abroad is nothing new in China. The Chinese Communist Party has long under-stood the power of good foreign press, examples of which can be found throughout its history. For example, in the mid-1930s the Chinese Communist Party invited American journalist Edgar Snow to China to report on the civil war. The book that Snow later wrote on Mao Zedong's struggle with the Nationalist forces, *Red Star Over China*, depicted the Communist leader as a hero. The book was a worldwide success. After founding the People's Republic of China in 1949, the regime kept inviting selected journalists and academics to visit (selected parts of) China and write about it. Furthermore, they soon created English-, French-, Spanish- and Japanese-language publications to inform foreigners about develop-ments in China and to propagate the blessings of Communism. The latter, of course, dominated the contents of these publications; problems or drawbacks were never mentioned. Even during the Cultural Revolution, magazines such as *Beijing Review*, *China Reconstructs* and *China Pictorial* found their way to foreign readers all over the world. The images projected over the decades by these magazines and other publications include those of China as a peace-loving country, a victim of foreign aggression, a socialist country (stressed in the Maoist era), an anti-hegemonic force, a developing country and – especially from 1978 onwards – a cooperator.[4]

In the early 1970s, when the Chinese leaders wanted to end China's international isolation, they started to propagate 'ping-pong diplomacy' and pandas, thus making way for the new image of a more outward-looking China. A real new image, however, only began to emerge in the late 1970s, after China's new and charismatic leader, Deng Xiaoping, introduced the 'open-door policy' and economic reforms. His pragmatic approach, summarized by the now famous one-liner 'it doesn't matter if the cat is white or black, as long as it catches mice', appealed to foreign audiences all over the world. Deng's public diplomacy was very effective, all the more so because it was supported by actions to open up and modernize China. Foreign businessmen and tourists crowded to China's door and investments surged. In 1985 Deng was chosen as 'Man of the Year' by the international *TIME Magazine*.

But in 1989 the Tiananmen crisis severely damaged China's new and favourable reputation abroad. The predominant image from Tiananmen was that of a lone protester, standing in front of a row of tanks, clinging on to a handbag – a strong, long-lasting image, all the more so when it was chosen as the World Press Photo of 1989. Immediately after Tiananmen, Chinese leaders were not very interested in what the outside world was thinking of them. They were too busy stabilizing the country. Soon, however, they understood that they had to break through the isolation and they hired one of the largest public-relations firms in the world – Hill & Knowlton – to help repair China's image. Two years later, the internal situation seemed under control and China's new leader, Jiang Zemin, sat firmly in the saddle. The Chinese regime began to step up its efforts to sway international opinion by increasingly reaching out to foreign audiences in order to promote trade and investment and to further China's standing in the world.

In sum, one could say that the concept of public diplomacy – their proponents would call it propaganda[5] – was a well-established part of the Chinese Communist Party's diplomatic handbook. With the exception of the immediate post-Tiananmen period, and parts of the Cultural Revolution period, China has used the instrument to create a favourable impression with foreigners of China and its achievements.

China's present public diplomacy goals

In the pre-Deng Xiaoping period, public diplomacy had the relatively limited goal of creating a favourable image of an otherwise autarkic country. However, the task of public diplomacy since Deng put forward his 'open door policy' at the end of the 1970s has become more complex and demanding. Current public diplomacy still has to boost the legitimacy of the Communist Party as China's central ruler, but in addition has to lure foreign investment to the country and make China's rise palatable to the region and the world at large. On top of that, negative news and images have to be redressed. China's leaders seem to understand that their public diplomacy efforts need to be supported by corresponding actions in order to be credible and thus successful. That does not stop them, however, from propagating images that they cannot live up to, such as in the field of human rights. Looking in more detail at China's public diplomacy, three major goals can be distinguished.

First, China wants to be seen as a country that works hard to give its people a better future and seeks understanding for its political system and policies. The image stressed is that of a developing country in the middle of a slow but fundamental economic transition, confronted with enormous challenges to which no easy responses exist. In other words, the world may not expect China's leaders to take radical steps in political and economic reform, as rash policies will destabilize the country and bring misery to the people. China's efforts to inform the public of its policies via websites, white papers, magazines and scholarly exchanges should be seen in this light.

Second, China wants to be seen as a stable, trustworthy and responsible economic partner, a rising economic power that does not have to be feared. This is the crux of China's policy of good neighbourliness, part of the 'Peaceful Rise of China' strategy and well illustrated by its balanced diplomacy in South-East Asia. With its charm offensive during the Association of South-East Asian Nations (ASEAN) summit meeting in Indonesia in October 2003, China clearly strove to convince neighbouring countries that both sides will gain from an economically strong China, that they will all attain 'co-prosperity'.[6] At the same time it wanted to show the West that China is trusted in the region. In this field the Chinese government clearly supports its public diplomacy with actions. Over the last decade, China has doubled its foreign direct investment to ASEAN, initiated a road map to a Chinese-ASEAN Free Trade Area by 2010, and concluded a bilateral swap agreement with ASEAN countries. Furthermore, it has softened its stand on the dispute over the Spratley Islands in the South China Sea.

Third, China's leaders want China to be seen as a trustworthy and responsible member of the international community, capable of and willing to contribute actively to world peace. The most recent and obvious illustration of this policy is Beijing's current role as host and chair of the six-party talks on North Korea. China's increasing multilateralist cooperation is another example. But there are opposing actions as well: until recently China traded nuclear technology with countries such as Iran, North Korea and Pakistan; and Beijing still threatens to use military force against Taiwan if the island takes steps towards independence.

Last but not least, China wants to be respected as an ancient culture with a long history. The increasing number of international cultural events that China organizes all over the world should strengthen this image. Beijing's contribution to the closing ceremony of the 2004 Olympic Games in Athens was another illustration. The act was mainly composed of traditional cultural images such as dragons, the figure of the monkey king and Chinese opera, stressing the image of China as an ancient culture.

Assets and liabilities

China's biggest liabilities that hamper 'selling' the country are: its human rights' records (including the Falungong issue); its minority policies (including the Tibet issue); and China's unification (the Taiwan issue). China recognizes them as liabilities and addresses them by public diplomacy: policies are explained in white papers, articles, on websites and during press conferences. Although public diplomacy with regard to these issues does not seem to be very successful – all the more as it is hardly supported by positive policies or actions – it is nevertheless considered internationally as a big step forward that the authorities no longer keep silent about these sensitive issues as they used to until the early 1990s. In that sense, the simple step of making these issues discussable, thus creating the hope that they will also be negotiable, has already yielded profit for the Chinese side.

China's biggest assets when selling the country are its (ancient) culture and its economic success. Beijing is well aware of the latter, and as discussed earlier has developed careful public diplomacy to allay suspicions of a rising China. Looking at how China exploits its culture or 'soft power', one finds an ambiguous approach. Joseph Nye defines 'soft power' as 'the influence and attractiveness a nation acquires when others are drawn to its culture and ideas'.[7] China's policy-makers certainly use the popularity of Chinese culture outside their borders to promote international relations and tourism, but mainly focus on harmless, apolitical, traditional culture, including Chinese cuisine and acupuncture. At the same time, however, a new generation of Chinese artists, writers, filmmakers and actors, combining traditional arts with modern ideas and developments, are conquering the world. They are attracting and dazzling foreign audiences and winning international prizes. In 2000, the Chinese author Gao Xinjian was the first Chinese to win the Nobel Prize for Literature. The Chinese film *Crouching Tiger, Hidden Dragon* has become one of the biggest non-English-language box office successes. The Chinese actress Gong Li is celebrated at major film festivals. Chinese painters such as Fang Lijun and Zhang Xiaogang are invited to exhibit in major galleries and museums around the world. Many cultural expressions, however, such as books, poems, films, visual art works as well as theatre performances are considered subversive by the regime and are subsequently denounced and domestically forbidden. This part of China's growing soft power thus seems ignored by China's leaders.

It is not only the Western world that is attracted by China's cultural expressions. South-East Asian youths in particular are fascinated by Chinese films, fashion and pop music. Furthermore, mainland Chinese consumer brands have become popular in the region, as has the study of the Chinese language.[8] Related to this growth of China's soft power in South-East Asia is the rise of ethnic Chinese groups in the region. Formerly often anti-Beijing, these communities have now come to accept a modernizing and successful China.[9]

Target groups

The Chinese distinguish between target countries and target groups and fine-tune their message or tone accordingly. During a conference of the Information Office of the State Council in 1991, it was already acknowledged, for example, that foreigners and overseas Chinese are 'different' and that 'publicity should not be carried out the same way that it is at home'.[10] Each of the above-mentioned goals involves one or more specific target group. The 'China's Peaceful Rise' message is aimed primarily at the Asian region, whereas public diplomacy with regard to China's human rights situation mainly targets Europe and the United States.

One of the more general target groups on which China is focusing is the enormous group of overseas Chinese communities. In the US alone there are 2.4 million overseas Chinese. They play a role in promoting Chinese culture and lobbying for political interests. Over the past three years China has set up more than 80 pro-China associations among overseas communities across the world and has supported the convening of regional conferences in a drive to form a united global network of such organizations.[11] Beijing sponsors and promotes a great number of economic, educational and cultural activities through such organizations, with the aim of keeping these groups on China's side and stimulating them to invest in China.

The instruments

China uses the same public diplomacy instruments as other countries: the media, internet, events and projects, celebrities and publications, but the way that they are used sometimes differs, if only for the fact that in the Chinese case many of the 'instruments' are state-controlled. This is a particularly important factor when we look at the domestic media as an instrument.

China's domestic media were until recently the main instruments to inform the outside world about China. There have been English-language Chinese newspapers and journals targeted at foreign audiences since the early years of the People's Republic of China. China also has an English-language television channel that can be received all over the world. The Chinese have their own 'Voice of China', called China Radio International, with broadcastings in all of the major world languages. The official Chinese news agency, Xinhua, has an English-language service. These organizations are all state-owned and controlled, and although in some cases the possibilities for journalists and editors to bring their own news and messages has somewhat increased, much of the content of the programmes, newspapers and magazines is still dictated by official policy lines.

Nowadays, in addition to its own media, China's public diplomacy makes more and more use of international media. A large number of foreign correspondents are accredited to Beijing, Chinese leaders often give press conferences during foreign visits and a new generation of Chinese diplomats has started to address the foreign press.[12] A good example of the latter is China's Ambassador to the Netherlands, Mrs Xue Hanqin. Shortly after her arrival in The Hague she gave several interviews to the Dutch press and wrote a week-long diary for one of the Netherlands' major newspapers.[13] The interviews and diary favourably impressed people, with the result that for the first time a wider audience than just the diplomatic community in The Hague knows a Chinese Ambassador to the Netherlands.

The Chinese are learning fast about how to deal with the press. In February 2000, for example, a suicide bomber killed himself in Tiananmen Square. A few years earlier silence would have followed, but this time it took only a few hours for the police to hand out press releases describing the bomber as a deranged farmer who was angry about a tax-dodging fine. This way they anticipated Western speculations that the man would be a political dissident or Falungong supporter. Chinese leaders also go out and talk to the Western editors and press agencies. When meeting Ted Turner of CNN, Minister Zhao expressed his concerns about biased news coverage of China: 'I told him that CNN is not objective – that it spends seven minutes showing trash on the streets of China and only three minutes on the flowers we plant'.[14]

Furthermore, China makes effective use of the possibilities of the internet. You do not have to speak Chinese to spend an afternoon surfing the Chinese internet, visiting accessible and sometimes beautifully designed websites in English or even several other languages. Newspaper archives are easily accessible and you can download new and old articles for free. Many of these websites are developed specifically for the purpose of propaganda/public diplomacy and are controlled by the Information Office. The Tibet website and the three-dimensional x3dChina website for showcasing China's culture opened in October 2003 in New York by Minister of the State Council Information Office Zhao Qizheng, are good examples of this policy.[15]

The importance of publications as a means to reach out to a wide audience has decreased with development of the internet. Once in a while you will still find little English booklets – for free – on Chinese topics, ranging from the Chinese Constitution or marriage law to big construction projects, but their share in the information flow has almost dissolved. As mentioned earlier, China devotes much attention to explaining its policies in white papers, the most remarkable being China's EU Paper, which was published in October 2003, making China the first non-European country to publish a serious and official vision on the European Union and to take Europe seriously as an entity.

Not to be underestimated is the power of the fourth instrument that China increasingly uses: events. With the aim of increasing its visibility in the world, China has become an eager organizer of big events. In the 1990s China hosted the Asian games and the UN International Women's Conference. In 2001 Shanghai spared no expense to impress participants in the APEC Summit, and in 2001 Beijing finally won its bid for the Olympic Games of 2008, which the regime, as well as outside observers, see as a major chance for China to show its capabilities to the world. It will also offer an ideal opportunity to capitalize on worldwide interest in China's ancient culture. The same will be true of the World Exhibition of 2010, to be held in Shanghai.

At the same time, China organizes many smaller events that are dedicated to Chinese culture or international trade. Examples for culture are Chinese Culture Weeks in the US (2000), Berlin (2001), and in St Petersburg (August 2003), the latter carefully planned on the occasion of the 300th anniversary of St Petersburg, to which many international guests and press were invited. A good example for international trade is the 2001 ten-city tour of the Chinese Ambassador to Washington under the banner 'A National Conversation with the Chinese Ambassador'. The tour was sponsored by US firms and the US Chamber of Commerce and was supposed to be about 'the many opportunities to do business in China', but some complained that it was just as much used as a platform to present Chinese views on political issues to the audiences.[16]

Another instrument that should be mentioned consists of the Chinese gardens and theme parks that have opened in many Western countries. They are usually of a non-political character and owned by Western companies or institutions. In the US, however, a 'Splendid China' theme park was opened, which is supposedly owned by the Chinese government and should convey the message that China attaches great value to the Tibetan and Uyghur cultures within its borders.[17]

Finally, there are innumerable exchanges among schools, universities, chambers of commerce, twin cities and so on.

The inner working of China's public diplomacy system

In developing and deciding upon China's public diplomacy activities, a major role is reserved for the State Council Information Office. In late 1991 at a National Work Conference on External Propaganda, the State Council Foreign Propaganda Office – or External Publicity as the Chinese nowadays prefer to call it – was established. Propaganda and publicity work had previously been the task of the Foreign Propaganda Office of the Chinese Communist Party. The declared task of the new State Council Foreign Publicity office was:

> to promote China as a stable country in the process of reform, a China that takes good care of its population, including the minorities, and works hard to reduce poverty.[18]

The creation of this new office coincided with the end of the period of post-Tiananmen isolation. The Chinese government started issuing a steady flow of white papers clarifying China's policies on such critical issues as ethnic minorities, human rights and national defence, and educational and cultural exchanges were resumed. But China's public diplomacy only got a real kick-start when Zhao Qizheng became Minister of the Information Office of the State Council and started his 'information' and 'publicity' work in 1998. He called upon China's overseas information officials:

> to publicize China's economic and social achievements and explain China's official positions and policies on issues more fully to foreigners, to create a more favourable image of China in world opinion.[19]

Since Zhao took over, a sea change in the way that Beijing deals with official information has occurred. A few examples of his change of style:

- he more than doubled the frequency of press conferences;
- he urged Chinese officials to be more accommodating towards journalists;
- he reinstated the use of English at press conferences;
- he introduced in Beijing the risky Western-style approach of speaking off the record.

Zhao's unorthodox style as official spokesman on foreign policy was marked at once, but he made a lasting impression when in 1999 he decried the US *Cox Report* that accused China of stealing military technology. During the press conference he used a computer to show the audience how all of the information that China was accused of having stolen from the US could be found on the internet.

Apart from the State Council Information Office and Foreign Publicity Office, China's Ministry of Foreign Affairs is the other major player in the field of public diplomacy. In 2000, China's Foreign Ministry established its first media centre to smooth relations with an international press, which it knows is critical for how the world perceives China's policies. It also operates an extensive and accessible website. Even more important, however, is that the Ministry is gradually giving the diplomats at its embassies more freedom to get involved with foreign audiences. The Chinese Minister of Foreign Affairs, Li Zhaoxing, mentioned a series of 'innovations and breakthroughs' in Chinese diplomacy in March 2004, among them the awareness of being active and creative in foreign work and 'assuming a deeper hue of emotion',[20] examples being China's aid to Algeria and Iran after the earthquakes that shook these countries in 2003 and its aid in cash and medicine to Vietnam, Thailand and Indonesia. According to Minister Li, 'it conveyed

China's sincerity in its policy of "good neighbourliness and partnership" towards its Asian neighbours'.[21]

Besides drawing closer to foreign audiences, the Chinese Foreign Ministry is also keen to reach out to domestic audiences. Within the Ministry of Foreign Affairs, the term 'public diplomacy' is even used for publicity work aimed at domestic audiences. In order to shorten the distance between Chinese diplomats and the ordinary Chinese people, the Foreign Ministry gives lectures, organizes internet discussions and invites people to visit the Foreign Ministry. In spring 2004 the Ministry of Foreign Affairs organized a (domestic) public diplomacy conference, which was attended by diplomats and scholars.[22]

China's public diplomacy strategies: the case of Tibet

Do these examples of public diplomacy activities by China mean that the Chinese government has developed a grand public diplomacy strategy, or, to speak in Chinese terms, a five-year plan for public diplomacy? Nothing points in that direction, but it is evident that the Chinese government does devote serious attention to the issue and that it has developed rather comprehensive plans for action. First, it makes choices: the government has identified a number of issues on which it wants to focus, such as human rights, Tibet, minorities, being a trust-worthy power, environment, culture, and so on. Second, it selects target groups for each topic and fine-tunes its message to a specific audience. Third, it uses various instruments to get the message across, such as the press (radio, newspapers, TV), the internet, white papers, cultural events and theme parks.

A good example of a comprehensive strategy to influence international public opinion is the strategy on the issue of Tibet. This is a relatively well-documented case, as classified documents on the external publicity strategy regarding Tibet were leaked from Beijing and various pro-Tibet organizations follow developments closely.[23] In documents prepared for a meeting of Chinese government officials to review the external publicity strategy regarding Tibet in 1993, the following statement was made:

> Looking at it in a bigger picture, the external propaganda work on the question of Tibet has bearing not only on the progress and develop-ment of Tibet, but also on the image of China as a whole in the world, as well as the creation of a good international environment for the reform, open policy and the construction of the modernization of all China.[24]

Public diplomacy on the issue of Tibet was thus considered to serve multiple domestic and international goals. The 1993 documents identified the US and France as the two nations that were most hostile to China on Tibet, and then went on carefully to list target groups. Appropriate actions and activities were developed for each target group. Target groups were listed as:

1. Tibetans living abroad: the campaign played upon the 'deep feeling for their homeland';
2. reporters, diplomats, international scholars and Tibetologists: for these groups the (then) External Propaganda Office annually organized visits to Tibet;
3. the foreign media: the documents advised to: 'select some relatively objective and fair-minded persons and journalists to visit Tibet and only request them to report objective facts. Being truthful to facts is very convincing. The number of people doesn't have to be large, but the selection must be well made';[25]
4. decision-makers, intellectuals and scholars: they were to be reached by a white paper;
5. the general public: the Office planned to send abroad Tibetan singing and dancing troupes, exhibitions and lectures by Chinese Tibetologists, to publicize important Tibetan religious events internationally, and to publish books.

Ten years later, the strategy is not that different: foreigners are still invited to visit Tibet; Tibetan cultural groups still go abroad; and websites and publications still try to win support for China's Tibet policy. The tone of China's public diplomacy with regard to Tibet, however, has been adjusted. Minister Zhao Qizheng of the Information Office of the State Council now stresses the importance of non-politicized publicity and has called for Tibetologists to play an important role in publicity work.[26]

This case serves to illustrate that China devotes much time and money to developing well thought-out and detailed public diplomacy strategies to tackle problems with regard to its international image. The strategy with regard to Tibet has been carried out for more than ten years and is reviewed and adjusted on a regular basis.

The limits of China's public diplomacy

No matter how well China is doing in transforming its traditional diplomacy and developing public diplomacy, sometimes things still go utterly wrong. This is when China gets into the old Communist cramp of maintaining full control of society and concealing unfavourable information from the public, thus not only hampering the growth of China's soft power but also damaging cautious international impressions that China is moving towards a more open society. The most recent example was the SARS crisis in summer 2003, when China hoped to limit the damage by playing down the gravity of the situation. This seriously backfired: international and domestic indignation was enormous and criticism was severe and put pressure on the Chinese leadership. But China learned fast and in April 2004, when new SARS cases occurred, China's leaders immediately disclosed the state of affairs and took swift and effective action.

The limits of China's public diplomacy are defined by the fact that diplomacy is a highly centralized and state-controlled affair – a form of modernized propaganda. In that sense the case of China seems to fit Manheim's idea of strategic public diplomacy perfectly: 'It is, within the limits of available knowledge, the practice of propaganda in the earliest sense of the term, but enlightened by half a century of empirical research into human motivation and behaviour.'[27] Connected to this notion, but not within the scope of this chapter, is the interesting question of to what extent China owes its relatively successful performance in the field of public diplomacy to the fact that the authorities can build on a long tradition of domestic and international publicity work and propaganda.

In developing its public diplomacy, China seems trapped between its aim at perfection in image projection and the structural lack of openness of its society, as well as its inability to give up control. Furthermore, the Chinese regime will need to match its words with actions. As long as political dissidents are arrested and detained for their political ideas or liberal newspapers and magazines are shut down, no public diplomacy will be able to change China's image as a country where human rights are violated.

For the time being there do not seem to be many possibilities for developing public diplomacy in the modern or 'network' sense. That is not to say that people-to-people exchange does not take place at all. The Chinese People's Association for Friendship with Foreign Countries (CPAFFC) and the Institute of Foreign Affairs (IFA), for example, organize all kinds of activities labelled 'People-to-People Diplomacy'.[28] In a speech on the occasion of the fiftieth birthday of CPAFFC in May 2004, Chinese President Hu Jintao said:

The Chinese government will always support non-governmental efforts to promote mutual understanding between its people and other peoples.[29]

In reality, however, organizations such as CPAFFC are not yet independent, although their freedom of action may gradually increase. In sum, one could say that the room for dialogue and the engagement of China's own population is expanding along with the slowly but steadily increasing number of non-governmental organizations and the need and freedom for people to speak out on international issues.

Conclusion

China may not (yet) have a 'grand public diplomacy strategy', but looking at the scope and variety of Chinese public diplomacy and considering how well-thought-out many of the actions are, one cannot but conclude that China is doing well and is even ahead of many Western countries in public diplomacy. China, however, needs public diplomacy more badly: China is 'suspected' for many reasons in many parts of the world. Asia worries about China's economic and political rise; Europe mainly about China's violations of human rights; and the US worries about both. China's leaders are concerned about China's image and standing in the rest of the world and devote much attention to creating more understanding for China's policies. They distinguish between themes, target groups and instruments and attune one to the other. They learn from their mistakes – as in the SARS case – and they are aware of their limitations: if something big is at stake, they enlist the help of international companies, as with the 2008 Olympic Games bid.[30]

Most of China's diplomacy, including its public diplomacy is, if not government-directed, at least government-controlled. Furthermore, it seems to build on decade-long experiences with domestic propaganda. These experiences and the state's command of public diplomacy instruments lie at the root of both China's successes and shortcomings with regard to public diplomacy. On the one hand, they enable China's leaders carefully to design and attune messages and actions and make sure that they are carried out as dictated. On the other hand, they hamper the development of a modern model of public diplomacy that is based on open dialogue and the policy networks of independent actors.

Notes

1. See the chapter in this book by B. Hocking; and Jarol B. Manheim, *Strategic Public Diplomacy and American Foreign Policy: The Evolution of Influence* (New York: Oxford University Press, 1994).
2. This debate varies from the question of to what extent a rising China will harm the economy of the United States, to the question of whether or not China has a long-term strategic plan to defeat America; named after the book by Bill Gertz, *The China Threat: The Plan to Defeat America* (Washington DC: Regnery Publishing, 2000).
3. 'Beijing Lashes Out at Western Media Coverage of China', *Agence France Presse*, 22 August 2003.
4. For a first step in the analysis of national images projected by *The Beijing Review* in the period 1958–2002 and the *Government Work Reports* in the period 1954–2000, see Hongying Wang, 'National Image Building and Chinese Foreign Policy', *China: An International Journal*, vol. 1, no. 1, March 2003, pp. 46–72.
5. It could be argued that every message put forward to influence others is propaganda, but in this chapter the word 'propaganda' is used to refer to China's publicity work of the early decades of the People's Republic of China until the late 1980s, when the information put forward by the Chinese government was most of the time false.
6. See, for example, Evelyn Goh, 'A Chinese Lesson for the US: How to Charm South-East Asia', *The Straits Times*, 31 October 2003; and Jane Perlez, 'The Charm from Beijing', *New York Times*, 9 October 2003.
7. Joseph S. Nye, *Soft Power: The Means to Success in World Politics* (Cambridge MA: Perseus Publishing, 2004).
8. Jane Perlez, 'Chinese Move to Eclipse US Appeal in South [corrected as 'South-East' on 19 November 2004] Asia', *New York Times*, 18 November 2004; and Eric Teo Chu Cheow, 'China's Rising Soft Power in South-East Asia', *PacNet* 19A, 3 May 2004, www.csis.org/pacfor/pac0419A.pdf.
9. Cheow, 'China's Rising Soft Power in South-East Asia'.
10. Xinhua News Agency, 2 November 1991.
11. 'Beijing Wooing Overseas Chinese Away from Taiwan: Officials', *Taiwan Security News*, 30 May 2002.
12. See, for example, Liu Xiaoming, 'Remarks at Farewell Reception for Ambassador Li', 29 January 2001, www.china-embassy.org.
13. See, for example, interview of Xue by Garrie van Pinxteren, 'Xue praat ook over mensenrechten' [Xue also discusses human rights], *NRC*, 30 August 2003; and interview of Xue by Anne Meydam, 'In China is een hoop te verbeteren' [There is much to be improved in China], *Trouw*, 9 September 2003. The diary (*Hollands Dagboek*) by Han Xueqin was published in *NRC* during autumn 2003.
14. Agence France Presse, 'Beijing Lashes Out at Western Media Coverage of China', 22 August 2003.
15. See 'Partnership Formed on Chinese Culture', *China Daily*, 22 October 2003, chinadaily.com.cn and www.x3dChina.com.
16. See, for example, William R. Hawkins, 'Chamber of Commerce Needs a Philosophy Seminar', US Business and Industry Council, 15 May 2001, www.unsustainable.org.

17. See 'The Case Against Florida Splendid China', update of 17 March 2003, www.caccp.org/case.html.
18. Xinhua News Agency, 2 November 1991.
19. 'Biographic Profile: Zhao Qizheng', 11 July 2003, www.chinaonline.com/refer/biographies.
20. 'China's Diplomacy has Drawn Closer to Ordinary People in Recent Years', *People's Daily*, 19 March 2004.
21. 'China's Diplomacy has Drawn Closer to Ordinary People in Recent Years'.
22. 'Academic Seminar on China's Public Diplomacy', 19 March 2004, www.fmprc.gov.cn.eng
23. See, for example, the websites of China Information Network, www.tibet-info.net; and Tibet Online, www. Tibet.org.
24. 'China's Public Relations Strategy on Tibet: Classified Documents from the Beijing Propaganda Conference', www.caccp.org/bp.html, doc no. 8, p. 36.
25. 'China's Public Relations Strategy on Tibet', Summary Speech, p. 45.
26. 'More Great Study Works on Tibet Demanded', *Peoples Daily*, 13 June 2000, http://english.people.com.cn; see also Tibet Information Network, 'Propaganda and the West: China's Struggle to Sway International Opinion on the "Tibet issue"', *TIN Special Report*, 16 July 2001; and Jeremy Page, 'China Buffs Image in Tibet with Beauty Contest', Reuters, 24 August 2002.
27. Manheim, *Strategic Public Diplomacy and American Foreign Policy*, p. 7.
28. 'Diplomacy with Foreign Dignitaries: Personalities Build Up China's New Image', *People's Daily*, 1 January 2004.
29. Speech of 21 May 2004, www.xinhua.cn.
30. The Beijing 2008 Olympic Games Bid Committee hired Weber Shandwick Worldwide to promote Beijing to the International Olympic Committee. For more information, see 'Beijing 2008', case studies, www.webershandwick.co.uk.

6
Revolutionary States, Outlaw Regimes and the Techniques of Public Diplomacy

Paul Sharp

Public diplomacy, the process by which direct relations are pursued with a country's people to advance the interests and extend the values of those being represented, appears to be an idea whose time has come. The consensus is that it is made necessary by economic interdependence, possible by the communications revolution, and desirable by the rise in democratic and popular expectations. Even the emerging civilizational wars, which some argue are disrupting this picture, do not tell against public diplomacy, in fact quite the reverse. In the aftermath of the events of 11 September 2001, governments, it is now customary to argue, will have to conduct more public diplomacy and become better at it.[1] However, this consensus about the importance of public diplomacy is not matched by a similar consensus regarding the consequences of its use for what remains an international society of states. Are governments merely to work harder at getting their message out to target markets in the same way that private enterprises seek to boost their sales? Or, in so doing, are they participating in the further disaggregation of existing social structures and the replacement of the constricted and constraining communications of states by real conversations between peoples?

This chapter will try to shed light on these questions by noting a simple point and then examining some of its implications. The point is that many of the techniques associated with public diplomacy today have their origins in the activities and antics of the revolutionary diplomacy conducted by those who wished to live outside the prevailing international order or to overthrow it. The *Anschluss* by which Nazi Germany absorbed Austria in 1938, for example, can be seen as a spectacularly successful example of public diplomacy operating at all levels of a society and employing a mix of official, semi-official and unofficial agents to convince a people and their government that their political destiny lay in a radically new direction. Similarly, Bolshevik public diplomacy in the aftermath of the Russian Revolution, through a process of collaboration with sympathetic locals in other states, sought to get a variety of messages to different targets within their respective societies. Indeed, targeting or appealing to the people (or some people) rather than to their governments lay at the heart of early Bolshevik diplomacy.[2]

Accordingly, this chapter looks at some examples from the 'dark side' of public diplomacy: the Bolsheviks' efforts to secure peace between the October Revolution and the end of the First World War; the Libyan search for unions and followers after the 1969 *coup d'état* and through consolidation of the *Jamahiriya* in 1980s; Iran's attempt to ignite a revolution of the pious against blasphemy in the Khomeini years; and, finally, some public diplomacy aspects from the other side of the hill of what has become known as 'the war on terror'. These snapshots will make the following points. First, that at the level of ambition at which revolutionaries usually function, public diplomacy is effective primarily in expressive and destructive terms. This should give pause to those who advocate a greater place for public diplomacy in wars on terror and the democratic state-building projects associated with them. Counter-revolutionary public diplomacy is likely to be ineffective and even counter-productive, not least because of the illiberal assumptions about human beings on which much of it seems to rest. Second, however, we should not expect any decline in public diplomacy. In an era where identity projection and social network creation are both becoming cheaper, while the execution of substantive policies is getting more expensive, governments will increasingly be drawn to public diplomacy, even in great contests like the war on terror. They scarcely dare do otherwise but, if they are wise and good, their public diplomacy will be reactive and defensive, not creative and assertive.

The public diplomacy of the Bolsheviks and the Berne mission

If there is an archetypal image of revolutionary, public diplomacy, it is that of Karl Radek hurling stacks of leaflets and newspapers onto the platform at German soldiers, in their own language, exhorting them to desert, revolt and insist that their commanding officers make peace, as the train carrying the Bolshevik delegation to the peace talks between

Russia and the Central Powers pulled into the station at Brest-Litovsk in 1918. It was one aspect of a diplomacy designed to precipitate a general and simultaneous peace among the great powers as an overture to world revolution, simply by going public. Other elements of this revolutionary diplomacy are well known. In addition to establishing contacts and relationships with key focus groups, local leaders and organizations that might share their values in the army and society as a whole on the other side of the trenches, the Bolsheviks ensured, if only just, that their own delegation reflected revolutionary Russian society from the top to the bottom. A worker, a peasant and an ordinary soldier were all added at the last minute.[3] In line with the decision to publish all of the secret treaties with Russia's former allies, the Bolsheviks presented their own part in the negotiations at Brest as an exercise in openness, directed not only at the Central Powers' delegations and the governments and peoples that they represented, but at the governments of Russia's former allies and their peoples. Thus, reports of the negotiations on the Russian side were accompanied by class analyses and commentaries about what was going on, the 'real' motives of the other side, and how this all fitted into the big picture of unfolding world historical events.

Brest, however, was a failure for both the revolutionary and public aspects of Bolshevik diplomacy. When he could not reach agreement with the Central Powers, Trotsky attempted to withdraw Russia unilaterally from the war.[4] This was, indeed, revolutionary in terms of established diplomatic practice, but it was a useless piece of statecraft. As Lenin had expected all along, Germany and its allies merely resumed their advance and Russia was sucked back into the dance of the Great Powers, negotiating terms for military assistance from its former allies.[5] As an exercise in public diplomacy, the results of Brest were no better. Wheeler-Bennett maintains that the Central Powers' initial willingness to allow fraternization among ordinary soldiers and circulation of newspapers containing Bolshevik propaganda allowed the ideological contagion that destroyed Germany one year later into the heart of the empire.[6] Given the performance of German troops on the eastern front for the balance of the war and for some months after, however, this seems unlikely. Exhaustion precipitated Germany's collapse and rendered it susceptible to a number of contagions, of which Bolshevism was only one. What Brest best illustrates is the pressures on revolutionary states to resocialize into 'business as usual' at high political levels.

More interesting is Senn's account of the Bolshevik mission in Berne between the October Revolution and the end of the war, because it provides a glimpse of public diplomacy activities that bear more than a family resemblance to those being advocated today, and it provides a useful sense of their significance in the overall scheme of things. The Berne mission was one of four that the Bolsheviks succeeded in establishing after the revolution, aided by the decision of the other Great Powers to retain their representation in Russia.[7] Although the least important, it was valuable because of Switzerland's position in the centre of Europe as a neutral and because of the large community of revolutionaries established there. From the start, the mission's focus was not on bilateral relations and what Lenin called 'purely diplomatic work', since not much could 'be accomplished in that direction'.[8] One official's characterization of relations with the host government was: 'They ignore us. We also ignore them'.[9] This was not quite true, but bilateral relations were largely confined to the issue of who should control the Tsarist legation and its archives, and handling complaints about the mission's conduct made by the Swiss and other, usually Entente, embassies. The main challenge was to inform Europe about events in Russia without being accused of conducting propaganda. The latter had been a Swiss condition for the mission's acceptance. As a result, one of the officials noted later that informational work had always been 'more important. We did not appear at meetings and we did not publish under our own names'. Rather, members of the mission tried to keep the Swiss and others informed about what was going on in Russia: 'This was the real purpose of our representation'.[10]

To this end, the Bolshevik diplomats were well funded. Lenin had told the Berne legation: 'You have much money...We will give *more and more without accounting*'.[11] Full- and part-time staff were hired from reliable people among the Russian and the international revolutionary communities to establish a press office. They translated official statements, speeches and press articles from Russian into the major languages of Switzerland and Western Europe, and they collected information from the West European press to be relayed back to Russia in direct reports, digests and summaries. Brochures were produced based on materials being sent from Russia and the other missions, using nominally independent agencies that had been set up to avoid annoying the Swiss.[12] Staff also sought opportunities to give interviews to sympathetic papers and journals, and funding was provided for Swiss trade union members to visit and study in Russia. With the possible exception of the 'front' organizations for publications, most of the mission's activities would be regarded as normal public diplomacy today. Even the publication fronts reflected the best practices of the time and circumstances, for all of the belligerent powers' missions used this device and the Swiss tolerated it.[13]

The Bolshevik mission's achievements, however, were modest. Revolution might have been in the air, but the Bolshevik diplomats had little role in supporting, never mind coordinating, it. Rather, they played the role of observers, even in the final days when a general strike was called, partly to protest at a proposal to close the mission. Their days were absorbed by the routine of what was broadly consular work, for example, securing permission for a variety of nationals to enter and leave the country, and seeking information on behalf of expatriates regarding their families back home. The mission's most tangible public diplomacy success occurred when pieces from the German version of its digest began to appear regularly in the Swiss press and occasionally in other European newspapers. In his final report, however, the head of mission ranked this below a far more conventional triumph: securing control of the Tsarist legation and the standing associated with that.[14]

The public diplomacy of Qaddafi's Libyan *Jamahiriya*[15]

The Bolsheviks, for all their radicalism, were of our world. By this, I mean that the world of states and their system of relations was not alien to them. Both were to be transformed and transcended from within, for, in the Bolsheviks' understanding, the same history that had produced the states and nations by which classes were divided and exploited had also produced the forces and consciousness that would overturn them. Trotsky thus appeared at Brest, not as a stranger trying to make sense of an alien world, but as someone who believed that he understood that world better than its upholders. The Bolsheviks would play its diplomatic game and exploit it to their own advantage even as they worked to loosen its underpinnings. The same cannot be said about Qaddafi's Libya for, until recently at least, the modern state system did not interest him. Qaddafi is a wilful and volatile individual from a minor tribe, for whom the idea of states was an alien and comparatively recent imposition. His own state – Libya – was one of the more obviously artificial manifestations of that imposition, and the idea of Libya coexisted uneasily with other conceptions of identity: tribal; religious; and, indeed, national. It helps to keep all of this in mind when examining a foreign policy that otherwise seems eccentric and, at times, irrational.

The most obvious manifestations of this eccentricity were Qaddafi's attempts to unite Libya with richer, larger and more powerful neighbours that would have absorbed it.[16] To a point, he may have felt like

Mussolini, cursing the gods for placing a leader such as he at the head of a people such as they. His offer to assume the Egyptian vice-presidency with full responsibility for the armed forces certainly suggests that he was interested in a broader platform for his ambitions.[17] However, the expectation that anyone should accept such an offer was unusual in itself and was compounded by the volatility of Qaddafi's efforts in this regard. The failures of merger attempts with states of the Arab Mashraq, with which Libya shared a radical orientation, were accompanied by intense recriminations and followed by attempts at mergers with far less sympathetic states in the Arab Maghrib.[18] Failures here were followed by renewed attempts in the east, and, as a backdrop to both, Libya worked steadily to create some sort of Islamic community of interest with the non-Arab states in the Sahara and to its south. These initiatives may be seen as emanations of Qaddafi's personality as he scrambled to become a bigger player. However, if one takes as Qaddafi's starting point, not the attempt to build bigger blocks of power by combining states, but his sense that all of the Arab states were in some sense arbitrary creations that stood in the way of Arab unity, then this sheds a different light on his efforts. His challenge was not to build lasting alliances or mergers of Arab states, but to loosen the political framework within which Arabs found themselves and to build new relations between them based on Qaddafi's conception of the *Dar ul Islam* of the Muslim *Umma*.[19]

Such an interpretation is particularly helpful in making sense of Libya's public diplomacy. Qaddafi is well known for his own theatrical contributions in this regard, arriving, for example, exotically garbed and escorted at meetings of the Arab League, the Organization of the Islamic Conference and what was then called the Organization for African Unity. During a state visit, he appeared unannounced on the stage of a cinema in Tunis to announce the union of Libya and Tunisia, forcing his hosts into a hurried explanation of what was really meant by 'union'.[20] On a visit to the former Soviet Union, he asked to pray in Moscow's great mosque, which was closed, and to recite Koranic verses in a local Muslim cemetery.[21] On one occasion, at an international conference on 'Combating Imperialism, Zionism, Racism and Fascism', he threatened to resign his position as the guide of the *Jamahiriya* to become the commanding officer of a revolutionary army that would liberate the entire world.[22]

Eccentric though these interventions undoubtedly were, they were also all measures directed not so much at governments as at foreign publics and, of course, people at home. More conventionally, Libya used the proceeds of its oil wealth to buy influence and to create a reservoir of sympathy and support for its own projects, not just among the populations of neighbouring countries, but in the United States, Europe, and among the camps of the Palestinians scattered around the Levant and in Libya itself. The assistance agreements that Libya concluded, especially with African states, would typically include funding for centres of Arabic and Islamic learning. Qaddafi also provided financial support for movements such as black Muslim organizations in the US, Islamic groups in the Philippines, and radical Palestinian groups, offering to bring their members to Libya for education and training. Particular individuals and institutions were also targeted, including the brother of a US president, the head of the Los Angeles Police Department's bomb squad, and Georgetown University.[23]

The targeting of publics, which most of these efforts entailed, cannot be separated from Libya's use of terror. However, they were also bound up with Qaddafi's larger project of transforming the political relations of Arabs, Muslims and indeed all people, both within Libya and in the wider world. The transformation that he sought rested on a vision of Arab tribal relations stiffened by the pieties of a particular brand of Islam and strengthened by Western technologies. To achieve them, however, required the sustained mobilization of people into new forms of political life, which bypassed older, alien and traditional sources of authority and power.[24] Qaddafi thus sought to replace government by involving everybody in the consideration of public questions through a system of local committees and congresses that reported and made submissions upwards to a general congress at the national level.[25] Within this system, distinction between domestic and foreign relations was intentionally broken down. In their local committees, people were invited to discuss foreign policy issues and submit resolutions on them to higher bodies. They were called upon to demonstrate against embassies and in support of policies and, on at least two occasions, people marched (or rode in motorcades) to Libya's borders and threatened unsanctioned crossings in support of unions with their neighbours. The Libyan Foreign Ministry was increasingly sidelined by a new body, the Foreign Liaison Bureau, which in its turn was forced to compete for influence over Libya's foreign policy with still later creations like the Secretariat of Justice, the Islamic Call Society, divisions of General and Military Intelligence, and the Secretariat for External Security. Echoing the putative seizure of power by people's committees at home in 1973, in 1979 Libyan nationals abroad were called upon to seize their embassies and to transform them into People's Bureaus, a process that came full circle when American nationals in Tripoli were, that same year, invited to march on the American embassy and transform it along the lines of the Libyan model.[26]

In its form, Libyan efforts matched the most recent thinking on what public diplomacy should involve, namely attempts by multiple government and quasi-government agencies to target peoples and people, at home and abroad, with a view to engaging them with one another and mobilizing them for common projects.[27] People were to be won over to Libyan values, by working with them and recruiting them, rather than merely broadcasting at them, with a view to making the world a friendlier place for Libyan interests. In fact, it was almost a complete fraud. In the trinity of 'freedom, socialism and unity' for which Libyans, Arabs and Muslims were being mobilized, unity came first.[28] When popular sentiment, as expressed through the committees, showed the slightest sign of getting out of line, Qaddafi insisted on either reasserting his control or scrapping the process in favour of another way of mobilizing people. When individuals, organizations or countries that he had formerly supported began to disagree with, or stand in the way of, his own shifting sense of strategic direction, Qaddafi could turn quickly and violently against them. Such flexibility made for poor public diplomacy in the sense of creating anything like stable constituencies of sympathy, and there is little in its recent diplomatic 'revolution' to suggest that Libya's commitment to the technique has evolved beyond its essentially instrumental and shallow origins.

To judge Libyan public diplomacy, however, is not the same as to assess its effectiveness. One clear success in conventional foreign policy terms was Libya's contribution to the roll-back of Israeli influence in Africa in the late 1970s and early 1980s. Offers of Libyan assistance in return for breaking relations with Israel were accepted by several states south of the Sahara. Each of these agreements included a request to establish and fund centres of Islamic and Arabic learning. The contribution of these centres to the basic objectives of Libyan policy, however, is problematic. Their success in recruiting and mobilizing host nationals into organizations such as the Islamic Legion sometimes caused a break in relations with the host governments. And there is no example of a state, with the partial exceptions of Sudan and Chad, being won over to Qaddafi's camp for any period of time, or with any appreciable benefit to Libya and its people. Such an assessment, however, ignores the more revolutionary priorities informing Libyan foreign policy. Revolutionaries are not driven by reasons of state alone, even when they find themselves in charge of states. At least three achievements may be noted in this regard. First, Qaddafi's struggle to mobilize the Libyan people and keep them mobilized, while failing in terms of his declared objective of creating a unified Arab nation as the bearer of Islam to the world, have helped to keep him in power for over 35 years. It did so in the way that all authoritative requests to keep busy, try harder and stay engaged discipline people by wearing them down. The public diplomacy of Green Marches and embassy takeovers played its part in maintaining this control. Second, Libyan public diplomacy provided compensation for its lack of substantive success by allowing the regime in general and Qaddafi in particular to express themselves. Like the Bolsheviks, Qaddafi was burdened with a great message about how the world should be, but, unlike them, he lacked the resources for putting it into practice through a more substantial foreign policy. Describing his vision, acting it out, and getting those he controlled to do likewise served as a substitute for some of these deficiencies.

Finally, the 35 years that Qaddafi has been in power have witnessed continuing pressure on the sort of shared assumptions and values that help sustain the international society of states. Qaddafi, the Arab nationalist and romantic revolutionary, did not subscribe to these assumptions, even though he greatly benefited from some of them. His survival, after indirectly admitting Libya's direct responsibility for at least two terrorist outrages and directly admitting that Libya has tried to develop nuclear weapons, for example, is testimony to the continuing vitality of diplomacy's prudential ethic and governments' continuing respect for internal sovereignty. Nevertheless, insofar as Libyan public diplomacy helped to mobilized all sorts of people into taking part in international affairs in new and sometimes terrible ways, it has also played its part in maintaining pressure on international society. It will be an irony, but not a surprise, if the prodigal is successfully rehabilitated, but the role of future Libyan public diplomacy in that exercise remains to be seen.[29]

Iranian public diplomacy under Khomeini

The similarities between Libyan and Iranian public diplomacy are apparent, but superficial. Both operated in Islamic idioms and aspired to transform the entire world into a pious community living according to God's will. Both sought to mobilize people at home and abroad in pursuit of this end and possessed the sort of financial resources that made efforts in this regard possible. And both – the Iranians in particular – shared with the Bolsheviks the problem of what to do once the wider revolutions of which they saw themselves as part of had failed to materialize. Whatever the Ayatollah Khomeini thought about states as the products of man's limited ideas that would have to be ruled by *faqih* until the twelfth imam arrived, Iran, however, was a real country (certainly by the standards of Libya) with a material and cultural power of its own based on its historic identity and geographical circumstances.[30] It had Iranian interests separate from those of its new masters. It also had specifically Iranian ambitions as a great power, and the potential to achieve them.

Iran's advantage over Libya in terms of external weight, however, was diluted by three factors. First, the intense relationship between foreign and domestic affairs that was common to both was less easily controlled in Iran than Libya. From the embassy seizures to the recent demonstrations both for and against reform, the sentiments of Iran's mobilized population – young people, the bazaar, and religious tendencies – always had the potential to exert their own influence upon events. Second, the Iranian leadership never aspired to the sort of personalized regime achieved by Qaddafi. Even in Khomeini's heyday, the opacity of his pronouncements gave plenty of opportunities for argument. He might declare the contest with America to be 'a struggle between Islam and blasphemy', but factions around him could argue about whether this called for the export of the Islamic revolution under the guidance of one man, or its consolidation at home by a collective leadership. Iranian diplomacy, and its public diplomacy in particular, was frequently driven by the need to hold a circle around the most bitter of arguments about doctrine, and hence policy, at home. Finally, there existed a disjuncture between the actual distribution of Iran's external cultural influence and the area where it wished most to be influential. Qaddafi could plausibly present himself as one of the Arabs and Muslims that he aspired to lead. Iran, in contrast, shared neither the cultural identity nor the denominational identity of most of the people that it sought to influence in the Levant and the Arabian peninsula. Its cultural community lay in the other direction and, with the important exception of Iraq, Shi'ite communities abroad were nearly always minorities.

The net result of this particular combination of assets and constraints was that Iranian public diplomacy was more restrained than that of Libya, fitting, as it did, into a much more conventional, albeit revisionist, statecraft. The imperative to export the revolution or perish was thus customarily expressed in terms of the example set by Iranian nationals in their conduct abroad and by the latter's inherent powers of attraction. In a 1980 New Year message, Khomeini spoke of Iran exporting Islam:

> through the youth, who go to other countries where a large number of people come to see you and your achievements. You must behave in such a way that these large gatherings are attracted to Islam by your action.

Ali Khamenei, the current Ayatollah, spoke of Iranian diplomats in the same terms, as 'apostles of the revolution' who would best 'demonstrate the role of the Islamic Republic of Iran' by adopting 'an Islamic approach'. Iran had no intention of intervening in the internal affairs of other countries, claimed the Iranian Foreign Minister, Mir-Husayn Mussavi, for what was happening in other Islamic countries was a revolt of the Muslim masses.[31] What the rhetoric of restraint in practice entailed was relatively low levels of support for the terrorist, religious, cultural and social service arms of subnational groups of co-religionists like Hezbollah and Amal in the Lebanon. Local religious leaders were invited to congresses of the network of Friday prayer leaders in Tehran, but the objective of these and other activities was to increase potential clients' local influence, to demonstrate that Iran was in the fight against Israel and the US, and to make life difficult for those two opponents of the Iranian revolution. It was not to mobilize these clients for some grander project of Iranian or Shia provenance; still less to provoke spectacular propaganda of the deed in the Qaddafi mould. Indeed, the most spectacular activity in these terms – the kidnapping of Western hostages in the Lebanon in the late 1980s – exposed a rift between those like Ali Akbar Mohtashemi, who saw the publicity value of the hostages in terms of keeping them, and those like Hashemi Rafsanjani, who sought a demonstration of Iranian power and goodwill by letting them go.

The two major exceptions to this relative restraint were the riots and armed assaults undertaken throughout the 1980s by Iranians performing the pilgrimage to Mecca – the *haj* – and Khomeini's *fatwa* calling for Salman Rushdie's execution. The tone for the former was set by Khomeini's reply to Saudi King Khaled's complaint about disturbances in 1981. The demonstrations, in the king's view, had been inconsistent with the requirements of both Muslim piety and Iranian interests. Khomeini is reported to have replied that the pilgrimage had always been linked to politics, and that the separation of politics and religion was a device of the two superpowers that had no place in Islam.[32] However, the extent to which these eruptions were actually orchestrated by Iran remains unclear. Given the decline in such incidents after Khomeini's death, it is reasonable to suppose that it was on this one, and exceptionally painful, issue of the holy places that Khomeini was prepared to put his personal stamp upon Iran's public diplomacy, to the extent of seeking radical consequences from it in the region. The Rushdie affair, in contrast, continued long after Khomeini had died, serving as a rallying point for defenders of his revolution in its purist form and their supporters abroad. As a matter of public diplomacy, however, it was a disaster that forced both the Iranian government and its diplomats to tie themselves in knots explaining how the death sentence in the *fatwa* did not entail that anyone had to be killed, while senior clerics promptly contradicted them.

Conclusions: public diplomacy and the 'war on terror'

What, then, do these three snapshots of three very different revolutionary – and hence outlaw – states have to tell us about their public diplomacy and perhaps public diplomacy in general? Rather than provide answers, they illuminate two related problems. First, there is always a great deal going on in the international relations of such regimes about which students and practitioners of diplomacy in the West know very little. We focus on how these regimes present themselves towards us on the issues in which we are interested and in terms with which we are familiar. We occasionally obtain glimpses of political and cultural competitions of which we are barely aware, such as Iran's competition with Turkey over the lingua franca and alphabet to be adopted in the former Soviet republics in Asia, or the appearances of Taliban diplomats at prayer meetings in the Gulf states. More recently, we have been confronted by the spectacle of horrific images posted on the internet by shadowy organizations of uncertain standing that seek to shock 'us' and credential themselves before potential supporters. The extent to which this may be regarded as public diplomacy, let alone effective public diplomacy – there is already talk of decapitation 'fatigue' – remains unclear. What is clear is that a better understanding of this wide range of glimpsed activities requires more intelligence work and the development of greater area expertise. However, we are all familiar with how difficult it is to get people to pay attention to intelligence and expertise, even when they are available, both on matters that they judge to be peripheral and on those that seem to demand an instant and dramatic response. One of the fundamental challenges facing public diplomacy therefore remains that of getting one's own people to take seriously the terms in which others see the world.

Second, however, the extent to which all this activity should be characterized as public diplomacy, to be countered as such, is by no means clear. In the current 'war on terror', the US and its friends have claimed that Iran, the Taliban, Al Jazeera and at times practically every other government and media outlet in the Middle East are conducting a purposeful battle for the hearts and minds of a variety of stylized entities ranging from 'the Arab street' and the Pashto village *hujra*, to American liberals and European anti-Semites. It is a battle in which public diplomacy, propaganda, subversion and intimidation all play their part, and the West is said to be losing. More resources for and attention to the struggle at hand are needed.[33] An internet search on public diplomacy, however, will yield a host of entries from Western governments, institutes, retired foreign service officers' (FSO) associations, journalists and academics discussing the need for more public diplomacy, but one sees little evidence of public diplomacy from the 'other side' directed at 'us'. Iraq's public diplomacy before the recent war, for example, adopted an obfuscatory, legal and forensic approach at the UN, coupled with point-by-point refutations and expressions of defiance at news conferences. There was little to report until the Iraqi information minister began his virtuoso performance in the final days of the regime. In their exchanges with the US over nuclear weapons and delivery systems, North Korea and Iran have almost entirely restricted themselves to the traditional conception of public diplomacy as public reporting of official positions.[34] The relative absence of these countries from the internet reminds us both of the great imbalance of power that exists in this dimension of public diplomacy and the low tolerance of the strong for feelings of insecurity.

In fact, the glimpses that we do get of public diplomacy on the other side of the hill suggest a similar concern about the difficulties of getting their views of the world across to us and shaping our attitudes on, for example, the relative merits of the positions of the Palestinians and the Israelis in their conflict.[35] A more extended, yet still brief, view of the problems faced by the other side was provided by the efforts of the Taliban's mission in Islamabad to conduct public diplomacy in the weeks between the al-Qaeda attacks of 11 September 2001 and the destruction of the Taliban regime by the US and its allies a few months later.[36] The idea of Taliban diplomacy, let alone public diplomacy, has the quality of an oxymoron to Western sensibilities, but in fact the Taliban were highly adept at both when they were conducted on friendly territory and directed at sympathetic audiences. Their Islamabad embassy, together with other Afghan political, religious and social service agencies, directed their efforts not merely at the Pakistani government and diplomatic corps, but also at provincial and tribal authorities, religious schools, political parties and other non-state bodies. In other words, they exemplified the sort of multilevel engagement with coalitions and constituencies about values as well as projects that are advocated in recent studies of public diplomacy and its potentials.[37] And on familiar territory, the Taliban's public diplomacy was, as far as we can judge, as effective as anyone else's.

However, domestic outrages and the onset of war increasingly required the Islamabad mission to present a public face of the Taliban to the wider world in general, and the West in particular. Background interviews and open-air press conferences achieved some transitory success in arousing interest in, and perhaps sympathy for, the mission itself, if not for those that it represented. The Taliban ambassador reputedly suffered from stage fright until he got into his stride, and the first secretary was famously reported as wishing that the media would go away so that the mission could get on with its work. Diplomats are diplomats everywhere, it would seem, even if they have only recently ceased to be *mujahidin*. The impression, however, is that like many governments and diplomatic missions elsewhere, the Taliban diplomats felt under pressure to respond to something, the demands of the mass media as articulated by the Islamabad press corps, which they did not particularly equate with the world of publics and their opinions. Meetings with students, appearances at the Friday prayers of distinguished clerics to take up collections, and discussions with Afghan refugees and their leaders in the frontier zone were far more to their liking.

If this broad range of activities that is to be countered by the 'war on terror' is not revolutionary or outlaw public diplomacy, however, then the question becomes, what is it? The possibility exists that it is nothing less than a dimension of life – human relations in all their subnational, national, international and transnational forms – and life only, rolling along in these different regions of the world. If this is so, then what needs to be countered is not the efforts of outlaws and revolutionaries to shape our publics, but the friendly milieu of ideas and beliefs in which they make their respective cases at home. This, however, is a tall order, for such an effort would have to be directed not at the policy of another country or movement, but at the dense patterns of life and ideas that sustain it. This would be hard to accomplish, even by revolutionaries from within who are part of the way that life is lived and understood in a particular country. Our historical examples suggest that the revolutionary use of public diplomacy is effective primarily in shaking belief in existing social structures and hindering the operations of their institutions. Furthermore, efforts in this regard seem to have been effective only as multipliers of corrosive forces already acting, and even then they have required deception and coercion to be fully effective. For revolutionaries, there appears to be sufficient encouragement in all of this for them to try public diplomacy, at least until they acquire a stake in existing power arrangements. Until then, they are playing against the odds and for very high stakes on the basis of their certainties about how the world works and what ought to be done about it.

However, these ought not to be sufficient grounds for those opposing revolutionaries to attempt a similar sort of public diplomacy on these sorts of issues. In addition to being overly ambitious, an emphasis on what we might call counter-revolutionary public diplomacy may get in the way of more conventional diplomacy. By emphasizing the presentational aspects of an encounter or negotiation, the search to discover substantive positions and opportunities for accommodation may be hindered. The actual motives, reasons and intentions of an adversary may be interpreted as tactics, and publics that were not paying a great deal of attention may be alienated by clumsy attempts to attract their attention and shape their world-view.[38] By taking a multilevel approach to contacts, a counter-revolutionary public diplomacy will reduce the chances of identifying, working with, or building up anyone who can negotiate authoritatively.

Most importantly, such attempts at public diplomacy will undermine the very values that they purportedly seek to advance among a wider global audience. There is something fundamentally illiberal about regarding human beings in terms of great lumps of humanity that can be nudged and shaped into beliefs, values and patterns of behaviour that accord with some conception of our own values and interests. This is not to say that such attempts cannot be effective, still less that governments can always resist the demand to make such attempts. When they try them, however, governments do not replace conventional diplomacy with opportunities for genuine dialogue between peoples, but with the techniques of mass marketing and political warfare. The pressures to do so are a symptom of broader trends in international relations and world affairs, over which revolutionaries, governments and even the agents of mass media and information technology exercise little control. Faithful to the revolution though they undoubtedly were, even the 'devoted specialists' of the Taliban diplomatic service found that people were knocking on their door and they had to respond, for like us they lived in an era in which no response is a response and may even be newsworthy.[39]

However, at least on the new 'high' politics of international terrorism – the public diplomacy of states – while being aware of and taking account of these trends, it should not serve as an agent of them. The similarities of what the Bolshevik mission in Berne attempted, Libyan diplomacy espoused, and the Taliban mission in Islamabad became rather good at, and what some proponents of public diplomacy that goes beyond the high-impact/low-reach strategies of traditional public diplomacy are advocating, is striking. In adapting the techniques of revolutionaries and outlaws to their own purposes, the governments of liberal democratic states would do well to keep in mind the purposes for which these techniques were originally developed. Unlike revolutionaries and outlaws, governments and those that they represent share a stake in the legitimacy and authority of institutions being respected, not in these institutions being undermined.

Notes

1. See, for example, Margaret D. Tutwiler, 'US Image Abroad Will Take Years to Repair, Official Testifies', *The New York Times*, 5 February 2004; and the US government's attempts to coordinate public diplomacy, first through the State Department (1999) and more recently through the White House Office of Global Communications, http://www.whitehouse.gov/ogc/aboutogc.html.
2. See John W. Wheeler-Bennett, *Brest-Litovsk: The Forgotten Peace, March 1919* (London: Macmillan, 1966); Alfred Erich Senn, *Diplomacy and Revolution: The Soviet Mission to Switzerland, 1918* (Notre Dame IN: University of Notre Dame Press, 1974); and Arno J. Mayer, *Political Origins of the New Diplomacy, 1917–1918* (New York: Yale University Press, 1959).
3. Wheeler-Bennett, *Brest-Litovsk*, p. 84.
4. *Statement by Trotsky at the Brest-Litovsk Peace Conference on Russia's Withdrawal from the War*, 10 February 1918.
5. Lenin, *Decree on Peace*, delivered at the second All-Russia Congress of Soviets of Workers' and Soldiers' Deputies, 26 October 1917, published in *Izvestiia*, 27 October 1917.
6. Wheeler- Bennett, *Brest-Litovsk*, p. 93.
7. The Bolshevik missions were found in Berlin, Stockholm, London and Berne.
8. Lenin in Senn, *Diplomacy and Revolution*, p. 111.
9. Holzman in Senn, *Diplomacy and Revolution*, p. 47.
10. Berzin in Senn, *Diplomacy and Revolution*, p. 181.
11. Senn, *Diplomacy and Revolution*, pp. 16 and 112.
12. Senn, *Diplomacy and Revolution*, p. 125.

13. Senn, *Diplomacy and Revolution*, p. 145.

14. Berzin in Senn, *Diplomacy and Revolution*, p. 181.

15. In 1969 a group of army officers known as the Revolutionary Command Council seized power in Libya and established the Libyan Arab Republic. Muammar Qaddafi soon established himself as the leader of the new regime. In 1977 the country's title was changed to the Socialist People's Arab Libyan Jamahiriya. The term *Jamahiriya* suggests a state ruled by and for all of its people.

16. Libya attempted union with Egypt, Syria and Sudan by the Tripoli Charter in 1969; Egypt again by the Benghazi Declaration in 1972; Tunisia in 1973; Syria again in 1981; Syria and Egypt in 1984; and, following the failure of that, Morocco, also in 1984.

17. Martin Sicker, *The Making of a Pariah State: The Adventurist Politics of Muammar Qaddafi* (New York: Praeger, 1987), p. 50.

18. Mashraq, land in the east, or where the sun rises; Maghrib, land in the west, or where the sun sets.

19. *Dar ul Islam* means the abode of Islam or peace; *Umma* is the community of all Muslim believers.

20. Sicker, *The Making of a Pariah State*, p. 69.

21. Sicker, *The Making of a Pariah State*, p. 107.

22. Ronald Bruce St John, *Qaddafi's World Design: Libyan Foreign Policy, 1969–1987* (London: Saqi Books, 1987), p. 45.

23. Sicker, *The Making of a Pariah State*, p. 113.

24. Bruce St John, *Qaddafi's World Design*, p. 128; and three volumes of Qaddafi's own *Third Universal Theory* or *Green Book*.

25. For details see Bruce St John, *Qaddafi's World Design*, p. 126.

26. Sicker, *The Making of a Pariah State*, p. 113.

27. B. Scarcia Amoretti, 'Libyan Loneliness in Facing the World: The Challenge of Islam?', in Adeed Dawisha (ed.), *Islam in Foreign Policy* (Cambridge: Cambridge University Press, 1983), p. 54.

28. The original slogan of the Revolutionary Command Council, which had seized power.

29. See *US News and World Report*, 25 May 2004, for British Prime Minister Blair's visit to Libya.

30. R. K. Ramazani, 'Khumayni's Islam in Iran's Foreign Policy', in Dawisha, *Islam in Foreign Policy*, p. 16. A *faqih* is an expert in Islamic jurisprudence.

31. All quotes from R. K. Ramazani, *Revolutionary Iran: Challenge and Response in the Middle East* (Baltimore MD: Johns Hopkins University Press, 1986), pp. 19–20.

32. Ramazani, 'Khumayni's Islam in Iran's Foreign Policy', p. 26.

33. See, for example, White House Office for Global Communications, *Apparatus of Lies: Saddam's Disinformation and Propaganda 1990–2003*, White House, http://www.whitehouse.go/ogc/apparatus/printer.html; and *Iraqi Propaganda Targets Citizens*, ABC World Today, 27 February 2003, http://www.globalsecurity.org/org/news/2003/03022.

34. See, for example, Boris Johnson's interview with the Iranian ambassador to Britain, 'It's Simple, No Democracy, No Nukes', in *The Daily Telegraph*, 24 June 2004.

35. David Hoffman, 'Beyond Public Diplomacy', *Foreign Affairs*, vol. 81, no. 2, March/April 2002, p. 85.

36. Paul Sharp, 'Mullah Zaeef and Taliban Diplomacy: An English School Approach', *Review of International Studies*, vol. 29, no. 4, October 2003.
37. See, for example, Mark Leonard and Vidhya Alakeson, *Going Public: Diplomacy for the Information Society* (London: Foreign Policy Centre, 2000).
38. See, for example, reactions to the new US government-funded Arabic-language satellite TV channel, Al Hurra, on BBC News, 13 February 2004, http://news.bbc.co.uk/2/hi/europe/3486109.stm.
39. Iranian Foreign Minister Mir-Husayn Mussavi's phrase, cited in Ramazani, 'Khumayni's Islam in Iran's Foreign Policy', p. 21.

7
The EU as a Soft Power: the Force of Persuasion

Anna Michalski

Introduction

The intra-European row that broke out in the build-up to the war in Iraq brought home the fragility of the European foreign policy regime. Existing and future member states publicly demonstrated their diverging positions regarding the appropriate stance to take in relation to the United States. For outside observers, this seemed to prove the futility of seeking to establish a common foreign and security policy among the member states of the EU, which continue placing national priorities before shared European objectives. From this perspective, the EU would forever remain a political dwarf despite its status as an economic giant.

However, in December 2003 at the summit in Brussels, EU member states, albeit with different intensity and emphasis, showed by adopting the European Security Strategy[1] that they are still willing to reaffirm the EU as a formidable international actor. On the same occasion, they also displayed a remarkable resolve (despite frequent displays of differences in perceptions of aims and structure) to their commitment to beef up the Union's defence potential by adding real military capabilities to the nascent European Security and Defence Policy through the establishment of the European armament agency and an 'EU cell' in NATO. However, despite the recent emphasis on the military dimension, the EU will remain above all a civilian 'soft' power, arguably the first of its kind, and definitely the foremost international actor that is not a state in the traditional meaning, yet that is much more than an international organization or regime.

Scope of analysis

This chapter builds on a well-known thesis of the EU as a 'post-modern' polity which, because of its particular constitutional construction and historical evolution, has developed into a political regime based on a strong normative component. It analyses the implications of the EU's specific 'post-modern' nature, which forces it to base any policy regime on transnational negotiation and consensus-building governed by institutional rules and procedures, on a particular mix of conventional and European public instruments and, above all, on strong compatibility with deeply-seated values and attitudes among the European public and elites. In this context, the power of persuasion becomes an existential requirement for the EU's popular legitimacy and credibility. Used well, it can contribute to the EU's 'meta-narrative'[2] by providing a sense of belonging to the same community of values. It is argued here that the normative component of the EU's 'constitutional' construction (values, norms and principles) constitute, within the constraints of its institutional and political structure, the backbone of the European foreign policy doctrine. Despite this shared foundation, the effectiveness of the EU's external activities has until now been hampered by its comparative inability to persuade both domestic (national) audiences and the international community of the nature of its existence and its vision of world order. In other words, although there is no doubt about the EU's capacity and know-how in a number of individual areas (such as development assistance, humanitarian aid, international trade, peacekeeping and reconstruction), it is seen as a weak actor (and sometimes non-existing) in the domain of international politics and an easy target for external pressure or diverging national interests of the member states.

This chapter analyses the strategies[3] – primarily of the European Commission and, to a lesser extent, the Council Secretariat – in communicating with national elites and publics and external audiences. Because of the evolution of the Common Foreign and Security Policy (CFSP) and the increasingly louder public claims for transparency and accountability, the Commission is increasingly also turning to domestic EU audiences in addition to its traditional external interlocutors to explain and argue in favour of EU external action, ultimately seeking broader support for an independent European external policy. Analysis therefore concerns two dimensions of public diplomacy: one concerning a domestic European audience; and one directed to audiences in countries outside the EU.

In their efforts to convince the outside world of the strengths of the normative foundations of European foreign policy, the Commission and the Council employ strategies of cognitive persuasion that are reminiscent of concepts and methods used within public diplomacy. Despite this, the concept of public diplomacy is not employed, not even recognized, among the majority of officials who were interviewed for this research, nor is it found in any of the Commission's or Council Secretariat's policy papers or other types of communication. Notwithstanding, these two institutions' endeavours to create a basis of legitimacy and international identity for the EU by persuading external and internal audiences of the strength of the normative component of its policy objectives and actions fit neatly into the conceptual framework of public diplomacy. This chapter focuses on how these values, norms and principles are integrated into policies and how they are instrumentalized in the EU's information and communication strategy. It analyses the strategy's significance in the internal political dynamics of the EU and in the creation of an independent European identity in the context of international politics.[4]

External policy and normative power

In the absence of clearly stated 'interests', the EU's external relations policies are often designed to correspond to values and principles underlying the European integration process and to forward norms that are vital to EU policy regimes. Indeed, the expression of shared values, principles and norms for a long time represented a kind of political settlement among the EU member states – a kind of substitute for a proper constitution. This 'constitutional' settlement is formulated in the following terms: *basic principles*, such as peace, democracy, the rule of law, respect for human rights, the member states' right to equitable institutional representation and diversity; *conceptualized ideas* underpinning European policy regimes, such as sustainable development, social market economy, the single market, the area of freedom, security and justice or more recently in the neighbourhood policy; and *procedural and rule-based norms*, such as good governance and institution-building. The normative element of the EU has been studied by scholars[5] who argue that the EU, besides being a civilian power with the capacity to wield economic and remunerative instruments, is also developing into a normative power where its ability to shape conceptions of what is 'normal' in international relations by the force of ideas and normative principles is decisive for its influence on world politics.[6]

In the same line of thinking, the EU constructs the foundation of its foreign policy on the basis of principles and norms in order to employ them in a variety of contexts: in *strategic policy doctrines* such as Agenda 2000[7] making the Copenhagen criteria operational and the *acquis communautaire* in the framework of enlargement, or the European security strategy in the area of security and defence; in the form of *normative conditionality* in regional partnerships around the world (such as with Mercosur and with the Cotonou agreement); or in terms of *procedural and institutional rules* of the game in various contractual relations with third countries. The 'normative' component is important in legitimizing the EU's soft power, but unless it is effectively communicated to external and internal audiences, much of its potential impact will be lost. In fact, the ability of the EU to diffuse its norms, thus influencing what is considered 'normal' in international politics, is decisive for the impact of the EU's normative 'soft' power. The strength of the EU's normative power is decided by its ability to shape other actors' perceptions of the appropriate cognitive content of international politics. Scholars have pointed to several different modes of diffusion of the EU's normative power.[8]

The internal dimension of EU communication and information

By virtue of its position as the framer and executor of EU policies and on the receiving end of most of the criticism levelled against EU institutions, the Commission undertook to reform its communication and information policy in 1999 under the incoming Prodi administration. The first step was to reorganize the Directorate-General, DGX, which was responsible for all communication and information activities and opinion surveys, into a leaner service, DG 'Press', whose activities were to focus on the spokesman service and its target audience, the Brussels press corps (one of the world's largest, counting some 1000 journalists).[9] Reform was set to concentrate on some centralized functions, such as coordination of the activities of the representations in the member states, and to seek a coherent approach to communication and information within the Commission. Above all, reform was based on decentralization to the services (line DGs) and the Commission's representations and delegations in the member states and third countries, which should have a direct stake in the elaboration and implementation of the communication and information strategy. As a consequence of the successful public information campaign preceding introduction of the new currency, the euro, on 1 January 2002, the Commission also realized that only in partnership with other European institutions (mostly the European Parliament) and in particular with the member states would it be possible to reach out to large sections of the European public.

In 2002, DG 'Press' published a report on an information and communication strategy for the EU.[10] The report reads as an invitation to the member states to join the Commission in its efforts to bridge the European public's scepticism and lack of knowledge about the EU. The Commission argues that 'the time is now right for a coherent and comprehensive information and communication policy for the EU which will improve public perceptions of the Union and of its role'. This strategy aims at improving the 'perceptions of the EU, its institutions and their legitimacy by enhancing familiarity with and comprehension of its tasks, structure and achievements and establishing a dialogue with the general public'. Information and communication should no longer be regarded as a sort of 'secondary appendage to or supplementary constraint on the EU's activities' and a strategy to this end is a 'precondition for the success of the EU's policies and initiatives'. For this reason, services preparing a new initiative should assess the communication needs and requirements at an early stage and no major initiative should be designed without a communication plan. The Commission recognizes, however, that the implementation of a strategy of this kind would not be easy, since it amounts to no less than a 'genuine cultural revolution', and that the 'acquisition of a new communication culture will depend on a coherent and methodical reconstruction of the EU's image'. In this critical assessment the Commission refers both to its own record of putting more emphasis on dimensions other than communication in various kinds of policy initiatives and on the member states' habit of not recognizing their own input and responsibility for EU legislation or other measures on the European level.

In operational terms, the strategy relies on voluntary partnerships with the member states to which the Commission allocates resources from the Prince Fund to four annual policy priority areas: enlargement (2001); the future of the EU (2002); the area of freedom, security and justice (2003); and the role of the EU in the world (2004). In return, the member states commit themselves to formulate national campaigns around a central storyline based on three central messages:[11] (1) 'the EU is a pledge of greater liberty, prosperity and security for Europeans; (2) the EU promotes a model of society inspired by solidarity and dynamism and respecting diversity; and (3) the EU enables us to play a world role matching our values and commensurate with our weight'.[12]

Today, some time after the launch of the EU information and communication strategy, the experience is thus far positive in relation to those member states that have chosen to enter into partnership with the Commission.[13] Other members, for instance Sweden, have not yet opted for partnership, often because of the perceived incompatibility in the Commission's approach with the national tradition of public communication. One lesson that the Commission has drawn both on the basis of existing partnership agreements and on the euro campaign is that cooperation with member states implies loss of control over formulation of the central 'European message'. Messages become 'nationalized' to fit the domestic arena. DG 'Press' assesses, however, that this risk is worth taking, since without cooperation with national authorities and a certain deformation of the original message the impact on national public opinion will be very limited. The decentralized partnership strategy is therefore here to stay, at least for some time, and will be adapted to changing national circumstances and evolving European policy priorities.

DG 'Press' expresses more concern regarding the reluctance of national politicians to include a European dimension into their communication with domestic audiences. There is a feeling in the Commission that their reluctance to admit the full extent of the European dimension of their work is a great hurdle for building public legitimacy of the EU. The national political level is often seen as the stumbling block for enhancing the EU's legitimacy and credibility. This can partially be explained by the national concentration of audio-visual media, which reports European news from a domestic angle, often reinforcing the sentiment of competition or conflict rather than cooperation and longer-term commitment. National politicians, being dependent on the audiovisual sector's coverage of news and political commentaries, play into this, making nuanced and factual reporting of 'European' news less appealing. The weakness of the European dimension of broadcasting is recognized by the Commission, but attempts to create European television channels have up to now met with only modest success, and those that do exist concentrate on news coverage, such as EuroNews, or have a specific cultural/intellectual content such as Arte. National regulations for broadcasting and language barriers are the most cited reasons for lack of progress in this area. The EU has until now concentrated its effort on encouraging cooperation in the production of audiovisual material and the technological aspects of broadcasting. It is interesting to note in this context that the internet has emerged as a medium that is suitable for European-wide news coverage and a number of providers of news and commentaries have emerged in recent years (European Voice, EU Observer and New Europe, to mention a few).

The Commission recognizes that it has only weak instruments to influence national public opinion and is therefore dependent on existing national channels and opinion formers. Its strength lies in its knowledge about European affairs and policies, which it tries to offer to the member states through partnerships. DG 'Press' is slowly building relations of trust with the information and communication authorities of the member states, which could with time bring about more fruitful and closer cooperation in the endeavour to reach out to European citizens.

EU external communication

Political and institutional paradoxes

The EU, being an unfinished political system, displays an uneven, sometimes seemingly arbitrary, division of competences that defy traditional political models. This is particularly salient in the area of foreign and security policy and in defence, in which integration was for a long time considered taboo. In the early 1990s, the common foreign and security policy (CFSP) was formally added to the EU's competences and is still considered very sensitive for national sovereignty as it has remained firmly in the hands of the member states. The logic in CFSP is therefore intergovernmental, implying that the Commission has to share the right of initiatives with the member states and has a much weaker stake in the implementation of EU action than in the common policies, while member states have no obligation other than procedural and moral to comply with actions or stances adopted.

In the common policies, which also include external trade, humanitarian assistance and development policy, the Commission has a special role as the institution responsible for putting forward proposals for EU initiatives, managing programmes and budgets, as well as ensuring the external representation of the Union (primarily in external trade) in international organizations (such as the WTO) or in negotiations with third parties. To assist it in drawing up policy initiatives and implementing policies, the Commission has created around it many policy networks that range from technical expert committees, to administrative and diplomatic networks, NGOs and socio-economic interest groups. In the area of development and humanitarian assistance in particular, interaction with NGOs and civil society fulfils a number of functions: (1) as a source for expertise and opinion different from that of the member states, driven by values and societal concerns rather than national interests. Consultation between the Commission and NGOs is a two-way process where both parties try to influence each other, and constitutes for the Commission, at least in certain cases, an alternative source of support; (2) as a symbiotic relationship – an epistemological community – through which ideas and values can be diffused, as well as making the implementation smoother and more efficient by anchoring new or revised policy approaches prior to their formal adoption. Member states' experts, civil servants and the academic community are also part of these networks; (3) as an interlocutor with third-country governments, thereby facilitating the implementation of policies. It is significant that the Commission's experience of establishing longstanding epistemological communities and civil society networks of this kind in the member states has led it to seek a similar development in third countries, in Africa through the Cotonou agreement, in the Mediterranean region through the Barcelona process, and in Central and Eastern Europe prior to accession.

However, the Commission's relations with NGOs are not always harmonious, as the breakdown of the Doha development round in September 2003 shows. In the run-up to the summit, the EU was accused of pursuing a self-interested and contradictory agenda by arguing in favour of extending global free trade while not opening up its agricultural markets or limiting agricultural subsidies with a trade-distorting impact. In terms of communication, the breakdown of the Doha development round in Cancun clearly shows the difficulty in getting across a message internationally, which seems to involve the EU's complex policy compromises working at counter-purposes.

Over the last ten years, the Commission's role in external relations has widened as a result of the creation of the CFSP, but perhaps even more as a result of the internationalization of many Community policy areas, such as the environment or consumer protection, and because of enlargement of the EU. The Commission shares the task of shaping EU foreign policy with the Secretary-General of the Council and High Representative (HR) of the CFSP, Javier Solana. Upon his arrival to the post in October 1999 hopes were high that the EU would agree on clear foreign policy strategies with which member states would consistently comply. Despite increased resources in terms of staff, infrastructure and great personal involvement, a potent and coherent CFSP is still lacking, as member states are reluctant to give up national prerogatives and traditional positions in international politics.[14] The most glaring recent example of disunity was the Iraq crisis, but the problem of an obvious discrepancy between lofty ideals as expressed in EU declarations and concrete action is notorious. For instance, despite having a human rights' clause in free trade agreements with developing countries, the EU has never invoked it against Tunisia, Egypt or Israel, as its member states' traditional ties and sensitivities with these countries have hitherto blocked any move towards sanctions.[15] On the political level, the task of communicating an EU foreign and security policy is obviously undermined by incoherence of policies and inconsistency in the application of rules.

As the High Representative's task is to represent the member states in the framework of the CFSP and to work towards reaching consensus among them, the Council Secretariat has not seen the need in the same way as the Commission to communicate with audiences outside the circle of member states' diplomats and experts. In accordance with their respective mandates, the Commissioner for external relations (Relex), Chris Patten, and the CFSP's High Representative, Javier Solana, have cooperated closely in order to draw up strategies and action plans in the framework of CFSP, the latter responsible for presenting the political dimension of the undertaking and the former for committing financial resources and planning implementation on the ground. This cooperation has proven that the considerable experience of the Commission in terms of reconstruction (social, economic, institution-building, civil society, and so on) is indispensable to the diplomatic efforts of the High Representative.[16] The Commission has also brought with it know-how about managing the EU's budget and drawing up legislation in order to get large-scale projects approved by the European Parliament. In addition, knowledge, instruments and networks built up and employed by the Commission in other areas, such as development, humanitarian aid and trade have assisted the EU's foreign policy undertakings in various parts of the world. Incentives to bridge the institutional separation between the communitarian and the intergovernmental dimensions of the EU's external relations' competences are strong. To that end the draft constitutional treaty of the European Convention proposed the creation of the office of a European foreign minister who would be appointed by and receive instructions from the EU member states in the European Council, but would at the same time be a vice-president of the Commission, overseeing all external relations policies.[17] Since the failure of the member states to agree to treaty reform at the European Council in December 2003, the unified institutional representation of the CFSP remains an unresolved issue, and so does the problem of finding a solution to the EU's inability to speak with one voice in international politics.

Communication in the field of external relations

Since the arrival of a new college in the second half of 1999, the Commission has sought to make its internal organization more coherent and efficient in the area of external action. The Relex Commissioner, Chris Patten, was made responsible for coordinating the Commission's activities in this field and for streamlining management of Community funds and programmes. There was also a general drive towards decentralization as part of the Commission's internal administrative reform. This drive included efforts to decentralize the communication and information policy away from a centralized function down to the relevant services. In the case of external relations, this meant that DG 'Relex' was given an overall coordinating role for drawing up a communication strategy and liaising with other services in the external relations' field, including the Council Secretariat (although cooperation has remained quite noncommittal between the two). It also meant that the Commission's delegations abroad (123 in third countries and representations in five international organizations) were charged with enhanced responsibility in the fields of communication and information, by being given the task of identifying external target audiences, designing communication and information programmes and actions, and reporting back to headquarters on the impact of these efforts and the general image of the EU in the country. In recent years, officials have observed a trend towards increasing interest and queries about EU policies directed to the Commission delegations abroad, which have become the central contact points for foreign interests and coordination among member states in the fields directly related to EU policies. On a more general level, the Commission has noted the imperfect knowledge about the EU, its institutions, functioning and policies in third countries. It has therefore reconfirmed the major role played by the delegations in terms of information and explanation, which they often carry out in conjunction with member states' diplomatic representations.[18] However, apart from various examples, mostly from Africa, of cooperation between the Commission and the member states in terms of joint representations and national diplomats seconded to Commission delegations, there are as yet no real attempts among the member states' embassies and representatives of the European institutions (the Commission and representatives of the High Representative (when applicable)) to streamline contacts with third countries according to an EU-inspired communication policy.[19]

A new structural element in the Commission's approach is the importance given to the communication dimension at an early stage of the elaboration of policy initiatives – today no new initiative is contemplated without also integrating this aspect. Communication is much more than before considered a strategic dimension of any policy initiative. Besides aiming for greater coherence between policy areas, communication should be coordinated in order to fit into a larger framework, to help overcome the impression of fragmentation and oversegmentation that sometimes appears in the Commission's policy initiatives because of strong administrative barriers between Directorates-General and the wish of Commissioners to enforce their own profiles.

Values and norms

With the significance of European values and norms at the heart of this chapter, it is time to take a closer look at their central function in the formulation of the EU's external relations policy.

On the principled declaratory level, the EU treaties proclaim that the CFSP should have as its objective to develop and consolidate 'democracy and the rule of law, and respect for human rights and fundamental freedoms', and that development policy should be guided by the same principles. The constitutional treaty adopted by the European Convention in July 2003 similarly refers to the values and interests of the Union – peace, security, sustainable development, free and fair trade, human rights and the observance of rule of law in the international system – which it should seek to uphold in its relations with the wider world. These and other basic documents such as the various declarations on human rights and democratization constitute the normative content on which the Union's external relations are built and which it seeks to promote externally in contractual arrangements with third countries, with strings of conditionality attached. These normative concepts are also used internally as policy tools to achieve coherence between policy areas and geographical regions, by mainstreaming contractual relations (such as regional cooperation agreements) and strategic communication (country strategy papers) and in dialogue with third country governments, NGOs, EU member states and international organizations.[20]

In terms of communication, this normative, value-based component permeates the Commission's activities in the external relations' field, with slight variations according to the policy area in question. DG 'Relex',[21] with the overall responsibility for coherence, puts emphasis on the EU as a peace project, which has brought prosperity and stability to Europe and acts as an anchor for democracy and human and fundamental

8888

rights in the world. The historical reasons behind European integration, its foundation on a voluntary transfer of sovereignty from its member states, its success in forging common policies on the basis of institutional and procedural principles, despite its imperfect and incremental constitutional structure, tell a story that invites others to emulate it. Being founded on the political will of historically warring nation-states, and having developed an approach to institutions and policy-making based on law, provide it with a notion of universality that is attractive to other countries and peoples. Presenting it as a transferable concept of postmodern political governance based on universal 'benign' values and soft power instruments, it is felt inside DG 'Relex' that European integration is regarded with increasing interest and benevolence by third countries as an alternative to balance other, more aggressive models of power in the new world order – there is a demand for 'more' Europe.

DG 'Relex' recognizes that communication with the general public in member states is the weak element of the Commission's strategy and realizes that the 'fact-and-figures' approach that prevailed in the past is not the appropriate way to carry out public communication. In view of the focus of the EU's information and communication strategy in 2004 on the external relations' dimension, the Commission aims at presenting concrete and people-focused 'success stories' to the European public. These are often presented in information material, building on examples from successful development projects in the third world or human relief efforts throughout the world in order to raise awareness of the impact of EU policies and to demonstrate that tax payers' money is well spent.

As Pascal Lamy took office as Commissioner for external trade in autumn 1999,[22] he prompted DG 'Trade'[23] to reflect on its communication strategy in order to elaborate a set of values and principles that the Commission would like the Union to promote abroad through regional or bilateral trade agreements with third countries and by defending them in international fora and organizations. Simultaneously, vocal public concerns concerning globalization and the impact of international trade on domestic policy areas prompted DG 'Trade' to reach out to a larger public than the customary audience of trade experts. DG 'Trade' has therefore set itself a twin objective, on the one hand to make the European public aware of the EU's position as the foremost commercial power in the world and to inform it about the purpose of the common commercial policy, while on the other it seeks to explain the EU's positions on globalization and its responses to the challenges that globalization poses to European societies. On the basis of quantitative and qualitative opinion surveys, DG 'Trade' therefore decided to pursue the following themes: (1) the EU as the foremost commercial power in the world has an interest in forwarding global free trade; (2) it works for 'controlled' globalization by encouraging sustainable development, protecting shared European values and supporting multilateral negotiations on the international level; and (3) it promotes the inclusion of developing countries into the international trade system in order to help them benefit from globalization. On this basis, DG 'Trade' developed the following messages destined for the European public: (a) the EU has a responsibility to support the formalization of rules aiming at regulating the effects of globalization, by giving support to WTO-based regulation of international trade; (b) the EU's stance in international trade aims at promoting the European model of society by protecting Europeans' interests in public services, the environment, public health, consumer protection and cultural diversity; and (c) the EU endeavours to open markets for European companies and to defend their commercial interests by managing trade disputes on the international level.

The Cancun experience of September 2003 constituted something of a communication failure for DG 'Trade', since its messages to external audiences about the benefit of international trade for all countries and the importance of a multilateral trading system were not persuasive enough to dispel the criticism that was brought against the EU by certain countries and NGOs. An appraisal of the current approach to multilateral trade is currently under way and might result in the Commission suggesting that the regional approach be given priority in the future while still pursuing multilateral negotiations where appropriate.

In development policy,[24] the value-based content is centred on respect for human rights, democracy and the rule of law. In this area, through the Cotonou agreement – the EU's framework agreement with countries in Africa, the Caribbean and the Pacific (ACP) – the Commission has put in practice a number of elements of principle, such as using trade as a means to bolster economic development and insisting on institution-building, good governance, the participatory approach to bolster civil society and measures to fight against corruption and poverty. Despite administering substantial funds on the basis of a more altruistic approach than the United States and most EU member states, DG 'Dev's' activities are not known to the large majority of the European public. Part of this lack of visibility can be explained by the wish of Commissioner Nielsen, supported by Commissioner Patten as concerns external relations in general, to keep a low profile until the administrative and management failures that caused the Santer Commission's fall had been sorted out. Now, as many necessary steps have been taken, DG 'Dev' is ready to adopt a more self-assertive approach to communication with the European public, focusing on presenting successful projects. Against this backdrop, DG 'Dev' is concerned that with politicization of the EU, it will be increasingly difficult to resist the pressure to turn development policy into a strategic foreign policy instrument.

The message of the EU's humanitarian aid is highly normative, representing 'an expression of the values of humanity on which the EU is founded and is a concrete demonstration of worldwide solidarity to the people in need'.[25] It is conducted on the principles of impartiality, non-discrimination and neutrality, by giving aid to whoever is in need, including 'forgotten crises'. Arguing his opposition to the proposals of the constitutional draft treaty on these principled lines, the Commissioner for humanitarian aid, Poul Nielsen, tried to counteract what he saw as a dangerous juxtaposition of foreign policy and humanitarian aid that might endanger the impartial nature of the EU's aid effort.

This normative component is reflected in the efforts of the Humanitarian Aid Office (ECHO)[26] to step up a major communication operation in 2004 directed to the European public, in particular young people. ECHO argues that this normative, principled stance is in accordance with the expectations of the public, which supports EU action in the humanitarian field, although ECHO as such remains little known.

ECHO was previously reluctant to communicate directly with internal or external public audiences and had little direct access to them, as it acts as a donor, letting NGOs take care of the actual distribution of aid. Recently, however, ECHO decided to add an obligation to recognize the origin of aid in its contractual arrangements with partners, by including a 'visibility' budget line to prompt the use of EU logos and other forms of symbols indicating the Union as benefactor. This measure was taken in order to make beneficiaries aware of the origin of aid and as a duty to inform European taxpayers where their money is going. ECHO's insistence on impartiality and neutrality is central to human relief operations, as the safety of aid workers depends on the donor's reputation and trust. It considers recent incidents where soldiers have been involved in the distribution of aid as a dangerous and deplorable development, resulting in a clear risk to future humanitarian activities. As a matter of policy, ECHO's officers in the field refrain from making political statements in public and pronounce themselves only on matters of a practical or functional nature.

Audiences, channels, instruments of communication

All DGs active in the field of external relations have in recent years widened the scope of their information and communication activities from targeting almost exclusively expert-oriented audiences to addressing also the European public. The theme of the EU's communication strategy 'Europe and the World' is acting as a stimulus for Commission services to undertake activities in this field. This major drive is grounded in the realization that in order to enhance the EU's popular legitimacy, the Commission must actively try to explain and justify to the European public EU action in all areas, including external relations. In adjusting its message to fit the European public, DGs active in the field of external relations attempt, on the basis of opinion surveys and other sources, to address public concerns, such as the fear of globalization and its (negative) influence on social justice and the environment, in order to pursue them in addition to the normative component of European foreign policy (human rights, democratization, rule of law, and so on). Another reason for reaching out to the public at this point in time is the sentiment among the Commissioners that their efforts to 'clean up the house' have resulted in more efficient management and implementation of EU policies and programmes that justifies a more assertive style of communication. However, despite recent advances, several officials in the Commission still think that the Commission could be even more proactive in its communication, 'selling its case' more confidently, in particular on the political level.

In their public communication efforts, all DGs make increasing use of modern information and communication tools, primarily by improving their websites. For instance, DG 'Trade's' website attracts more than 2.27 million consultations per month (November 2001). Electronic mailings are also used to contact numerous correspondents: through its database DG 'Trade' can reach at least 75,000 addresses, and in the year 2001 it sent out at least 100 different messages to these recipients. DGs also aim at targeting multipliers (such as journalists, civil servants, academics and the organized civil society) in third countries through conferences, seminars or organized visits. The European Union Visitors' Programme (EUVP), set up jointly by the Commission and the European Parliament, is dedicated to enhancing knowledge about and goodwill towards the EU among opinion formers from countries outside the Union. Created in 1974, the programme administers study tours in the EU (to EU institutions and two member states of choice) for over one hundred visitors per year (in 2003 the EUVP managed 165 visits).[27] Foreign journalists are considered particularly important multipliers, and to that effect dedicated study tours and seminars are organized every year for groups of journalists. The Commission's delegations play a specific role in this process, since they recommend which journalists should be invited and follow up on coverage of the EU in the national press or television that might result from the visit.

In terms of building cognitive awareness and support for the ideas and world-views of the EU, the Commission seeks to encourage dialogue with civil society within as well as outside the EU through a variety of different kinds of links and networks. They can take the shape of interest-based networks with groups that have a direct stake in a policy (such as the environment, social rights, trade, or humanitarian aid), with which the Commission interacts in a two-way communication process. Other networks act as implementing agents for the Commission (such as with humanitarian aid and development), while others again are encouraged directly by the Commission as part of international trade and cooperation agreements that stipulate dialogue with civil society (for instance, the Cotonou agreement). The Commission also influences international debates on issues such as economic development, international trade and finance, which take place in international organizations such as the UN, the World Bank, WTO, the OECD and so on. The nature of the Commission's influence in these bodies is directly dependent on the form of policy competence that it holds in the EU, so the Commission has much stronger influence in the elaboration of the EU's stance on international trade, environmental protection or development than in, for instance, international finance (although with the introduction of the euro, a common international representation of the EU could be envisaged in the future). With regard to the political dimension of foreign policy and defence, the High Representative has not yet achieved a similarly central position for the EU in, for instance, NATO or in the UN Security Council, but again in view of recent developments, common positions on issues such as proliferation and armament, or in view of relations with certain countries such as Iran, will be increasingly likely in the future.

The evolving European foreign policy and the significance of communication

Despite many efforts in the last 15 years to forge a genuine European foreign and security policy, the failure of EU member states to speak with one voice in international political settings compromises the Union's ambitions to become an independent power in the world. The lack of overall coherence and commitment to European interests that have hampered the elaboration of policy responses, instruments and resource deployment is the most serious impediment to the EU's external identity and further demonstrates Europe's weakness in the context of serious international crises.

As a response to the failure to adopt a European position in the political posturing in the run-up to the war in Iraq, the EU member states adopted the European Security Strategy in December 2003. The strategy is influenced by the perceived need for the Union to become a 'hard' soft power in order to be able to hold its own in international politics and present a credible alternative to counteract (by persuasion) the prevailing world order influenced by aggressive unilateralism. However, in order to become a foremost international actor carrying a message of multilateralism founded on universal values, the Union will imperatively have to communicate coherently and forcefully to the outside world and match its good intentions with concrete action (including military if necessary). This requires a degree of political will and commitment on behalf of the member states, and mutual trust among them, that is not present in the current state of affairs in Europe.

Until now, the EU has built credibility within various functional areas of external action (such as trade, development, humanitarian aid, and, in a different fashion, enlargement), mostly because of the non-political character of these policies. There is a striking paradox in that as the EU seeks to politicize foreign policy by increasing the coherence between the functional areas and the 'political' CFSP, endowing itself with 'hard' power capabilities and enhancing its international profile, it will at the same time put the credibility of the 'functional' policies at risk. Nonetheless, it is beyond doubt that the confusion surrounding the EU's foreign policy objectives reduces its overall credibility as an actor and makes the task of communicating its wider intentions difficult, both in regard to the international community and to domestic EU audiences. The EU therefore seems to have no other choice than to politicize its international identity further.

In terms of public legitimacy, the EU is dependent on 'earning' the goodwill and support of the European public by demonstrating its capacity to speak with one voice on the international scene and matching its good intentions with concrete action. There is no underlying legitimacy for the EU to tap into (as is the case for most nation-states) and the permissive consensus from earlier decades is wearing thin among increasingly sceptical publics. The challenge is to make the normative content of European integration match the European interests that will first have been agreed among the member states. These interests need not cover all areas of international affairs, but should concentrate on some important issues where agreement on a common position is possible, where a European stake is clearly demonstrable and where the EU's involvement makes a difference. If the EU member states were ready to agree on European interests, and from there derive shared foreign policy objectives and priorities, communication with the European public and audiences abroad would be more effective and its identity greatly enhanced.

Conclusion

Rather than drawing any firm conclusions on a policy area that is bound to undergo profound political and material transformations in the near future, we will return to the initial subject matter of this chapter, namely the EU and public diplomacy.

It is an obvious statement to make today that the EU (the member states and the European institutions) does not have a shared public diplomacy strategy in the American sense, primarily because of the lack of political consensus on the EU's overall objectives and interests. If, on the other hand, we regard public diplomacy as a novel form of communication with different groups of society, then the EU is abound with examples – we could argue that the EU already possesses many of the required ingredients to mount a viable public diplomacy strategy. From this perspective it is interesting to note that the EU, in particular the Commission, has used the normative content of the Community pillar in building cognitive communities to persuade internal and external audiences of its ideas and perceptions of world order – much as it did to justify the creation of the common policies. The Commission has been quite successful in building credible functional regimes in trade, development policy and humanitarian aid, supporting them with an increasingly sophisticated normative content and techniques of diffusion. But the EU as a whole (the High Representative, the Commission and the member states) has not succeeded in forging a credible over-arching foreign policy regime, or speaking with one voice, which is an obvious requirement for any political entity wanting to promote its values on the international scene. From this perspective, the EU therefore seems far from being politically capable of conceiving and upholding a coherent public diplomacy strategy, and there are also question marks surrounding the member states' willingness to commit to such a strategy, since it would entail limitations on the pursuit of national interests and priorities and would certainly raise questions of democratic accountability.

From the functional, sector-specific perspective, however, the picture is quite different, as the normative content of the existing functional regimes is quite strong and reflects directly the EU's own constitutional set-up. In the past, however, the Commission was reluctant to communicate beyond the quite narrow circles of experts, interest groups and NGOs active in the related areas. Faced with an increasingly sceptical public, the Commission has realized that it needs to justify its actions and policies in the area of external relations with the populations of the member states, as well as with publics in third countries, in order to build a positive public image, promote European values and ultimately enhance the EU's legitimacy. The impact of the EU institutions' efforts is, however, dependent on the willingness of national political elites to support European interests and positions, both in the national arena and in international settings. If member states could agree on a set of European 'interests' and bring coherence to European policy competences and representation, the EU would be able to forge a proper international identity. It has enough 'actorness' to communicate principles and ideas about the nature of international relations and to persuade others of its perceptions. Were it to endow itself with enough instruments and resources to live up to its principles and objectives, the EU could become a strong international actor as well as earning the popular legitimacy at home on which it is so dependent. A public diplomacy strategy could be put in place using many of the techniques already deployed in the Community policy areas, but adding the endorsement at the national political level that is missing so badly today. Closer cooperation in third countries between member states' embassies and representations of EU institutions (Commission delegations or the High Representative's representatives) in communicating European objectives and policies would also greatly assist in enhancing the EU's international identity.

Notes

1. *A Secure Europe in a Better World: European Security Strategy*, presented to the European Council, Brussels, 12 December 2003.
2. See Peter van Ham, *European Integration and the Postmodern Condition: Governance, Democracy, Identity* (London: Routledge, 2001).
3. This chapter does not discuss the activities undertaken by the European Parliament in this field.

4. It is beyond the scope of this research to investigate the effects of these strategies on either internal or external audiences, or to evaluate the Commission's actions in the field of communication from the perspective of professionalism of the trade.
5. Ian Manners, 'Normative Power for Europe: A Contradiction in Terms?', *Journal of Common Market Studies*, vol. 40, no. 2, pp. 235–58.
6. Ian Manners argues that there are five 'core' norms (peace, liberty, democracy, the rule of law, and human rights and fundamental freedoms) and four 'minor' norms associated to the constitution and practices of the EU (social solidarity, anti-discrimination, sustainable development and good governance); see Manners, 'Normative Power for Europe', pp. 242–3. It would be possible to add 'market economy' to the last category [own remark].
7. European Commission, *Agenda 2000: For a stronger and Wider Union*, COM(97)2000 final, Brussels, 1997.
8. Manners notes six different ways to diffuse, by: 1) contagion (unintentional diffusion); 2) the informational mode through strategic communications; 3) the procedural mode through institutionalized contractual agreements with third parties; 4) transference through exchanges of goods, aid, trade or technical assistance; 5) overt diffusion through the physical presence of the EU abroad; and 6) a cultural filter leading to the construction of knowledge by third parties on the basis of EU norms; see Manners, 'Normative Power for Europe', pp. 244–5.
9. www.forum-europe.com.
10. European Commission, *Communication from the Commission to the Council, the European Parliament, the Economic and Social Committee and the Committee of the Regions on an Information and Communication Strategy for the European Union*, COM(2002) 350 final/2, Brussels, 2 October 2002.
11. These messages are derived from the Treaty on the EU, articles 2 and 6.
12. European Commission, *Information and Communication Strategy for the European Union*, p. 12.
13. The following assessment is based on an interview in the Commission's DG 'Press', Brussels, 7 October 2003.
14. See for instance, 'Follow my Leaders', *Financial Times*, 12–13 July 2003.
15. Judy Dempsey, *Financial Times*, 3–4 April 2004.
16. The EU has had some clear policy success, for instance in Macedonia and in the reconstruction of the former Republic of Yugoslavia. Common European positions have also been adopted on Iran and the Middle East.
17. It is, however, noticeable that the two incumbents argued in hearings organized by the Convention that coherence and effectiveness can be achieved through close cooperation between the Relex Commissioner and the High Representative without a formal merger of the two offices.
18. European Commission, *Communication from the Commission to the Council and the European Parliament concerning the Development of the External Service*, COM(2000) 456 final, Brussels, 18 July 2000.
19. The Commission has sought to take the lead in the EU troika in countries where the Presidency has a weak representation and the High Representative has no personal envoy.
20. See, for instance, *Communication from the Commission to the Council and the European Parliament: The European Union's Role in Promoting Human Rights*

and Democratization in Third Countries, COM(2001) 252 final, Brussels, 8 May 2001.

21. Interview at DG 'Relex', 7 October 2003.
22. Interview at DG 'Trade', Brussels, 7 October 2003.
23. Under article 133 of the treaties on European Union (TEU), the Commission is responsible for conducting negotiations with third parties on trade-related issues in order to conclude bilateral, regional or multilateral agreements. Although the Council of trade ministers remains the ultimate decision-maker, the Commissioner for trade and DG 'Trade' have great influence in defining the Union's trade interests and the direction of trade policy and ensure a unified voice for the EU in international fora.
24. Interview, DG 'Dev', Brussels, 18 September 2003.
25. The European Convention, the Secretariat, *Note from Commissioner Nielsen on Humanitarian Assistance: Working Group VII – 'External Action'*, Brussels, 21 November 2002.
26. Interview at ECHO, Brussels, 9 October 2003.
27. Giles Scott-Smith, *Mending the Unhinged Alliance: Public Diplomacy, the European Community Visitor Programme, and Transatlantic Relations in the 1970s*, unpublished manuscript, Middelburg, 2004.

Part III
Improving Practice

8
Culture Communicates: US Diplomacy That Works

Cynthia P. Schneider

The State Department has discovered jazz.
It teaches folks like nothing ever has.
Like when they feel that jazzy rhythm,

They know we're really with 'em.
That's what we call cultural exchange.

No commodity is quite so strange
As this thing called cultural exchange... [1]

Introduction

From the earliest days of the American republic, diplomats have recognized the value of cultural diplomacy. In a letter to James Madison penned from Paris, Thomas Jefferson described its goals in words that still apply today: 'You see I am an enthusiast on the subject of the arts. But it is an enthusiasm of which I am not ashamed, as its object is to improve the taste of my countrymen, to increase their reputation, to reconcile to them the respect of the world and procure them its praise'. [2] Cultural diplomacy, 'the exchange of ideas, information, art and other aspects of culture among nations and their peoples to foster mutual understanding', [3] forms an important component of the broader endeavour of public diplomacy, which basically comprises all that a nation does to explain itself to the world. Since much of cultural diplomacy consists of nations sharing forms of their creative expression, it is inherently enjoyable, and can therefore be one of the most effective tools in any diplomatic toolbox. Cultural diplomacy is a prime example of 'soft power', or the ability to persuade through culture, values and ideas, as opposed to 'hard power', which conquers or coerces through military might.[4]

It is not difficult to understand the potency of cultural diplomacy. What is more persuasive: a démarche delivered by an Ambassador to a foreign minister urging greater liberalization and emphasis on human rights, or films or music that express individuality and freedom? Compare the impact of Michael Moore's *Fahrenheit 9/11* to the impact of John Kerry's stump speeches. For Vaclav Havel, music was 'the enemy of totalitarianism': in 2000 at a White House Millennium evening devoted to jazz, Havel described how listening to jazz kept hopes of freedom alive in the darkest days of oppression in communist Czechoslovakia.

A consensus has emerged that American public diplomacy is in crisis. At least that is what the numerous task forces convened since '9/11' to study the dilemma of how to improve US public diplomacy would suggest.[5] Surprisingly, these studies give little attention to the category of cultural diplomacy. Given the success of cultural diplomacy during the Cold War, one might have expected the United States to turn to cultural diplomacy in the wake of '9/11' to increase understanding between America and the Arab/Muslim world. But the early success of cultural programmes sowed the seeds for their demise. Without the threat of the former Soviet Union, cultural and public diplomacy programmes suffered increasing cutbacks until the home of cultural diplomacy, the United States Information Agency (USIA), was dissolved and its functions and people absorbed into the State Department. Cultural diplomacy is not a partisan issue; it has both Republican and Democratic supporters and detractors. Walter Laqueur, among others, warned of the long-term danger of diminishing cultural diplomacy:

> Nor can it seriously be argued – as some have – that these tools of US foreign policy are no longer needed now that the Cold War is over and America no longer faces major threat . . . far from being on the verge of a new order, the world has entered a period of great disorder. In facing these new dangers, a re-examination of old priorities is needed. Cultural diplomacy, in the widest sense, has increased in importance, whereas traditional diplomacy and military power . . . are of limited use in coping with most of these dangers.[6]

Laqueur's warning was heeded neither by the Clinton nor the George W. Bush administration. Short-sighted cost cutting and euphoria over the crumbling Berlin wall led to drastic reductions in the scope and effectiveness of cultural and public diplomacy programmes.

The integration of all public diplomacy activities into the State Department in 1999 dealt cultural diplomacy a near-death blow. By 2000 the total budget for all public and cultural diplomacy activities amounted to less than eight per cent of the State Department budget, or approximately one-third of one per cent of the Pentagon budget.[7]

This chapter examines the reasons behind the decline of cultural diplomacy in the United States from the 1990s to the present. Following a brief history of cultural diplomacy in the US, a comparison is made between US practices in cultural diplomacy and those of other countries. Successful and failed strategies for cultural diplomacy are analysed. Finally, there is a discussion of the specific challenges facing the United States in the post-'9/11' world, as anti-Americanism peaks all over the globe, and the potential and limitations of cultural diplomacy in meeting them.

American culture and understanding America until the Cold War

Long before cultural diplomacy was employed by the US government, American cultural expression was influencing audiences throughout the world. Invariably, non-Americans have recognized the power of American culture more than have Americans. The Dutch historian Johan Huizinga identified art and literature – specifically Walt Whitman and film – as the strongest bearers of America's message.

> Anyone who wishes to understand America must first carry over his concept of Democracy from the political and social field to the cultural and generally human. The best way to do this continues to be reading Walt Whitman ... There is no stronger promoter of democracy in this sense than the cinema. It accustoms the nation, from high to low, to a single common view of life.[8]

Through both his use of language and his themes, Walt Whitman, the so-called 'bard of democracy', trumpeted the values of equality and individual freedoms in verses such as 'One's Self I Sing'. Whitman's distinctive combination of lyricism and blunt honesty created a poetic voice, whose no-nonsense language matched his favourite theme, the common man. In his preface to *Leaves of Grass* (1855), Whitman addressed the fundamental principle of equality in America.

> Other states indicate themselves in their deputies ... but the genius of the United States is not best or most in its executives or legislatures,

nor in its ambassadors or authors or colleges or churches or parlors, nor even in its newspapers or inventors...but always most in the common people.

If Whitman's poetry revealed the essence of American democracy, the novels of two of his contemporaries, Mark Twain and Harriet Beecher Stowe, revealed its dark underbelly – slavery. In *Huckleberry Finn* and *Uncle Tom's Cabin*, these authors bring to light one of the greatest strengths of creative expression generally and cultural diplomacy specifically – dissent. A critical role of the artist in any society is to question the status quo, but for the United States, grounded in the protection of civil liberties, dissent and opposition to government policies have special meaning. Huckleberry Finn embodied civil disobedience in choosing to protect the runaway slave Jim, a principled stand that set him at odds with the law. In *Huckleberry Finn*, Mark Twain created the prototype for countless heroes who buck the system, from Gary Cooper in *High Noon*, to Will Smith in *Enemy of the State*.

Like all great works of literature, *Huckleberry Finn* has provoked multiple interpretations and controversy. It was banned in the northern states in the 1870s for 'racism' (the word 'nigger' appears over 200 times), and in the southern states for being too sympathetic to blacks. In the former Soviet Union, *Huckleberry Finn* was used as an example of the injustice and inequalities in America. After the fall of the Iron Curtain, the interpretation of *Huckleberry Finn* in the new democratic Russia seamlessly evolved to one that resembled the traditional American view of Huck as the hero struggling against an unjust world.[9]

Probably the most influential book of the nineteenth century, Harriet Beecher Stowe's *Uncle Tom's Cabin*, first published in 1852, came to epitomize the cruel oppression and degradation of slavery. A best seller with more one million copies in circulation, *Uncle Tom's Cabin* was later adapted to protest colonial imperialism in Asia in one of the masterpieces of American cultural interpretation, Rogers' and Hammerstein's musical *The King and I*. The musical included the play within the play, *The Small House of Uncle Thomas*, based on Eliza's flight, one of the most dramatic scenes from Stowe's novel. What was this poignant scene from the 1850s doing in a musical about Thailand produced in the 1950s? During the Cold War, 'slavery' was a buzzword used to refer to communism. In the context of the King of Siam's court, the vignette about family reunification from *Uncle Tom's Cabin* renounced the practice of slavery in the King's harem, specifically the bondage that prevented the King's wives from marrying for love and having their own families.[10] At the same time, *The King and I*, despite its patronizing tone of Western superiority, opposed colonization and Western imperialism, and defended the independence of Siam. Identified with the cause of freeing slaves and reuniting families, America appears as a progressive power that champions both modernity and freedom.

Diplomacy that worked: cultural diplomacy during the Cold War

The works of Whitman, Twain and Stowe give a taste of how creative expression can help to shape the image of a nation and to communicate its values, but it was during the Cold War that America harnessed the power of culture as the stealth weapon against the US's enemy – the former Soviet Union – and its ideology – communism. The US government, through the State Department and other agencies, among them the CIA, orchestrated an unprecedented dissemination of American thought and creative expression throughout the world. The revelation of CIA funding for cultural initiatives, a story broken in *Ramparts* magazine in April 1967, contributed to the eventual demise of significant cultural programming by the US government.[11] Despite some tainted funding – a mistake that should not be repeated – cultural programmes, from the huge gathering of intellectuals—the Congress for Cultural Freedom[12] – to more intimate artists' and writers' exchanges and to music programmes on Radio Free Europe, helped to turn Europeans away from socialism and communism and opened the door of Western culture and lifestyle to Soviet artists and citizens.

In general the Cold War cultural programmes were brilliantly adapted to their targets. For example, the exchanges of both people and works among American and Russian writers, artists, and scholars that began shortly after Stalin's death in 1953 appealed to the inherent Russian respect for the intelligentsia and for cultural expression, while challenging some basic beliefs about their own society and ours. The best and the brightest from the two countries, including Arthur Miller, Joyce Carol Oates, and John Steinbeck from the US, and Aleksander Kushner, Vasily Aksyonov, and Yevgeny Yevtushenko from the former Soviet Union, met to discuss their art and the environments in which it was created. American writers who participated recalled that their counterparts seemed most impressed – and amazed – by the freedom of speech accorded them as official representatives of their government. When Norman Cousins was asked at one meeting if the American writers would not get into trouble for criticizing the government openly, he astounded his Soviet interlocutor by replying that any government official who complained would be more likely to encounter difficulties.[13] Another American writer recalled the impact of the exchanges as follows:

> What I sensed they got out of visiting American writers was, to them, our spectacular freedom to speak our minds. I mean, there we were, official representatives of the US – sort of the equivalent of their Writers Union apparatchiks – who had no party line at all... and who had the writers' tendency to speak out on controversial issues... In other words, the exchanges enabled Soviet writers, intellectuals, students, *et al.*, to see that the 'free world' wasn't just political cant.[14]

In addition to the exchanges, Americans in both private and public capacities helped to distribute and translate dissident works within the Soviet Union and outside. USIA published the popular, coveted *Amerika* magazine which, despite Soviet efforts to limit its distribution, revealed the American lifestyle in images and text to the Soviet public.[15] Private groups and the US government translated and distributed Russian dissident writers and English-language classics, as well as political commentary by experts such as Brzezinski and Kissinger. Prominent dissidents such as Aleksandr Solzhenitsyn relied on these book programmes to receive literature and commentary from the West as well as the works of Russian dissidents banned in the Soviet Union.[16]

Cold War cultural diplomacy contains valuable lessons for today's challenges. Like many Middle Eastern countries, notably Iraq and Iran, Russia had a distinguished literary tradition that was closely identified with its national identity. By honouring Russia's literary giants of the past and dissident writers of the present, the US government gained important allies in Soviet society and through them was able to communicate broadly with the Soviet people. All of this was possible because US diplomats understood the importance of cultural expression to the Russians and respected their literary and artistic achievements.

As the United States seeks avenues for communicating with the Arab/ Muslim world, literary and scientific publications provide ideal vehicles. But the potential for 'book diplomacy' has barely been tapped. The State Department sponsors the translation of only about 20 books a year into Arabic, at a cost of a mere US$5000 per book for editions of about 3000.[17] The 'Book Program' that distributed to Solzhenitsyn and others was funded at up to one million dollars per year, but through the CIA.[18] Although such a funding source is unacceptable, the sum and the source demonstrate a commitment to cultural diplomacy that is absent today. While security risks prohibit American writers and artists from visiting Iraq at present, Iraqi writers and artists could be invited to the United States and other Western countries for frank exchanges modelled after those in the 1950s. The US tour by the Iraqi symphony orchestra in December 2003 and the visit of Michael Kaiser, President of the Kennedy Center, to Iraq to help rebuild Iraqi cultural institutions represent good first steps.

Arguably even more potent than literature in revealing the cracks in the communist façade and communicating the freedoms of the West was music, particularly jazz and rock 'n' roll. Western music penetrated the Iron Curtain through the nightly programming of *Music USA*, hosted by Willis Connover from 1955 until his death in 1996. Little known in the United States, Willis Connover truly *was* the 'voice of America' for much of the world. A Russian listener described the experience: 'Every night we would shut the doors and windows, turn on Willis Connover, and have two hours of freedom'.[19] Connover himself brilliantly described why jazz is the music of freedom:

> Jazz is a cross between total discipline and anarchy. The musicians agree on tempo, key, and chord structure but beyond this everyone is free to express himself. This is jazz. And this is America... It's a musical reflection of the way things happen in America. We're not apt to recognize this over here, but people in other countries can feel this element of freedom.[20]

In addition to the music itself, jazz's power as a cultural ambassador stemmed from the inherent tension created by black musicians travelling the globe trumpeting American values during the Jim Crow era. The musicians themselves did not shy away from exposing this hypocrisy.[21] When summoned to the State Department for a pre-tour briefing, Dizzy Gillespie declined, noting that 'I've got three hundred years of briefing. I know what they've done to us and I'm not going to make any excuse... I liked the idea of representing America, but I wasn't going to apologize for the racist policies of America'.[22] As was true of the authors who freely criticized aspects of America to their Soviet counterparts, musicians such as Louis Armstrong, Dizzy Gillespie and Charlie Parker brought abstract concepts of liberty to life by democratizing their concerts and insisting that ordinary people, not just elites, be allowed to listen. In addition, African American bands and dance companies toured Africa, forging close bonds with local performers and artists and igniting cross-fertilizations that benefited both.[23] Although jazz is widely recognized to have been an extremely effective tool for diplomacy, its presence has dramatically declined from its heyday during the 1960s when the State Department toured Ellington, Armstrong and Brubeck and their bands for weeks at a time, sending them to countries all over Africa, Asia and the Middle East, as well as to the Soviet Union and Eastern Europe. Today, the greatly diminished annual budget of US$840,000 for the Jazz Ambassadors programme funds concerts by eight jazz quartets.

Like jazz, rock 'n' roll enabled people living under repressive regimes to experience moments of freedom while listening, and it provided a unifying bond for young people all over the globe. Unlike jazz, it was not an American phenomenon, but rather English-speaking, with the Beatles, the Rolling Stones, and other British groups garnering world-wide followings. Andras Simonyi, the current Hungarian Ambassador to the United States and a guitarist, was profoundly influenced by rock 'n' roll, which he first experienced when he heard a recording of the Beatles's 'All My Loving' 40 years ago at the age of 11. In a speech entitled 'Rocking for the Free World: How Rock Music Helped Bring Down the Iron Curtain', delivered in various venues across America, beginning in the Rock 'n' Roll Hall of Fame in Cleveland, Ambassador Simonyi has tried to make Americans understand the strength of their own culture, and also to appreciate their freedoms. 'Rock 'n' roll was the internet of the 1960s and early 1970s. It was the carrier of the message of freedom ... Rock 'n' roll, culturally speaking, was a decisive element in loosening up communist societies and bringing them closer to a world of freedom.'[24] Simonyi's opinion is widely shared, and commentators of various nationalities and ages credit popular culture, especially rock 'n' roll, with helping to precipitate the collapse of communism.[25]

Jazz and rock 'n' roll had visual counterparts in abstract expressionist art; in films, such as *On the Waterfront, Rebel Without a Cause* and *Dr Strangelove*; and in the plays of Arthur Miller.[26] The inventor of 'action painting', Jackson Pollock, became an unlikely poster boy for American freedom of expression. The image of the man from Wyoming who took New York by storm with his new invention of paint hurled and dripped on a canvas fit perfectly, but Pollock was also an abusive alcoholic, an aspect of his biography that was omitted as his paintings toured Europe in exhibitions organized by the Museum of Modern Art.[27]

Until the fall of the Soviet Union and its empire, both public and private entities contributed to the shaping of the image of the US abroad. The jazz tours were organized by the State Department, but the exhibitions of modern art were toured by the Museum of Modern Art, and the films were distributed in Europe by their studios. Whatever their origin, these various modes of creative expression formed part of an overall portrayal of the United States as a country of individual freedoms, opportunity and tolerance. That visiting Americans exposed the cracks in the façade of the US, such as racism and McCarthyism, made the message of freedom all the more powerful. Given the earlier successes of cultural diplomacy, how can its virtual demise be explained? Arguably, cultural diplomacy has never recovered from the dual blow of the revelation of CIA support, and, with the fall of the Iron Curtain, the loss of the 'evil empire' against whose culture that of the United States was projected. Another problem has been confusion and disagreement over where responsibility for cultural diplomacy belongs within the US government.

The role(s) and position(s) of cultural diplomacy in the US government or 'déjà vu all over again'

From the first US government efforts at disseminating information about America abroad with the Creel Committee of 1917–19 until the present, there has been a consensus about the importance of promoting understanding of the United States to other countries, but how to accomplish that goal has been the subject of countless debates and studies.[28] The critical question is: how to separate or integrate the functions of diplomacy, information, cultural expression, and exchanges? Not long after cultural diplomacy was given its own agency – USIA, founded in 1953 – questions arose about the wisdom of separating cultural programmes designed to promote understanding of the United States and its policies from the State Department, where the policies were promulgated. Nonetheless, during the peak of the Cold War, both government and private initiatives flourished under President Eisenhower, who was personally committed to cultural diplomacy.[29] Soon after his inauguration in 1961, President Kennedy chose to maintain the separation between the state and USIA.[30] USIA's brilliant director at the time, Edward R. Murrow, exerted more influence than anyone in his position before or since, but even he expressed frustration with his famous plea to be 'present at the take off, as well as the crash landings' of foreign policy. A panel convened by the Center for Strategic and International Studies (CSIS) in response to concerns in the foreign policy community about the efficacy of public and cultural diplomacy recommended that cultural, informational and educational functions be united in a single agency, the Information and Cultural Affairs Agency, and that the Voice of America break off into a separate agency.[31] The panel's recommendations echoed those in the USIA Appropriations Authorization Act of 1973.[32]

Twenty-five years later, in 1999, USIA was integrated into the State Department. Although the rationale was efficacy, the drastic cuts in USIA's budget once cultural activities joined the State Department indicated that economy also played a role.[33] The abolition of USIA as an independent agency was part of a larger restructuring: the Foreign Affairs Reform and Restructuring Act of 1998, which also integrated the Arms Control and Disarmament Agency and some functions of AID into the State Department.[34] Although public diplomacy was described as a 'national security imperative' by then Secretary of State Madeleine Albright at the ceremony marking the consolidation, the precipitous decline in funding during the 1990s indicated that others in the government did not share her commitment.[35] After the 1994 Republican landslide, USIA and public diplomacy were caught in the crossfire between Senator Jesse Helms, Chairman of the Senate Foreign Relations Committee, and the Clinton administration over reductions in government expenses. Senator Helms targeted both the State Department and USIA, with requests for accountability and quantifiable evidence of their value.

The reduction in budget, personnel and effectiveness of public and cultural diplomacy that resulted from the consolidation reflected a profound misunderstanding of diplomacy in the post-Cold War world. In a world made smaller by globalization, and one in which non-governmental actors and organizations (NGOs) exert increasingly greater influence, public opinion matters more, not less. With the collapse of the Soviet Union and the opening up of the communist bloc, the need to communicate democratic values and ideas with people at all levels of society was greater than ever. Yet it was precisely at this moment that the United States shut the doors to its libraries and 'America Houses', and drastically cut the number of public and cultural affairs' officers all over the world, eliminating some posts entirely.[36] In a misguided effort to join the information age, libraries were replaced by 'Information Resource Centers'. In reality, this meant that books were thrown or given away to make way for multiple computer stations for internet research.[37] While access to the internet adds value, especially in totalitarian societies, it does not fully compensate for the thousands of books that filled the shelves of US embassies all over the world. Lamenting the closing of US libraries and cultural centres, Samer

Shehata, Georgetown University Assistant Professor and specialist in Arab Studies, recalled that 'The American Cultural Center in Alexandria [Egypt] was where I learned about Jefferson and Lincoln'.[38]

Confusion and disagreements over where to house cultural diplomacy within the US government point to fundamental questions about its role in foreign affairs. The establishment of USIA as a separate agency reflected the belief that cultural diplomacy should have independence from foreign policy. The consolidation of USIA into the State Department responded to the opposite impetus – the guiding rule of cultural diplomacy at present – namely that it should be linked to increasing understanding and support for US policies.[39]

Comparative practices of other countries

While the United States has struggled with the issue of culture in the service of government policy, other countries have separated the two both philosophically and bureaucratically. For example, the British Council, created in 1934, and the Goethe Institut, founded just after the Second World War, which are the cultural diplomacy agencies for the United Kingdom and Germany respectively, are subsidized by government, but exist as autonomous agencies.[40] In other cases, such as France and Mexico, for example, the cultural attaché is housed within the embassy structure, but nonetheless focuses on long-term relationship building, and not trouble-shooting for particular policies.[41] In Mexico, a country with a long, distinguished cultural history, the Fox government has linked cultural diplomacy and foreign policy more tightly than before in an effort to open Mexico up to the democratizing influences of international cultural figures and NGOs.[42] The former Soviet Union provides a prime example of cultural diplomacy that is explicitly linked to government policy. The goal of Soviet cultural offensives, however, was not to win America over to communism, but, with artists such as the dancers of the Bolshoi and Kirov ballets, to establish links in spite of the profound differences between the systems of the two countries. George Kennan, the renowned Russian expert, strongly advocated artistic and cultural exchanges between the United States and former Soviet Union, as a means of counteracting isolationism and increasing understanding between the two countries.[43]

From the start, the United States has eschewed the 'culture for culture's sake' approach that often governs cultural diplomacy elsewhere. Culture for culture's sake has no place in the US Information and Education Exchange Program. The value of international cultural interchange is to win respect for the cultural achievements of our free society, where that respect is necessary to inspire cooperation with us in world affairs',[44] according to a 1950 memorandum from the Bureau of the Budget that differs little from the utilitarian approach that governs US cultural diplomacy today. In contrast, some countries, such as the Netherlands, select arts professionals for the cultural outreach positions, but even in countries such as France, where the position of cultural counsellor at the French embassy in Washington is a coveted foreign service post, potential cultural initiatives are evaluated on the basis of quality, not political efficacy.[45]

In general, other countries have recognized the long-term, non-quantifiable nature of relationship building through cultural diplomacy to a greater degree than the United States. The former Soviet Union understood its value in establishing links even in an adversarial political situation, and Germany turned to culture to help restore relationships after the Second World War. France has deftly used its language and learning to reach peoples all over the world, including in the Middle East. Finally, for countries such as France and the Netherlands, culture provides a means to expand upon ideas and images created by the market. 'Tulips and wooden shoes' might attract tourists to the Netherlands, but Dutch cultural counsellor Jeanne Winkler enlarges upon that stereotype by showcasing avant-garde artists to emphasize the modern, creative dimensions of the Netherlands.[46]

Other countries have also matched their commitment to cultural diplomacy with significant funding. In a recent survey of cultural diplomacy in nine countries, the United States ranked last in per capita spending, lagging behind not only France and the United Kingdom, but also Sweden and Singapore.[47] France leads in spending on cultural diplomacy, with an annual budget of over one billion dollars.[48] The total sum of the US budget varies, depending on what activities are included. Estimates range from one billion US dollars[49] to 600 million dollars[50] to US\$184,359,000.[51] The latter figure, which excludes all broadcasting expenditures, compares unfavourably with budgets in the United Kingdom and Japan.[52]

Cultural diplomacy in the twenty-first century

After the demoralizing abolition of USIA, the future of cultural diplomacy began to look brighter at the end of the Clinton administration. In late November 2000, Clinton's White House and the State Department convened a star-studded gathering that sought to match the rhetoric about cultural diplomacy with more visible support. Opening with speeches by President Clinton and First Lady Hillary Rodham Clinton, followed by remarks by Nobel Laureate Wole Soyinka, former US Poet Laureate Rita Dove, Doris Duke Foundation President Joan Spero, Italian Cultural Minister Giovanna Melandri, cellist Yo-Yo Ma, and His Highness the Aga Khan, the White House Conference on Cultural Diplomacy reasserted the value and importance of cultural diplomacy. Unfortunately, however, even though the attendees included business leaders, government members, academia and the arts, the conference did not stem the tide of reduced funding, nor did it validate cultural diplomacy within the State Department ethos. As Edmund Gullion, former Dean of the Fletcher School of Law and Diplomacy, predicted, the State Department's culture subordinated public diplomacy, valuing the traditional 'cones' (fields of specializations) of politics and economics more highly.[53]

Anecdotal evidence further attests to the gradual diminution in importance of cultural programmes and those who promoted them. When I first spoke with my public affairs officer in August 1998, soon after I assumed the position of US Ambassador to the Netherlands, she proudly told me, 'We (the public affairs section) don't do culture; we do policy'. When I explained that with 150 other people doing policy, I wanted the public affairs division to concentrate on cultural diplomacy, she looked disappointed and confused. Her rejection of cultural diplomacy as a viable undertaking reflected the toll taken by years of demands for quantifiable results, with no compensatory appreciation for the long-term value added of increased understanding and relationship building.

Around the same time, US Ambassador John O'Leary had an analogous experience in Chile. When Ambassador O'Leary suggested that the American embassy in Chile provide transportation for Poet Laureate Rita Dove while she participated in a poetry festival in Santiago, he was told that such a gesture would violate regulations since Ms Dove was not travelling on official US business.[54] Yet in Chile, where literature and poetry are revered, Rita Dove, Poet Laureate, was an American hero. Even if Dove's visit had no official connection to the US embassy, the embassy and American presence in Chile would have gained by associating themselves with the Poet Laureate.

With only 2.7 million US dollars budgeted for cultural presentations in 2004, embassies only can achieve a viable cultural programme by leveraging private visits such as those of Ms Dove. Without an ethos inside the State Department that values such initiatives, and that rewards them through the promotion process, embassies will not take advantage of the opportunities afforded by private visits. Furthermore, without institutional support, cultural diplomacy is not systematic, but capricious and sporadic, reflecting the interests of individual ambassadors. Those chiefs of mission with an understanding of and commitment to cultural diplomacy will create a favourable climate within the embassy, and will encourage personnel to capitalize on opportunities presented by cultural leaders visiting the country or area. For example, during my tenure in The Hague (from 1998–2001), I hosted Michael Graves, Frank Gehry, Al Green and other jazz musicians, Dennis Hopper, as well as academic, business, and political leaders, none of whom were funded by the US government.[55]

The challenges of cultural diplomacy today

Never have the challenges of cultural diplomacy for America been greater than today, when public opinion about the United States stands at its lowest ebb. Opinion polls indicate that favourable views in Europe of the US have dropped by 40 percentage points or more in the United Kingdom, France, Germany, Italy and Spain.[56] Negative views previously held in the Middle East have spread to other Muslim populations, such as in Indonesia and Nigeria, where favourable ratings for the United States have dropped from 61 per cent to 15 per cent and 71 to 38 per cent respectively.[57] The negative opinions reflect views about the policies of the US government, most notably the war and occupation in Iraq, not the American people or the ideals of American society. While cultural initiatives can never compensate for opposition to policies, they can help to keep alive appreciation for American ideals, values, and contributions to culture and learning. Despite the opposition to American policies, most Muslim populations still believe a Western-style democracy would work in their country.[58] The interest in democratic society and in Western culture (and also science and technology) remains high: '80 per cent of Arabs and Muslims disagree with your policy, not your values', commented Hafez Al-Mirazi, bureau chief of Aljazeera satellite channel in January 2004.[59]

Post-'9/11' cultural diplomacy has had both successes and failures.[60] The television spots created under Under-Secretary of Public Diplomacy Charlotte Beers, a former advertising executive praised by Colin Powell for having convinced him to buy Uncle Ben's rice, fall into the latter category. Middle Eastern distributors and audiences recognized as propaganda the sunny view of lives of Arab Americans in the United States portrayed in the clips, and chose not to show the films. Senator Richard Lugar, among others, understood the fallacy of applying a Madison Avenue approach to public diplomacy. At a hearing on public diplomacy and Islam, he noted,

> The missing ingredient in American public diplomacy between the fall of the Berlin Wall and the September 11th attacks was not advertising cleverness. It was a firm commitment by the American people and the American leadership to all the painstaking work required to build lasting relationships overseas and advance our visions of fairness and opportunity.[61]

After a brief tenure of just over one year as Under-Secretary of Public Diplomacy, Charlotte Beers left the position for health reasons, to be succeeded by Margaret Tutwiler, former US Ambassador to Morocco and a veteran of Bush Senior's administration. Having stated in Congressional testimony in February 2004 that it will 'take us many years of hard, focused work' to restore America's standing in the world, Under-Secretary Tutwiler quit the top public diplomacy position after only a few months to accept a Wall Street offer.[62]

Despite multiple hearings and studies stressing the importance and the inadequacy of American public and cultural diplomacy, resources have not begun to match rhetoric. Less than three million US dollars per year is allocated to send American performers abroad, compared with France's budget for performances and exhibitions of over 600 million dollars.[63] Even smaller countries such as the Netherlands or Singapore dedicate larger funds to these activities.[64] The miniscule sum dedicated by the US government to performances can be explained only if one believes that the free market distribution of US popular culture does the work of cultural diplomacy. But the free market will not ensure that American artists reach target populations, such as those in the Middle East, nor will it guarantee that the US is even represented at major international arts festivals such as the Venice Biennale, where the US exhibition is funded privately. Furthermore, the tightening of visa requirements with the Patriot Act has thwarted hundreds of cultural exchanges, and is significantly diminishing the number of foreign students at US universities.[65]

While popular culture contributes – sometimes positively, sometimes not – to communicating American ideas and values, the most effective interface between government-sponsored cultural diplomacy and the free flow of popular culture has yet to be determined, or even analysed.

The recent initiatives by the US Broadcasting Board of Governors represent attempts to merge cultural diplomacy with popular culture. The United States has dedicated a disproportionate amount of its cultural diplomacy budget – hundreds of millions of dollars – to broadcasting, with mixed results. The Broadcasting Board of Governors has used the funds to launch new stations in the Middle East, both on radio – Radio Sawa – and TV – Alhurra. Broadcast on FM transmitters in Arabic and local dialects throughout the Middle East, including in Iraq, Radio Sawa alternates between contemporary Arab and Western music, with periodic news spots, aiming to appeal to the 60 per cent of the Middle East's population that is aged under 30. By giving Middle Eastern music equal billing, Radio Sawa implicitly signals its respect for local culture. Although Sawa has been criticized by some for being too commercial and too 'light', by all accounts it has a wide following.[66] Sawa's success, however, has come at the expense of traditional Voice of America (VOA) programming, which targeted a different audience – opinion-makers and the intelligentsia. This shift in broadcasting priorities was criticized by more than 500 VOA employees, who protested the reduction of quality news programming in a petition to Congress.[67]

The recently launched television station Alhurra is struggling harder to establish itself, partially because of the more competitive television market (over 100 cable channels), and partially because of inherent suspicion in the Middle East of government-sponsored media.[68] Airing an interview with President Bush as the inaugural event of the station did not help to alleviate these suspicions, but when Alhurra broadcast the Senate Armed Services Committee grilling Donald Rumsfeld over the scandal at Abu Ghraib, viewers witnessed a level of accountability uncommon in the Middle East.[69] Whether the 62 million US dollars invested in Alhurra were well spent remains to be seen; indeed, whether media can alleviate or compensate for unpopular policies is unproven.[70] A less costly alternative to creating a new television station in a market that is already flooded would be to provide programming for the numerous extant stations, a dire need met by private ventures such as Layalina Productions. Layalina will offer both news and content programmes, including a series targeted towards youth in which an Arab and a Western boy travel back in time to famous events in Arab and Western history.[71]

Despite minimal funding, there have been successful cultural initiatives launched in recent years. Examples are the Culture Connect programme, the Ambassador's Fund, and American Corners. The effective Culture Connect programme sends the best in American culture to places off the beaten path for an intense programme of concerts and master classes. In 2003, Culture Connect brought Yo-Yo Ma to Lithuania and Denise Graves to Venezuela and Poland. Funded at only one million US dollars per year, the Ambassador's Fund for cultural and historical preservation has had a positive impact that is disproportionate to its size.[72] Together with colleagues from their host countries, ambassadors serving in the developing world select historical preservation projects that meet local needs and priorities and finance them with monies from the Ambassador's Fund.

One of the many lessons since '9/11' has been that the closing of libraries and cultural centres was a mistake, but perhaps ultimately a fortuitous one. Access to libraries inside embassies is no longer possible in today's security climate, and American centres would be prime terrorist targets. Turning adversity to advantage, the State Department has launched American Corners. Numbering more than 130 and located primarily in the former Soviet Union, these pockets of America placed inside local libraries and cultural institutions offer access to the internet, plus videos, CDs and books about the US. The drawback of their small size is more than compensated for by the virtues of convenience and discretion. Visitors can drop into an American Corner any time that the host library is open – no need to make an appointment and no risk of exposure from visiting an American embassy. In addition to these three examples, individual ambassadors and public affairs officers continue to make 'cultural diplomacy lemonade' by squeezing the last drops of funding and creatively leveraging every opportunity.[73]

Conclusion

No amount of cultural diplomacy, however skilfully deployed, can win back world opinion in the face of policies that are resented and despised. Vigorous cultural diplomacy, however, can sustain appreciation for the values and ideals that are characteristic of America. Launching a forceful, energetic policy of cultural diplomacy would require leadership from the White House and the State Department as well as partnerships with the private sector, not to mention adequate funding. Soft power requires hard dollars. Even though such significant foreign policy experts as Walter Laqueur, George Kennan and Thomas Pickering have all argued for the importance of cultural diplomacy, in the current climate of insecurity about national security, cultural diplomacy is easily dismissed as too soft and peripheral to the real issues of security.

In addition, sufficient thought has yet to be given to the right balance of 'market' and public sector forces in using culture to shape world opinion. Previously, when aerospace products were the US's number one export, their sales were strategically targeted and supported by the US government, but the same is not true today of the current top export – cultural products.[74] Strategically investing in popular culture by targeting the distribution of desirable products would reap rewards in the court of world opinion.

Whether the United States will heed the advice of multiple panels about the importance of public and cultural diplomacy remains to be seen. As long as public diplomacy funding amounts to only one-third of one per cent of the military budget, Jefferson's vision of 'increasing the reputation' of his 'countrymen' and 'reconciling to them the respect of the world' will remain out of reach. But there may still be hope. After all, an American, Michael Moore, won the *Palme d'Or* at the 2004 Cannes Film Festival.

Notes

1. Iola Brubeck's lyrics for the satirical musical revue *The Real Ambassadors*, performed in 1962, from Penny M. von Eschen, 'Satchmo Blows Up the World: Jazz, Race, and Empire during the Cold War', in Reinhold Wagnleitner and Elaine Tyler May (eds), *Here, There, and Everywhere: The Foreign Politics of American Popular Culture* (Hanover and London: University Press of New England, 2000), p. 168.
2. Letter dated 20 September 1785, in John P. Kaminski, *Citizen Jefferson: The Wit and Wisdom of an American Sage* (Madison WI: Madison House, 1994), p. 6.
3. Milton C. Cummings, *Cultural Diplomacy and the United States Government: A Survey* (Washington DC: Center for Arts and Culture, 2003), p. 1, www.culturalpolicy.org.
4. Joseph Nye coined the phrase 'soft power'. See Joseph S. Nye, *The Paradox of American Power* (Oxford: Oxford University Press, 2002), pp. 8–9; and Joseph S. Nye, *Soft Power: The Means to Success in World Politics* (New York: PublicAffairs, 2004).
5. For example, *Finding America's Voice: A Strategy for Reinvigorating US Public Diplomacy*, report of an independent task force sponsored by the Council on Foreign Relations, chaired by Peter G. Peterson, 2003; *Changing Minds, Winning Peace: A New Strategic Direction for US Public Diplomacy in the Arab and Muslim World*, report of the Advisory Group on Public Diplomacy for the Arab and Muslim World, chaired by Edward P. Djerejian, 1 October 2003; Stephen Johnson and Helle Dale, *How to Reinvigorate US Public Diplomacy* (Washington DC: The Heritage Foundation, 23 April 2003).
6. Walter Laqueur, 'Save Public Diplomacy', *Foreign Affairs*, September/October 1994, vol. 73, no. 5, p. 20.
7. David J. Kramer, 'No Bang for the Buck: Public Diplomacy Should Remain a Priority', *Washington Times*, 23 October 2000, http://www/state.gov/r/

adcompd/kramer.html; and Ambassador Kenton Keith, 'US Public Diplomacy from MAD to Jihad', CERI conference on US Public Diplomacy, Paris, 3 June 2004.

8. Johan Huizinga, *America: A Dutch Historian's Vision, from Afar and Near* (New York: Harper & Row, 1972), pp. 240–41.
9. Information from Russian students in my 'Diplomacy and the Arts' seminar, autumn 2001.
10. Christina Klein, *Cold War Orientalism: Asia in the Middlebrow Imagination, 1945–61* (Berkeley CA: University of California Press, 2003), pp. 204–8.
11. Frances Stonor Saunders, *The Cultural Cold War: The CIA and the World of Arts and Letters* (New York: The New Press, 1999), pp. 381–3.
12. Frank A. Ninkovich, *The Diplomacy of Ideas: US Foreign Policy and Cultural Relations, 1938–1950* (Cambridge: Cambridge University Press, 1981), pp. 166–7.
13. Yale Richmond, *Cultural Exchange and the Cold War* (University Park PA: Pennsylvania State University Press, 2003), p. 158. On Soviet reactions to encounters with American freedoms, see also Frederick C. Barghoorn, *The Soviet Cultural Offensive: The Role of Cultural Diplomacy in Soviet Foreign Policy* (Princeton NJ: Princeton University Press, 1960).
14. Richmond, *Cultural Exchange and the Cold War*, p. 154, quoting Ted Solotaroff.
15. Richmond, *Cultural Exchange and the Cold War*, p. 148.
16. Richmond, *Cultural Exchange and the Cold War*, p. 137.
17. Information from Christopher Datta, Office Director for Special Projects, Bureau of International Information Programs, 13 July 2004.
18. Information from Christopher Datta, as before.
19. Ambassador Kenton Keith, in comments on the panel 'Keeping Culture on the International Stage', panel at the National Performing Arts Convention, Pittsburgh PA, 12 June 2004.
20. Richmond, *Cultural Exchange and the Cold War*, p. 207, citing Connover's statement in John S. Wilson's, 'Who is Connover? Only *We* Ask', *New York Times Magazine*, 13 September 1959.
21. Armstrong and Brubeck's 1962 musical revue *The Real Ambassadors* satirized the contradiction; see von Eschen, 'Satchmo Blows Up the World', p. 168.
22. Von Eschen, 'Satchmo Blows Up the World', p. 170.
23. Ambassador Thomas Pickering described the mutual benefits of the visit of the Alvin Ailey dance company to Tanzania when he was Ambassador there during the late 1960s in a speech delivered at Georgetown University at the conference 'Communicating with the World: Diplomacy that Works', 30 April 2003, available on the website www.culturalpolicy.org.
24. Bill Nichols, 'How Rock 'n' Roll Freed the World', *USA Today*, 6 November 2003.
25. For example, James G. Herschberg, 'Just Who Did Smash Communism?', *Washington Post*, Sunday 27 June 2004, pp. B1 and B5; Thomas Fuchs, 'Rock 'n' Roll in the German Democratic Republic, 1949–1961', in Reinhold Wagnleitner and Elaine May (eds), *Here, There, and Everywhere: The Foreign Politics of American Popular Culture* (Hanover and London: University Press of New England, 2000), pp. 192–206.
26. On film, see Lary May, *The Big Tomorrow: Hollywood and the Politics of the American Way* (Chicago IL: University of Chicago Press, 2000), especially

pp. 175–265. On the propagandistic anti-communist films of the 1940s and 1950s, see Stephen J. Whitfield, *The Culture of the Cold War* (Baltimore MD: Johns Hopkins University Press, 1996), pp. 127–51.

27. Saunders, *The Cultural Cold War*, pp. 252–78. Saunders elaborates the connections between leaders at the Museum of Modern Art and the CIA, but no proof of direct CIA support for MOMA's exhibitions in the 1950s is known.

28. Ninkovich, *The Diplomacy of Ideas*; Charles Frankel, *The Neglected Aspect of Foreign Affairs* (Washington DC: Brookings Institution, 1965); Hans Tuch, *Communicating with the World in the 1990s* (Washington DC: USIA Alumni Association and the Public Diplomacy Foundation, 1994). See also footnote 5.

29. Cummings, *Cultural Diplomacy and the United States Government*, pp. 8–9.

30. *International Information, Education and Cultural Relations: Recommendations for the Future* (Washington DC: Center for Strategic and International Studies, 1975), p. 77.

31. *International Information, Education and Cultural Relations*.

32. Dated 22 May 1973, cited from *International Information, Education and Cultural Relations*, pp. 50–2.

33. On the decline in public diplomacy funding, see Juliet Antunes Sablonsky, 'Recent Trends in Department of State Support for Cultural Diplomacy: 1993–2002', white paper in the Cultural Diplomacy Research Series, Center for Arts and Culture, 2003, www.culturalpolicy.org. See also Rosaleen Smyth, 'Mapping US Public Diplomacy in the Twenty-First Century', *Australian Journal of International Affairs*, vol. 55, no. 3, 2001, pp. 421–44.

34. 'The Public Diplomacy and Public Affairs Missions', www.fas.org/irp/offdocs/pdd/pdd-68-docs.htm, accessed 24 June 2004; see also http://ieie.nsc.ru:8101/nisnews/let5/easa.htm, accessed 29 June 2004.

35. http://www.wtcsglobal.org/cie/fedspeech.htm.

36. House Report 105–207 on the 1998 appropriations for USIA calls for eliminating 22 American and 96 foreign national positions, making a reduction of 1488 personnel since 1994. In addition, the budget dictates the closure of America Houses in Munich and Hamburg, and the USIA sections in the embassies in Nigeria and Papua New Guinea; see http://www.congress.gov/cgibin/cpquery/?&dbname=cp105&&r_n=hr207.105&sel=TOC. On the founding and value of the America Houses, see Manuela Aguilar, *Cultural Diplomacy and Foreign Policy: German–American Relations, 1955–1968*, Studies in Modern European History, vol. 19 (New York: Peter Lang, 1996), pp. 156–70.

37. John. N. Berry III, 'Librarians are Public Diplomats', *National Journal*, vol. 128, issue 12, 15 July 2003, p. 18.

38. Comments during speech at the conference 'Communicating with the World: Diplomacy that Works', held at Georgetown University, 30 April 2003.

39. Foreign service officer Joe Merante in a presentation on cultural diplomacy to my Georgetown seminar, 'Culture and Diplomacy', on 29 March 2004.

40. *Arts and Minds: A Conference on Cultural Diplomacy*, report of conference held from 14–15 April 2003, New York, Columbia University, pp. 35–44, http://www.culturalpolicy.org/issuepages/Arts&Minds.cfm. On German cultural diplomacy, see also Aguilar, 'Cultural Diplomacy and Foreign Policy', pp. 79–217.

41. *Arts and Minds*, pp. 35–39.

42. *Arts and Minds*, p. 39.
43. George F. Kennan, 'International Exchange in the Arts', *Perspectives USA*, no. 16, 1956, pp. 6–14, cited in Barghoorn, *The Soviet Cultural Offensive*, p. 342.
44. Aguilar, *Cultural Diplomacy and Foreign Policy*, p. 54.
45. *Arts and Minds*, p. 33.
46. *Arts and Minds*, p. 38.
47. Margaret J. Wyszomirski, Christopher Burgess and Catherine Peila, *International Cultural Relations: A Multi-Country Comparison* (Washington DC: Arts International and Center for Arts and Culture, 2003), p. 24; see www.artsinternational.org and www.culturalpolicy.org.
48. Wyszomirski, Burgess and Peila, *International Cultural Relations*, Table 2, p. 3.
49. Joseph S. Nye, 'Today, It's a Question of Whose Story Wins', latimes.com, 21 July 2004.
50. Christopher Marquis, 'US Image Abroad Will Take Years to Repair, Official Testifies', *New York Times*, 5 February 2004.
51. Wyszomirski, Burgess and Peila, *International Cultural Relations*, p. 24.
52. Wyszomirski, Burgess and Peila, *International Cultural Relations*, pp. 24–5.
53. Letter from Edmund Gullion to Frank Stanton, in *International Information, Education and Cultural Relations*, p. 81.
54. Oral communication, March 2003.
55. Cynthia P. Schneider, *Diplomacy that Works: 'Best Practices' in Cultural Diplomacy* (Washington DC: Center for Arts and Culture, 2003), www.culturalpolicy.org.
56. Pew Research Center, *America's Image Further Erodes, Europeans Want Weaker Ties*, 18 March 2003, pp. 1–2, http://people-press.org/reports/display.php3? ReportID=175.
57. Pew Research Center, *Views of a Changing World 2003*, 3 June 2003, pp.1–2, http://people-press.org/reports/display.php3?ReportID=185.
58. Pew Research Center, *Views of a Changing World 2003*, p. 5.
59. Delinda C. Hanley, 'Secretary's Open Forum Examines Public Diplomacy', *Washington Report on Middle East Affairs*, January/February 2004, vol. 23, pp. 75–6.
60. Carl Weiser, 'Report Lists Public Diplomacy Failures', *USA Today*, 16 September 2003, p. 13a; and John A. Paden, 'America Slams the Door (on its Foot)', *Foreign Affairs*, May/June 2003, vol. 82, pp. 8–15.
61. Richard Lugar, *Opening Statement on Public Diplomacy and Islam*, Senate Foreign Relations Committee Press Release, 27 February 2003, p. 2.
62. Christopher Marquis, 'US Image Abroad Will Take Years to Repair', *New York Times*, 4 February 2004.
63. Information on performances from Karen L. Perez and Joe Merante Bureau of Educational and Cultural Affairs, Department of State; and correspondence with Joe Merante, 29 June 2004. See also Wyszomirski, Burgess and Peila, *International Cultural Relations*, Table 2, pp. 3–5. On radio and TV, see Peter Slevin, 'Changes in US Diplomacy Sought: Efforts to Influence Islamic World Inadequate, Panel Says', *Washington Post*, 2 October 2003, p. A16.
64. Wyszomirski, Burgess and Peila, *International Cultural Relations*, Table 2, pp. 3–5.
65. Paden, 'America Slams the Door (on its Foot)'.
66. See www.radiosawa.com/english; Michael Dobbs, 'America's Arab Voice: Radio Sawa Struggles to Make Itself Heard', *The Washington Post*, 24 March

2003, p. C01; Eli Lake, 'Pop Psychology: How Lionel and J. Lo Can Help Bridge the Gap Between Us and the Arabs', *Washington Post*, 4 August 2002, p. B03; Jan Perlez, 'US is Trying to Market Itself to Young, Suspicious Arabs', *New York Times*, 16 September 2002.

67. Brian Faler, 'VOA Staff Members Say Government Losing Voice', *Washington Post*, 14 July 2004, p. A17.
68. 'Live from Virginia, It's Alhurra', NPR *All Things Considered*, 7 February 2004, www.npr.org/featurs/feature.php?wfld+1658915, 23 June 2004.
69. Steven A. Cook, 'Hearts, Minds, and Hearings', *New York Times*, 6 July 2004.
70. Hafez Al-Mirazi, bureau chief of Aljazeera satellite channel, in Hanley, 'Secretary's Open Forum Examines Public Diplomacy'.
71. Conversation with Leon Shahabian, Vice-President and Treasurer of Layalina, 14 July 2004.
72. The Ambassador's Fund was launched by Bonnie Cohen during her tenure as Under-Secretary for Administration at the State Department (1998–2001).
73. Schneider, *Diplomacy that Works*.
74. Cynthia P. Schneider, 'There's an Art to Telling the World about America', *Washington Post*, 23 August 2002, p. B3.

9
Making a National Brand
Wally Olins

Introduction

'If we were looking at the US as a brand we would say this is the time to relaunch the brand'[1] says Keith Reinhard, group leader of Business for Diplomatic Action (BDA). Reinhard is Chairman of DDB, an advertising agency within Omnicom – the world's largest marketing and communications business. BDA is very concerned that 'political developments – including opposition to the Iraq war – are eroding the global appeal of US brands from McDonald's to Microsoft and MTV'. So senior image-makers have embarked on an experiment in private sector foreign policy that is designed to rehabilitate the US national brand. Arguing that business can do things that governments cannot, the group is seeking to create a corporate united front that would counter anti-Americanism through means including the promotion of higher-quality cultural exports, says the *FT* article.

Through the appointment of Charlotte Beers (Under-Secretary for public diplomacy and public affairs until 2003), the US government has already tried and failed once recently to deal with what it sees as a rising tide of anti-Americanism, and now in traditional American fashion the private sector is having a whirl. According to the *FT* article, one of Keith Reinhard's private sector ideas is to create a 'public diplomacy' portal on the internet, which some people might perhaps see as a contradiction in terms.

This initiative, whether successful or not, underlines the new significance of branding as part of the national promotional programme. When I first talked and wrote about branding the nation and the nation as a brand in the 1980s, most commentators could barely conceal their bile. The idea they had was that branding the nation was the equivalent

169

of treating the nation like a washing-up liquid in a supermarket. When Blair's government launched a hastily prepared, ill-thought-through initiative on national branding in the late 1990s it was publicly pilloried: 'Cool Britannia' was difficult to live down and is still used by critics of national branding programmes as a model of 'how and why not to do it'. And yet the truth of the matter is that nations have always tried to create and modulate their reputations in order to create domestic loyalties and coherence and promote their own power and influence in neighbouring countries. There is in reality nothing new about national branding, except the word 'brand' and the techniques that are now used, which derive from mainstream marketing and branding techniques.

France and nation-branding

Elsewhere I have written about the way in which national branding as we know it today began with the French Revolution. It was the French who really started national branding in a big way. France's five republics, two empires and about four kingdoms (depending on how you count them) offer a fascinating case study of how creating and establishing identities has been highly influential in establishing their internal legitimacy, their hold on power and their influence on their neighbours.

In the kingdom of the Bourbons nobody was more glorious an autocrat than *le Roi Soleil* – Louis XIV. Versailles was erected as the physical embodiment of absolute power. Then, in 1789, came the first and most significant Revolution. Not only was the traditional nobility exiled and dispersed, the royal family executed, a Republic proclaimed, religion excoriated, and an entire social and cultural system turned on its head, but every little detail changed too. The tricolour replaced the fleur-de-lis, the 'Marseillaise' became the new anthem, the traditional weights and measures were replaced by the metric system, a new calendar was introduced, God was replaced by the Supreme Being and the whole lot was exported through military triumphs all over Europe. France was quite consciously and overtly rebranded, the first nation to enter on so self-aware a course. And the whole of Europe was profoundly influenced by it.

Only a very few years later another rebranding operation took place. General Napoleon Bonaparte made himself First Consul, then Emperor. Empire was a concept entirely new and hitherto completely alien to France. Napoleon crowned himself Emperor at his own coronation just like Charlemagne. He introduced new titles, rituals, uniforms, honours and decorations, not to speak of a new legal and educational system that was exported to all his dominions and that has had pretty remarkable staying power. The Napoleonic legal code remains the legal structure in much of Europe today. All this was commemorated and memorialized by a number of artists and writers, of whom Jacques-Louis David was perhaps the most gifted. Under Napoleon France wasn't big enough – the whole of Europe was rebranded. The accepted view among most historians is that this was Napoleon's idea. He may not have been concerned with all the detail, but his was the master plan.

The rebranding of France has proceeded sporadically and often violently ever since. Napoleon's Empire gave way to the restored Bourbons, who were overthrown and replaced by a bourgeois monarchy, which was followed by the Second Republic, which turned itself into a Second Napoleonic Empire. By the time the Third Republic emerged from the ashes of Napoleon III's defeat at the hands of Prussia, French politicians had become the world's specialists at branding and rebranding the nation. The Third Republic collapsed in defeat in 1940 and was replaced by Petain's Vichy. Under Vichy, France was rebranded yet again: the Republican slogan, or as branding experts would put it 'strapline', of *liberté, egalité, fraternité* was replaced with *travail, famille, patrie*. Although the Vichy regime is now regarded as an humiliating and shameful period in French history, there is no doubt that it was yet another national brand with, for a short time, a powerful and popular, political, cultural and social ideology.

After Vichy came the Fourth Republic and then the Fifth, which is France's current political and cultural incarnation. Of course it's true that there is continuity underneath the change. The French people and France itself continue to demonstrate many traditional characteristics. Nevertheless, the brand changes are not superficial, cosmetic or meaningless; they are real and profound. I cite the example of France because, of all the countries in the world, France is probably the one that has been most influential in the branding and rebranding of other nations. But similar observations can be made about almost but not quite every country.[2] The reason why nations continue both explicitly and sometimes implicitly to shape and reshape their identities, or if you prefer explicitly and implicitly to rebrand themselves, is because their reality changes and they need to project this real change symbolically to all the audiences with whom they relate. They want, as far as they can, to align perception with reality.

The French experience is far from unique. Almost every country you can think of from nineteenth-century Germany under Bismarck to twentieth-century Turkey under Ataturk has gone through a similar branding process – only nobody ever called it that. The dissolution of European colonial empires gave further impetus to the development of national brands. The Dutch East Indies, for example, became Indonesia, its capital Batavia became Jakarta, and a new language, Bahasa Indonesia, was constructed that was intended to enable the people of the different Indonesian islands to communicate with each other. New or newish nations such as Indonesia, and for that matter those even newer nations that have emerged since the dissolution of the former Soviet Union, have the same problems as the then new European nations of the nineteenth and early twentieth centuries: they have to build a national consensus – around language, presumed ethnicity, religion (sometimes), culture, sporting, artistic, commercial and military achievements. Some nations have a long but interrupted history, like Georgia, while others, such as Tajikistan or for that matter Iraq, have been carved out of the former imperium and therefore have difficulty in establishing legitimacy.

However they have emerged, it is evident that the urge to create nations remains extremely powerful. There were 51 nations in the UN in 1945 – now there are 191. So despite increasing globalization, the power of corporations, the increasing size and influence of super regions like NAFTA and more particularly the EU, the nation is a thriving entity. But nations now live in an increasingly competitive commercial environment. They do not simply compete on issues of political influence any more, but also compete commercially.

Projecting the national brand

There are now three areas in which nations are in direct and overt competition with each other. In each of these there are winners and losers, and each nation depends to a very considerable extent for its success on the clarity, emphasis and enthusiasm with which it projects its national brand. The three areas are: brand export; foreign direct investment; and tourism.

Export

It is, of course, a truism that we associate particular products and brands with certain nations. For cars, Mercedes, Audi and BMW are Germany and Germany is cars. VW, the initials of Volkswagen whose particularly unpleasant origins are now largely forgotten, is perhaps the ultimate symbol of the intense and long-lived relationship between Germany and the automobile. It was the Führer who early in 1934 commissioned

Dr Ferdinand Porsche to create a people's car (literally, a *Volkswagen*) that would cruise along the new *Autobahnen* conveying the German working classes towards their various recreational pursuits. The extent to which Germany and automobiles are currently perceived as a single entity is really quite astonishing. In a series of interviews as part of a study on national branding carried out in the early 1990s,[3] over 500 quite sophisticated and experienced purchasing directors of companies from all over the world were so overwhelmed by the automobile imagery of Germany that they barely mentioned any other types of German products and services. It appears that banking, pharmaceuticals, chemicals and even other kinds of engineering products exist – at least in terms of perceptions – only in the shadow of Germany's great, global motor industry.

If Germany for the world is the motor industry and the motor industry is Germany, is this advantageous or disadvantageous for German brands? Well, it seems that it is a bit of both. On the credit side, anything to do with engineering, efficiency, and a particular kind of stripped down quasi-Bauhaus style gets a boost. So apart from the world famous motor companies and organizations like Siemens and Bosch, other technical companies also benefit. There is a halo effect for organizations that make products, such as Braun, Miele and Gaggenau. On the debit side, however, German brands are disassociated from fashion – Jil Sander and Hugo Boss – from cosmetics and personal products – Lancaster and Nivea – from banking and financial services – Deutsche Bank and Allianz – and even, curiously, from high tech – SAP. Not surprisingly, none of the companies in these sectors go out of their way to emphasize their German origins. On the contrary, Hugo Boss talks about its European style, SAP half-heartedly pretends to be American, and so on. They all avoid an association with Germany because Germany means cars, and that, they believe, will disadvantage them commercially.

So a reasonable conclusion to draw is that if the nation's leading brands are based around too narrow a sphere of activity, those flagship brands in the sector may flourish, but the other brands in different sectors may find life more difficult. They will certainly not be able to wrap themselves in the national flag, and they may even decide to distance themselves entirely from their national origins. Where the perceived range of national brands is broader, the situation may be a bit different. France, Italy and Britain all have a wider range of perceived expertise in products than Germany. Gucci comes from Italy, but so does Ferrari. Jaguar comes from Britain, but so do Burberry and Scotch whisky. France has the TGV and Renault in engineering, it dominates perceptions of Airbus even though Airbus also has German, British and Spanish participation, yet France also dominates nuclear technology and of course an entire panorama of names in fashion, food and drink; Louis Vuitton, Hennessy, Dior and so on. This means that French high-profile brands can exploit the national brand of France over a much broader range of activities than their German counterparts.

In this context at least, the United States is like France, only more so. America, much the best-known nation in the world, although currently not necessarily the most popular, excels and is seen to excel over a very wide range of products and services, many of which are overtly associated with the nation. In technology, Apple, Hewlett Packard, Intel, Google and all the rest of them are clearly seen to be American in origin, although they are specifically related to Silicon Valley. Curiously we do not necessarily know or care where the products created in Silicon Valley are made – Apple computers are made in Cork, Ireland, among other places – but we do care where they originate. There is no doubt that American, specifically Silicon Valley, technology is highly regarded. Another kind of American product, the demotic, popular, perhaps populist products of Main Street USA – Coca-Cola, McDonald's, Wrigleys, Pepsi, Hollywood movies, Disney, CNN, MTV, Blockbuster and the rest – are also seen to be quintessentially American, even though some of them try hard to adapt to the local situation wherever they go. These products are perceived to be so much part of the American world that they are attacked or boycotted as an integral part of anti-US propaganda. Mecca Cola is a French-based Muslim cola brand deliberately intended to undermine Coke. It is an attempt to subvert the American way by mocking as well as emulating its American original. But an unintended by-product of Mecca Cola may be actually to reinforce the image of Coke, which remains 'The Real Thing'.

Certain American fashion products – Hilfiger, Gap, Levis (all three perhaps a bit tarnished now), Nike, Converse, Ralph Lauren, Donna Karan, Marc Jacobs and many others—derive part of their brand power from being seen to be American, at least in origin.[4]

Foreign direct investment

An increasingly interdependent global environment means that companies have to look outside their own borders to find cheaper places to get their products built. The first place to look is of course next door. That is why US companies built *maquilladoras* – US-financed Mexican companies paying Mexican wages for products shipped a few miles back across US borders for sale. A few years ago European companies did the same thing in southern Europe. Renault and other car companies set up factories in Spain and Portugal. Now that wages have gone up in the south, eastern Europe has come into fashion. Tiny Slovakia, which had never built a car, is now becoming home to French, Japanese and Korean motor companies. By 2010 Slovakia will be the world's largest car producer judged by head of population.

At one level this kind of investment policy is, of course, influenced by local legislation, tax breaks, regional funding, education level of employees, central and local government attitudes, transport infrastructure and so on; but at another, more emotional, level, is also to do with follow-my-leader, keeping up with the Jones's and just being fashionable. Like anything else, fashion plays a large, although unacknowledged, part in foreign direct investment, and this means that countries that promote themselves well can beat countries that do not – assuming that the hygiene factors are more or less equal.

Tourism

Tourism, the world's fourth largest industry and growing at about 9 per cent per year, is even more subject to whim. Some countries depend largely on tourism for their earnings and have developed a sophisticated tourist infrastructure. Many of the most unlikely countries are highly reliant on it. For instance, New Zealand's largest foreign exchange earner is tourism. The danger for countries that rely heavily on traditional tourism is that sun, sea and sand are in danger of becoming a commodity, driven by fierce competition on price, into attracting more and more people who often spend less and less money individually. So a country can end up getting large numbers of tourists that it cannot effectively cope with and who spend very little money per head. The alternative is for countries to trade up, differentiating themselves like consumer brands – emphasizing their art, culture, history, food, architecture, landscape and other unique characteristics through sophisticated imagery. That way the nation will aim to get fewer tourists, each of whom will individually spend more money.

All this points to a national branding programme coordinating brand export, foreign direct investment and tourism, backed by a cultural, sporting and commercial programme and all associated with political influence – public diplomacy in fact. And that is what the US-based Business for Diplomatic Action private initiative, mentioned in the introduction, is trying to achieve. Now, that the United States has suddenly become profoundly unpopular in many parts of the world and there is a real danger that American brands are suffering as American influence declines, a view seems to be emerging that all aspects of the national brand, including brand export, foreign direct investment and tourism, which are palpable, tangible and quantifiable, can be linked to those other factors such as culture, sporting and artistic activity and influence that do not lend themselves so easily to quantification – and that the whole should be promoted collectively. There are a few countries that through a combination of dramatic political change and the imperative to develop economically have demonstrated the massive impact that this kind of rebranding can achieve.

Spain, once a world power of the first rank, went into a long, self-destructive decline, culminating in the hideous Civil War in the 1930s. It degenerated into an isolated, autarkic, poverty-stricken, authoritarian anachronism, hardly part of modern Europe at all. Since Franco's death in 1975, it has transformed itself into a modern, well-off, European democracy. The reality has changed but so have perceptions. Spain appears to have carefully orchestrated and promoted its re-entry into the European family. The extent to which this has been explicitly managed is difficult to determine. Success always makes it easy to post-rationalize and rewrite history, but it certainly did not happen only through serendipity. The Joan Miró sun symbol was an identifier for a massive promotional programme that was closely linked to national change and modernization. Institutional and tourist advertising on a national and regional level, the creation of successful international business schools, the growth, privatization and globalization of Spanish companies like Repsol, Telefónica and Union Fenosa, the rebuilding and beautifying of major cities such as Barcelona and Bilbao, the self-mocking, sexually explicit, tragicomic films of Pedro Almodóvar and his contemporaries, political devolution, the Barcelona Olympics and the Seville International Exhibition of 1992 all underlined and exemplified the change and helped to alter perceptions.

This programme of activities, much based around individual initiatives, has rehabilitated and revitalized Spain, both in its own eyes and in the eyes of the world. Spain is among the best examples of modern, successful national branding because it keeps on building on what truly exists. It incorporates, absorbs and embraces a wide variety of activities to form and project a loose and multifaceted yet coherent, interlocking, mutually supportive whole. Many countries have examined the Spanish example and have taken notice of what has been done and how.

Poland is currently working on a major national branding programme.[5] This is not a quick fix. It is a serious long-term effort to project the changing reality of Poland and to bring perceptions of Poland into line.

Until very recently most western Europeans were unable to distinguish clearly the accession countries to the EU from each other. They did not know which was big, which was small, which was highly industrialized, which was relatively agricultural. They had difficulty in naming national figures and even in naming outstanding cities or tourist attractions. They could not say which countries were democratic. They could not even spontaneously name global leaders. In other words, not to put too fine a point on it, Poland together with most other central and east European countries were seen as a grey undifferentiated splodge. Very few people can spontaneously name Polish products or even Polish creative works let alone famous contemporary Poles.

Curiously this situation is not so different from Spain just a generation ago. Around the time of Franco's death in 1975 Spain was seen solely as a country for cheap holidays and wine, a poverty-stricken country of no cultural or commercial influence with an authoritarian leader.[6]

Like Spain in 1975, Poland in 2004 has staggering potential. It has beautiful cities like Wroclaw and Krakow; it has prime tourism sites such as the Mazurian lakes and Zakopane; it has a dynamic creative tradition in theatre, films, the arts, music and so on; it has the potential to produce global businesses; and above all it has the critical mass, with 40 million people, to make a real difference in Europe.

The reality of Poland is changing fast, but to win, Poland's image has to change so that perceptions are linked with reality. Poland the nation and Polish companies must invest money and time in creating brands that demonstrate to the world that in commerce, industry, the creative arts and sport, Poland is world class, and that is what the branding programme for Poland is intended to do. Have a look in ten years time to see if it works.

Conclusion

Poland is not the only former communist country seeking to project a new national brand. Virtually every country in central and eastern Europe is thinking about it, discussing it, planning it. Other countries are involved too: from New Zealand to Scotland national branding is on the agenda and, as pointed out at the beginning of this chapter, even the US is having a go at it. It is clear that over the last few years branding has emerged as a serious issue on the national agenda. But as nations are finding out, doing it is far from easy. Charlotte Beers in the US is not the only one who has tripped up. Peter Mandelson in the UK made the same kinds of mistakes a few years earlier. Trying to do too much too quickly is, however, only one of the issues.

If the national brand embraces tourism, foreign direct investment, brand exports, sport, the arts, cultural activities and so on, who runs it? Private sector or public sector – or both? Who in the public sector is in charge – the foreign ministry, the industry ministry, tourism, or the Prime Minister's office? Who pays for it? How are the different activities coordinated? The simple fact of the matter is, and I write here on the basis of much experience, that launching and managing a national branding programme is infinitely more complex, sophisticated, difficult and above all long term than managing a similar activity for a commercial organization. It takes years, and the pay-off is slow and not readily measurable. Politicians like quick, measurable results that get them votes, and that is one of the reasons why so many national branding programmes are taken up enthusiastically and then dropped.

In my experience, national branding programmes need to be managed between the public and private sectors through small, dedicated and highly coordinated groups that take a long-term view. It is essential to remember that the national/domestic audience has to understand and support the programme, and that means engaging and getting support from the media. There has to be a will on the part of significant organizations representing specific segments to take part in the programme. Cultural, tourist, sport, fashion, arts and other organizations must be prepared to cooperate with chambers of commerce and government, so that the national promotional effort is properly coordinated. All this takes time, money, enthusiasm and tenacity.

The focus for a national branding programme is usually a visual symbol, which is adopted by all of the organizations taking part in the programme that use it as an endorsing tool. Sometimes the visual symbol is immensely powerful – like Joan Miró's sun for Spain. But the symbol alone is not enough. It is the core idea that lies behind the symbol that has the real significance. What makes the country different? Many countries have difficulties in finding a core idea that is sufficiently clear and individual. Most nations in the West want to claim that they are tolerant, multicultural, friendly, welcoming and so on – but what else are they? What is it that actually makes them different? What is their personality or, as I prefer to put it, what is their core idea? Then there are technical issues. Who are the key audiences? What are the key areas of focus? Should the launch be low or high profile, should coordination among different bodies be close or loose? How much variation in messages should there be for different audiences? To what extent should there be overlap?

All these and the hundreds of other issues involved are highly contentious. National branding is now on the agenda. Its significance as a tool for promoting the nation is now understood. But nobody can really claim that we have sufficient experience to make it work effectively. It is all trial, error and experience. There is no doubt that a few countries have got it right – Spain and New Zealand come readily to mind. But many more have not made it work. Some countries, such as Paraguay, are only known by their neighbours, and for them an attractive national brand is important but not mandatory. For other countries, however, an attractive national image is an asset beyond price. Losing it, as the US has found, can happen quickly and easily, almost without anyone noticing. Getting it back, as the US will find, will not be easy.

Notes

1. 'America's New Brand of Anger and Resentment', *Financial Times*, 24 June 2004.
2. Wally Olins, *Wally Olins On Brand* (London: Thames & Hudson, 2004).
3. The company Wolff Olins and *Financial Times*, *'Made in . . . '* series of studies about perceptions of the UK, Italy and Germany.
4. Wally Olins, 'Polish Brands and the European Union', *Harvard Business Review Polska*, 2004.
5. My company, Saffron, is working on this project.
6. Wally Olins, *Wally Olins O Marce* (Warsaw: Fundacja Promocja Polska-Instytut Marki Polskiej, 2004).

10
Dialogue-based Public Diplomacy: a New Foreign Policy Paradigm?
Shaun Riordan

Introduction

As the earlier chapters of this book have made clear, public diplomacy is increasingly seen as a central element of broader diplomatic activity in the twenty-first century. But it remains controversial. Debate remains about whether it is really new, or whether it is merely a fancy name for traditional propaganda activities. This chapter does not directly address these issues, but rather focuses on more practical aspects of how public diplomacy can be undertaken. It argues that the new security agenda requires a more collaborative approach to foreign policy, which in return requires a new dialogue-based paradigm for public diplomacy. In the process, some of the theoretical issues may also be clarified. To get a handle on the practical aspects, the chapter begins by looking at two concrete cases: the struggle against international terrorism; and nation-building.

Building bridges to moderate Islam

Leaving aside issues such as the wisdom of declaring a 'war against international terrorism', for the purposes of this chapter the key objectives[1] of the confrontation with international Islamic terrorism might be defined as: the disruption of attacks, detention or killing of terrorists and the dismantling of networks; the reduction of the capacity to recruit; the reduction of the capacity to secure financing; and marginalization within Islamic society. Examination of these four objectives will clarify the centrality of public diplomacy to broader policy, and will elucidate something of its nature and the tools on which it must draw.

At first sight, the first of these objectives appears to relate primarily to security, military and policing policies. Yet it has an important element of public diplomacy. The successful disruption of terrorist operations and networks and the detention or killing of terrorists requires the collaboration of a broad range of foreign governments, and particularly governments in Islamic countries. These governments must be convinced, and not only coerced, to collaborate. But the effort to convince must extend beyond governments, and even political elites, if the collaboration is to be effective, stable and long lasting. The extent of collaboration will inevitably be constrained by what even non-democratic or semi-democratic governments perceive as acceptable to their broader societies. For example, the government of Pakistan has clearly had to balance its collaboration with the US in the 'war against terrorism' with what is acceptable to its broader society, including its own military and security elite. Furthermore, full collaboration by an Islamic government serves Western interests little if the price is a rise in Islamic fundamentalism among the broader society and a consequent weakening of the government, or even its ultimate substitution by an extremist alternative. Effective long-term collaboration against Islamic terrorism thus requires public diplomacy to win the support, or at least the acquiescence, of broader Islamic societies.

The other objectives – recruitment, finance and marginalization – are more obviously centred on public diplomacy, and are closely related. While there have been surprisingly few studies of why young men and women are willing to become terrorists, and in particularly suicide bombers, simplistic answers like poverty, poor education or the Israel/ Palestine dispute are clearly inadequate. Studies have shown, for example, that Hamas suicide bombers tend to come from above-average income families with above-average education.[2] Similarly, while al-Qaeda has sought to make capital out of the plight of the Palestinians, it has never been a core objective, nor does al-Qaeda recruit Palestinians. Rather, there is a complex of reasons and motives relating both to the perception of the West and of existing Middle Eastern regimes. Similar complexes of factors explain the ability of groups affiliated to al-Qaeda to secure financing and the necessary level of tolerance, if not active support, in Islamic societies. While we need far more effective and rigorous studies of what these factors are, it should be clear that a key element is the perception of the West – both of Western governments and society – in Islamic societies.

Thus the shared public diplomacy aim of the four objectives outlined above is to engage with broader Islamic societies in a way that changes their perception of the West. In blunt terms, a public diplomacy strategy that can convince them that the West is not the enemy and that Osama is; that democracy and market economies are neither incompatible with Islam, nor are tools of neo-imperialism; and that constructive co-existence with the West is possible, and is in the interest of all. This engagement with the 'Islamic street' will not be easy, and raises important issues of the form and content of the message and the tools and actors of the strategy.

Simply asserting the primacy of Western values – whether human rights, democracy or free markets – or of good intentions is unlikely to work. On the contrary, it runs the risk of provoking a reaction in which Western values are rejected because they are Western, and in which Islamic values are defined against those of the West. This does not imply that Western values must be abandoned in some form of moral relativism, or that all Western values are inherently incompatible with Islam. A series of polls, for example, have demonstrated that a majority of Arabs do favour democracy.[3] But the same polls also demonstrate deep attachment to 'Islamic values'. This implies that successful engagement must be built upon a genuine dialogue that accepts that Islam is different and has its own values and historical and cultural traditions; that the West does not have all the answers and that, while maintaining its own values, it accepts that not all of them are universally valid for everyone everywhere; and that there are many paths to democracy and civil society.

However, if the dialogue is to be successful in engaging with broader Islamic society and promoting a moderate approach to Islam, the agents of the dialogue must enjoy credibility and access. At first sight this may be the hardest part. Neither Western governments nor their agents (namely, diplomats) have either the necessary credibility or access. Their need to maintain good relations with existing Islamic governments and political elites further constrains their freedom of action. More credible agents will need to be found among non-governmental agents in broader Western civil society. The credibility of such non-governmental agents will be enhanced by the extent to which they are perceived to be independent of, and even critical of, Western governments. Equally important will be the extent to which they are able to build on existing relationships, or shared interests or problems between Western and Islamic societies. They will thus include non-governmental organizations (NGOs) and universities, which already have exchange programmes or relationships with local universities and NGOs. Associations of small and medium enterprises (SMEs) and chambers of commerce can develop relationships through promoting and fostering good commercial practice, including advising on lobbying for legislation to protect the SME sector in Arab countries against corrupt state-owned corporations. Sports clubs and associations can also be important, particularly given the shared passion for football.

Of particular potential in building bridges to moderate Islam are the Islamic communities in Western societies. But they also point to another aspect of successful public diplomacy. Many potential agents are reluctant to be associated with government. In as far as they are perceived to operate under government direction, or with government funding, their credibility and effectiveness can be undermined. Their involvement in a public diplomacy strategy can therefore be highly problematic. In the particular case of Western Islamic communities, these communities may have significant differences with their governments, not only on foreign but also on aspects of domestic policy, and differences between their own standing and the broader communities. Governments may therefore need to engage in a prior dialogue with their own Muslims about shared values and the basis of co-existence. Aside from the need to do this in any case in the interests of domestic racial and ethnic harmony, and its value in bringing domestic Islamic communities within a broad public diplomacy strategy, it could provide a powerful preparation for the dialogue with overseas Islamic communities, and a demonstration of the genuineness of the intent behind that dialogue. The more general point is that an effective overseas public diplomacy strategy may often have to be preceded by an equally effective domestic public diplomacy strategy.

Thought must also be given to the tools of public diplomacy. Government-sponsored conferences and seminars can be effective with existing political elites, but are unlikely to reach broader Islamic societies (although they can be effective tools for non-governmental agents). New technology, and in particular the internet and its offshoots such as email and chat rooms, offer cheaper and easy techniques for networking and building relationships to all public diplomacy agents, both governmental and non-governmental. But so far extremist Islamic groups may be making more effective use of them. For example, there is evidence[4] that extremist groups are using cookie and other e-commerce techniques to build profiles of visitors to their websites, with a view to identifying and recruiting potential agents of influence, or even terrorists. While there may be privacy concerns about Western governments using similar techniques to recruit agents of influence in Arab countries (although this should not be excluded in particularly difficult or hostile environments), such techniques, combined with more traditional polling techniques where these are available, can be of value in assessing the effectiveness of online public diplomacy. Greater sophistication is also needed in engagement with the media. While television and radio stations sponsored by Western governments, playing Western popular music, may attract audiences among younger sections of the population, there is evidence that their audience gives no credibility to, and even switches off, their news broadcasts. They also run the risk of reinforcing prejudices about Western popular culture (that it is corrupt, decadent, and so on). A more effective approach could be to use the media, and especially the Arab media such as Aljazeera, to launch dialogue and engagement. Once again this will be more effective if taken on by non-governmental agents rather than government spokesmen.

Promoting civil society

Another example that shows the power of alternative and more imaginative approaches to public diplomacy is nation-building. The West's record in this area is mixed. In what might be called 'soft nation-building', primarily in Eastern Europe where the state was in transformation rather than collapse, where the West had not been forced to intervene militarily and where civil society already existed, at least to some extent, there has been considerable success. A broad range of good-government, education, training and economic/commercial promotion programmes played a significant role in bringing these countries to the brink (and beyond) of EU membership. In what might be called 'hard nation-building', where the West has been forced to intervene militarily and subsequently to become an occupying power, where the state has effectively disintegrated, and where existing civil society is scarce on the ground, the West has been far less successful. Even in its European protectorates of Bosnia and Kosovo, the West has failed to create politically stable and economically successful states. Its pro-consuls, far from passing political power to local institutions, frequently feel compelled to seize it back, and the military presence looks set to continue for years yet. The situation in Afghanistan and Iraq is, of course, even worse. Without going into a detailed critique of Western efforts to nation-build in these countries, part of the problem has been the failure to recognize that democracy, respect for human rights and successful market economies emerge from concrete historical, social, economic and cultural conditions. Thus Western diplomats and international civil servants have put excessive emphasis on a top-down imposition of democratic and liberal values and practices, institutional and constitutional arrangements and physical security and policing. An alternative 'public diplomacy' approach would instead focus on the creation of civil society, the promotion of a stable and secure middle or professional class, giving people 'ownership' of both the economy and political institutions and creating the conditions in which indigenous political institutions could emerge.

Some of the building blocks in this approach should be obvious: exchange programmes and networking between universities and schools; promotion of an independent media, especially one that is critical of the West and thus more credible (to this end, exchanges and networking between journalists and journalists' associations); cultural events; sporting links; promotion of civil society activities that develop social capital; links and networking among political parties; and the role of religious organizations. An area that is often neglected, but that gives a flavour of the broader approach, is the promotion and protection of a vibrant SME sector. SMEs are, of course, important economically: some 60 to 70 per cent of new job creation in Britain is in the SME sector (the figures are similar in other countries). But they have a broader political and social importance as well. SMEs promote a feeling of ownership of the economy and its institutions in the broader society. Even those employed by SMEs, as opposed to their owners, have a greater sense of responsibility and interest in economic decisions than those employed by large corporations. Thus SMEs can also have an important role in promoting civil society and political participation, and an independently minded middle/professional class. They can be particularly important in motivating younger generations. However, in unstable societies, or those emerging from failure, SMEs are highly vulnerable to political elites that are primarily intent on promoting large corporations, whether multinational corporations promising foreign investment or corrupt local corporations linked to political and personal interests. Diplomats and international civil servants do too little to protect them, often under pressure themselves to focus on the interests of multinationals. The alternative approach would focus not only on greater institutional and regulatory protection of SMEs, but also on more active strategies to promote them, including roles as sources of information and advice, or even as 'guardians/tutors' for Western SME associations or even individual SMEs.

Once again, diplomats and international civil servants may not be the ideal agents for these activities. As government representatives, they are no more trusted in nation-building societies than they are in Islamic (or even their own) societies. Their bureaucratic and hierarchical working structures and cultures are poor preparation for the innovation and creativity that are needed (what might be described as the 'entrepreneurial spirit' of public diplomacy). An example of where this spirit was sadly lacking arose during the NATO bombing of Serbia. Hundreds of thousands of Kosovars were sitting for six weeks in refugee camps in Macedonia, a captive audience with nothing to do, and yet it occurred to nobody to initiate classes in citizenship or democratic political practice as preparation for their return. Diplomats also frequently lack knowledge of key areas or the practical skills needed (for example, economics and programme management).

What effectively amounts to the promotion of civil society in failed states requires the engagement of agents from the broader civil society in the West (with the incidental advantage of strengthening Western civil society), reinforced by the effective use of the new technology. Some will already be active (for example, NGOs and to some extent universities) and their activities primarily need coordination within a broader strategy. Other agents that have much to offer will never have thought of doing so and will need encouragement (such as SMEs, chambers of commerce, sports associations or schools). Others may need technical or even financial support to realize their potential. Key roles for governments will therefore be as coordinators, catalysts and advisers/supporters. Many relevant agents will be suspicious of governments' motives (if not perhaps as suspicious as in the case of Islamic societies) and will be reluctant to be seen as too close. Diplomats will therefore need to demonstrate tact and subtlety. Once again, a public diplomacy strategy abroad will require a prior public diplomacy strategy at home. This does not mean that diplomats and other government officials have no direct role. They should continue to engage with existing elites and training programmes aimed at civil servants, police, the military and the judiciary. But they need to realize that these activities, while necessary, are not sufficient, and that they need to collaborate with, and to bring into their thinking and decision-making, a broader coalition of non-governmental agents.

Beyond selling policies, values, and national image

On the base of these two brief case studies, we can now consider the lessons for the broader approach to public diplomacy in the twenty-first century. First, these are not the only issues that require a public diplomacy approach. Recent years have seen the emergence of a new international security agenda, including non-traditional issues such as environmental degradation, the spread of epidemic diseases, financial instability, organized crime, migration, and resource and energy issues. These issues are all interrelated. The threat that they pose to Western societies has been enhanced by the extent of interconnectedness and interdependence and changes in technology and human behaviour in a globalized world.[5] No single country, however powerful, or even regional grouping of countries, is powerful enough to tackle these issues alone. The threats that these issues pose can only be contained through collaboration with a broad range of partners from a broad range of different cultures. As with international terrorism, collaboration with governments and political elites will not be sufficient. Not only will the level of collaboration that these can offer be limited by the attitudes of their publics, but in some cases key issues do not lie within their control or competences, while in others they require changes in societal attitudes. For example, reducing the threat from epidemic diseases both requires the collaboration of medical professionals, who may not be directly linked to government, and changes in social attitudes and behaviour in the wider population. Similarly, tackling environmental degradation requires the collaboration of NGOs and commercial companies, as well as of governments. Thus a public diplomacy strategy aimed beyond governments to broader civil societies will be essential.

If this is so, then public diplomacy must move from being an optional 'bolt-on' to a central part of the foreign policy decision-making process. Ed Murrow, Kennedy's head of the US Information Agency (USIA), famously demanded to be in at the 'take-off', not only at the 'crash-landing'.[6] Murrow meant that he wanted public diplomacy, or better described presentational aspects, to be taken into account during the policy development stage. In other words, policy formulation should take account of how the policy could be sold later. The argument here is stronger. If tackling the major security issues requires collaboration at the global level with both governmental and non-governmental agencies, and if stable and effective collaboration can be secured only through engagement with broader foreign societies, public diplomacy becomes an integral and substantive, not just presentational, part of the policy-making process. Increasingly in the twenty-first century, diplomacy will be public diplomacy. There is little evidence so far of this move of public diplomacy to the centre of the decision-making process. The British Foreign Office (FCO), for example, has made a great show of taking public diplomacy seriously. It has created a Public Diplomacy Policy Department, which has produced a public diplomacy strategy.[7] All policy recommendations must include a section on public diplomacy implications. But the changes are bureaucratic rather than the profound change of attitude that is needed. In as far as these changes do bring public diplomacy into the 'take-off' in Murrow's sense, they are welcome. But it remains essentially a bolt-on, invoked only in the sense of how to sell policy better, rather than a substantive and integral part of the policy-making process.

The idea that public diplomacy is about selling policy and values, and national image, remains central to much theoretical and practical work on the issue. Seminars and conferences are organized on promoting Western values or 'selling democracy'.[8] President Bush appointed an expert from the marketing industry to head up US public diplomacy following '9/11'. Even authors like Joseph Nye treat 'soft power' as an exercise in winning the battle of ideas.[9] Brand consultants are making significant profits from advising governments on how to improve and sell their national image ('national branding' is becoming a research theme in its own right). But the examples observed of engagement with Islam and nation-building suggest that this may be a seriously mistaken approach. It is, for example, highly questionable whether a 'national brand' can be created, and whether efforts to do so are credible. The attempts to rebrand Britain in the late 1990s collapsed in the fiasco of the much-derided 'Cool Britannia'.[10] The strength of a country's image emerges from its cultural, political and economic plurality. Attempting to impose an artificial coherence, and to spin it to the rest of the world in the way that policy-makers or their consultants think profitable, risks undermining both richness and credibility. In the case of Britain, the effort to promote its modernity and youthfulness contradicted its traditional image that is so important to its valuable tourist industry. The FCO's public diplomacy strategy is reduced to meaningless platitudes such as that Britain 'is building dynamically on [its] traditions'. The national branding approach constantly wavers between overly simplified and non-credible claims and blandness, in which all countries (and regions and cities) seek to present themselves as combining innovation and tradition.

But the issue goes beyond applying inappropriate marketing tools to national promotion. Many commentators now recognize that public diplomacy, and indeed diplomacy as a whole, will increasingly be about ideas and values. We have seen that values and ideas are crucial both to engagement with Islam and nation-building. They are equally crucial to the other security issues identified above. But we have also seen that assertion of Western values as possessing unique and universal validity could be counter-productive. There has been a progressive breakdown of the consensus on universally accepted and applicable political, economic and social values, even among elites. To some extent this reflects the decline of political and intellectual domination by Western Europe. The Universal Declaration of Human Rights, for example, was a European document, written by Europeans at the end of what was essentially a European civil war (the Second World War) that was notable primarily for its non-respect for human rights. Non-Europeans were unable to participate because at the time they remained under the control of European colonies. It is questionable whether the same document would today be accepted as universal. Instead the association of Western values with US hegemony, and the perception by many in developing countries that these values are used as a tool to secure Western political and economic domination, lead to their rejection. Thus in the wake of the recent war, we have seen the resurgence of Islamic Sharia – rather than Western democratic – values in some parts of Iraq. In Africa we have seen African states prioritizing sovereignty and African solidarity over human rights in Zimbabwe. In a related phenomenon, the simple assertion of values, when such values are no longer universally accepted without question, risks provoking automatic rejection and the assertion of alternative value systems. Even where core Western values are clearly in the interests of the individual – such as right to life, freedom of expression, and equality of the sexes or ethnic groups – the perceived need of a group or nation to identify itself in opposition to the West can lead to their rejection.

If tackling the new agenda of security threats requires the collaboration of other governments and their broader civil societies, a successful public diplomacy must be based not on the assertions of values, but on engaging in a genuine dialogue. The messages of public diplomacy need to be more sophisticated and subtle. Public diplomacy must engage in dialogues with a broad range of players in foreign civil societies. This requires a more open, and perhaps humble, approach, which recognizes that no one has a monopoly of truth or virtue, that other ideas may be valid and that the outcome may be different from the initial message being promoted. If the aim is to convince, rather than just win, and the process is to have credibility, the dialogue must be genuine. This does not amount to abandoning core values. The aim remains to convince other publics of these values. But the effort to convince is set in a context of listening. Just as no individual will long suffer, or be convinced by, an interlocutor who endlessly asserts his views while never listening to those of others, so other governments and societies will not engage in collaboration if they feel that their ideas and values are not taken seriously.

Collaboration with non-governmental agents

As earlier chapters of this book have explained, governments and diplomats have progressively lost their monopoly over international relations. New ICT, by radically reducing the costs and increasing the speed of communication, has allowed a broad range of new actors to participate in the debate over, and implementation of, foreign policy, including subnational governments, global NGOs and less formal groupings of citizens. Not only does new technology allow these new actors to communicate and collaborate more efficiently, but it has also opened up a treasury of sources of information through the World Wide Web, which means that they are frequently as well, if not better, informed on key policy issues and geopolitical developments than governments and their officials. This is reinforced through the increasing privatization of technology that formally remained under exclusive government control. For example, the launch of commercial monitoring satellites means that these new actors can access the kind of keyhole imagery that was once the preserve of the Western military.[11] While those who argue that these developments imply the 'end of the state'[12] in international relations may protest too much, states have little option but to engage with these new actors in the formulation and implementation of foreign policy. As international relations increasingly operate not at a single inter-state level but through complex, multi-level and interdependent networks, governments and their diplomats must learn to operate in these networks.

But as we have seen, involving non-governmental agents in public diplomacy strategies is not just accepting an inevitable development in international relations, but relates to the most effective way of developing and implementing such strategies. While diplomats retain an important role in engaging in debate with other governments and political elites, they are often not the ideal, or are even counter-productive, agents for engaging with broader foreign civil societies. As government representatives, they can lack credibility. They often lack detailed expert knowledge of the key issues. Their key role of maintaining relations with existing governments can conflict with engaging with broader civil society, especially if the government concerned is corrupt or repressive and does not like the direction or possible implications of the engagement. Diplomats may not have natural ways of engaging with key elements of civil society: creating artificial channels of approach can increase suspicion of their motives, both with foreign governments and their civil society. In many countries, being seen as too close to foreign diplomats can be dangerous, either in career terms, or even physically.

Engaging with foreign civil societies is often best done by the non-governmental agents of our own civil societies. Unlike diplomats, they do have credibility, often to the extent to which they are seen as critical of their own governments. Many do have specialist knowledge of the key areas. They also have more natural ways of engaging with their opposite numbers, which arouse less suspicion of their motives. They are deniable in a way that diplomats are not, meaning that their engagement with civil society can be pursued in parallel to maintaining normal diplomatic relations with existing governments. Many of these potential non-governmental agents of public diplomacy have already been identified: universities and individual academics can be highly effective public diplomacy agents and already have highly effective networks; schools/colleges can engage foreign citizens during the formative years; NGOs, national and international, which provide a vivid example of the plurality and freedom of debate in Western society and many of which are already well plugged in to counterparts in other countries; journalists; political parties, which have already developed effective networks among themselves at a European level (the role of German political parties in promoting democracy in Spain was particularly notable), but have been more limited elsewhere in the world; citizen groups, ranging from babysitting collectives to local issue lobbies and parent–teacher associations; business associations and individual companies, especially at the SME level; youth movements, such as the scouts, girl guides or boys'/girls' brigade, which pioneered international networking in the first half of the twentieth century, and their modern counterparts; sports clubs; and offshoots of the internet such as chat rooms and usernets. The role of government and diplomats in relation to these non-governmental agents will be more as catalysts, coordinating their activities within a broader strategy, encouraging those not already engaged in such activities, and, on occasion, providing discreet technical and financial support. But governments must bear in mind that many potential agents will be reluctant to be seen as too close to, or acting at the behest of, government. Indeed, being seen to do so could undermine the very credibility that otherwise represents much of their added value. Governments will therefore need tact, openness and understanding. As noted above, effective public diplomacy at home may be an essential precursor to successful public diplomacy abroad.

A public diplomacy strategy along the lines outlined above has significant implications for the structure and culture of foreign ministries. Dialogue-based public diplomacy needs time to work; it does not produce instant results. Foreign ministries therefore need to develop a capacity for long-term policy thinking and geopolitical analysis. Western foreign ministries are notably weak in both. Overly hierarchical decision-making processes, and the consequent administrative burdens and premium on conformism rather than innovation or creativity, condemn officials to short-termism, both of policy-making and analysis.[13] Foreign ministries should learn from the experience of the private sector, which makes extensive use of the scenario planning techniques developed by Shell in the 1960s and 1970s,[14] as well as newer modelling techniques derived from network and complexity theory.[15] Drawing on these techniques, foreign policy machines should be restructured to allow the development of medium- to long-term objectives against various future possible scenarios, which can provide the framework in which a public diplomacy strategy to secure these objectives can in turn be developed. This will need a change of culture as well as structure. Western foreign ministries remain tied to a 'closed' paradigm of decision-making, in which policy is decided and then 'sold' to other governments. Policies once decided may indeed be changed, but only as a result of 'defeat' by foreign governments. This paradigm largely holds true even between close allies. But it is inadequate, and even counter-productive, if the aim is to secure the collaboration of a broad range of partners and their civil societies. Dialogue-based public diplomacy requires a more open decision-making process, in which broad policy objectives are set, but in which detailed policies emerge as part of the dialogue process. To return to an earlier point, dialogue means listening as well as talking, and accepting that you do not have all the answers and that others might have alternative valid solutions.

The move to a more open culture will also be required if foreign ministries are to collaborate with non-governmental agents of public diplomacy. Some moves have been made in this direction. The Director of the British Foreign Office's Human Rights Department has been seconded from Amnesty International. The FCO also created a Panel 2000, bringing together experts from a wide range of backgrounds to advise on its public diplomacy strategy.[16] A task force in the US has suggested establishing an independent, not-for-profit Corporation for Public Diplomacy to coordinate the activities of non-governmental agents.[17] But these steps will serve little if the hermetic, almost monastic, culture of foreign services is not broken open. Officials should also beware their almost instinctive tendency to respond to a problem by creating yet new coordinating committees. Apart from the risk of creating yet more bureaucratic structures, where the aim should surely be to create less, membership of formal government committees may cause significant ethical or political problems for many potential public diplomacy agents, while their bureaucratic nature may turn off others. Less formal network structures may prove more effective, cost-efficient and less politically sensitive. But network, as opposed to hierarchical, structures will again pose significant cultural and structural challenges to foreign ministries.

Practitioners as public diplomacy entrepreneurs

A major part of the new public diplomacy will fall to non-governmental agents, but embassies and diplomats abroad will continue to play an important role. They too will need radical changes of culture and structure, neither of which has significantly changed in the last 50 years. Diplomats will continue to have an important role in engaging political elites, in many cases including key journalists and commentators. To do so they will need to be more open and willing to go 'off-message' and to engage in genuine dialogue and debate. Their knowledge of the countries in which they are posted, which will remain of enormous importance, will need to be augmented by greater expert knowledge of the key issues to give them credibility. To perform this role successfully, they need to be encouraged to take, and rewarded for taking, risks. In the engagement with broader civil society, their key role will be as 'public diplomacy entrepreneurs', looking for and identifying opportunities for engagement, communicating them to the relevant non-governmental agents and, where necessary, facilitating the first steps in engagement. They will only be able to do this effectively if they are part of the informal network established with the non-governmental agents at home. They will also need to get out and about, and not only in capital cities. The current departmentalized embassies, and increasing micro-management from foreign ministries, pose serious obstacles to these public diplomacy roles. Larger Western embassies tend to spend too much time in self-administration, managing both personnel and large embassy estates, and talking to other diplomats. Premium is placed on the ability to handle the paperwork sent from headquarters, rather than local networking. Future embassies need to be slimmer and more flexible, less tied to prestigious buildings and with more structures around functional networks. In the future, five or six well-prepared and well-motivated diplomats with clear objectives, travelling constantly and linked to the foreign ministry network through their mobiles and laptops, will be far more effective than the current 30 to 40 diplomats bound to their desks. As RAND analysts have put it, we need a revolution in diplomatic affairs to match that in military affairs.[18]

Notes

1. For a similar list of objectives, see Niall Burgess and David Spence, 'The EU: New Threats and the Problem of Coherence', in Alyson Bailes and Isabel Frommelt (eds), *Business and Security: Public – Private Sector Relationships in a New Security Environment* (Stockholm and Oxford: SIPRI and Oxford University Press, 2004).

2. Alan B. Krueger and Jitka Malecková, 'Education, Poverty and Terrorism: Is there a Causal Connection?', *Journal of Economic Perspectives*, vol. 17, no. 4, autumn 2003.

3. Joseph Nye, *Soft Power: The Means to Success in World Politics* (New York: Perseus, 2004); Civility Programme, www.civility.org.

4. Michele Zanini and Sean Edwards, 'The Networking of Terror in the Information Age', in John Arquilla and David Ronfeldt (eds), *Networks and Netwars: The Future of Terror, Crime and Militancy* (Santa Monica CA: RAND, 2001).

5. For an analysis of this in relation to epidemic disease, see Jennifer Brower and Peter Chalk, *The Global Threat of New and Re-emerging Infectious Diseases* (Santa Monica CA: RAND, 2003).

6. Independent Task Force on Public Diplomacy of the Council of Foreign Affairs, *Public Diplomacy: A Strategy for Reform 2002*, www.cfr.org/pubs/Task-force_final2-19.pdf.

7. Foreign and Commonwealth Office, *Public Diplomacy Strategy*, www.fco.gov.uk.

8. For example, a British Council Conference entitled 'Selling Democracy' in February 2004. In the words of George Kennan: 'Democracy has, in other words, a relatively narrow base both in time and space, and the evidence has yet to be produced that it is the natural form of rule for peoples outside these narrow parameters', cited in Philip Bobbitt, *The Shield of Achilles* (London: Penguin, 2002).

9. Nye, *Soft Power*; and Joseph Nye, *The Paradox of American Power* (Oxford: Oxford University Press, 2002).

10. Mark Leonard, *Britain TM* (London: Demos, 1997).

11. Stephen Livingston, 'Diplomacy and Remote Sensing Technology', *iMP Magazine*, July 2001, www.cisp.org.

12. Jean-Marie Guéhenno, *The Decline of the Nation State*, translated by Victoria Elliott (Minneapolis MN: University of Minnesota Press, 2000).

13. Shaun Riordan, *The New Diplomacy* (Cambridge: Polity Press, 2003).

14. Kees van der Heiden, *Scenarios: The Art of Strategic Conversation* (Chichester: Wiley, 1996).

15. Paul Ormerod and Shaun Riordan, 'A New Approach to Geo-Political Analysis', *Diplomacy and Statecraft*, vol. 15, no. 4, December 2004; Robert Lempert, Steven

Popper and Steven Bankes, *Shaping the Next One Hundred Years: New Methods for Quantitative Long Term Policy Analysis* (Santa Monica CA: Rand, 2003).
16. Mark Leonard, *Going Public* (London: Foreign Policy Centre, 2000).
17. Independent Task Force (2002).
18. John Arquilla and David Ronfeldt, *The Emergence of Noopolitik: Towards an American Information Strategy* (Santa Monica CA: RAND, 1999).

11
Training for Public Diplomacy: an Evolutionary Perspective
John Hemery

Introduction: training in transition

In his chapter of this book, and elsewhere, Brian Hocking has distinguished between two phenomena in the contemporary international system: a state-centred group of actors operating in a more or less ordered hierarchy; and a more amorphous set of networks between peoples and institutions co-existing and interpenetrated with the first group. It is a system in transition, and governments are adapting their diplomacy to the change, with increasing attention being paid to public diplomacy. Training regimes are similarly in transition.

Public diplomacy – in the sense of engaging with publics – is as old as governance. All governments have programmes of national self-promotion built on distinct culture, geography, trading opportunities or other niche specializations. All are aware of the power of the media and the internet, and grapple with how best to use them to their advantage. All encourage their diplomats to get out into the society of the country to which they are posted and especially beneath its surface, where the beginnings of understanding can be found. Thus all governments, to the extent that they can afford it, train their diplomats to contribute to that essentially national effort.

Fewer foreign ministries yet prepare their diplomats to be players in or facilitators of the amorphous transnational networks. Those at the cutting edge of the profession recognize that they have to deal effectively with this emerging parallel universe in order to get the whole diplomatic job done. For many, however, this is not the proper work of a diplomat, or is only a subordinate part of the job. For some, lack of resources may prohibit any serious attempts at public diplomacy. Governments are thus at different stages in the evolution of their thinking on public diplomacy.

Training for public diplomacy varies accordingly. The conclusions presented here are drawn from a survey of diplomatic training programmes in some 20 countries on all continents, large states and small, developed and developing.[1] The results demonstrate a pattern of sorts, an evolutionary path in training for public diplomacy that is defined partly in terms of resources and partly of intellectual and professional approach. Interestingly, there appears to be no direct correlation between the sophistication of the approach to public diplomacy and scale of resources devoted to it, and the specific training – if any – of diplomats for the task.

Barriers to training

The principal obstacle for the poorest states is lack of resources, both human and financial. There may simply be no budget for training in the foreign ministry at all, much less for a programme of strategic outreach. Missions abroad are typically small, with perhaps only two or three diplomats to cover the whole range of diplomatic tasks. Without training or plan they can simply do their best, learning on the job. One counsellor from a small developing country observed that 'Nobody knows about our countries. We are not being heard, because we do not know how to use the system to reach out'.

The public diplomacy effort may also be hampered by limited communications' infrastructure at home, with only intermittent electricity and overloaded telephone exchanges. As this study has shown, making effective contact with the foreign ministries of a number of countries by telephone, email or post can be a long, arduous and ultimately fruitless process. If reaching in is difficult, reaching out is likely to be comparably problematic. Physical handicaps of this order relegate such states to an obsolescent and partial diplomacy, when just to promote their development they need to be fully and dynamically engaged in *both* diplomacies – state-centred and network-orientated.

Even where physical communication is not an obstacle, attitudes can erect effective barriers. The design of a mission's foyer can offer welcome or signal unwelcome; diplomatic staff can be made accessible, or hidden behind a defensive wall. Without encouragement from the ministry or training in dealing with the public and the media, hard-pressed staff in small missions may simply put up the shutters because it is the easiest way to contain political risk and limit the workload.

But where there is the will to communicate – that is, in the large majority of developing countries – so also there is enthusiasm for professional training to counter prevailing negative perceptions, and to project what is strong and positive about them. Providers of technical assistance might usefully offer developing countries' missions professional advice and training in public diplomacy strategy, media skills and marketing, in order to help them to deal as effectively as possible with the international media in the capital cities to which they are posted.

Effectiveness in this sphere can be as much a matter of organization and management as of skill or flair in public relations. It involves practical details, targeting and prioritization, such as making the most of national leaders' and other experts' visits to a foreign capital by planning and coordinating the timing and content of their speeches, and ensuring that they are connecting with the right audiences.

Conveying messages widely and coherently is an important multiplier for a poor country in competing for development assistance, as well as for international recognition. But programme design and training can be costly, and few donors regard foreign ministries as priorities for funding. Governments themselves consequently have to decide whether the opportunity cost of invisibility is greater than the cost of developing an effective public diplomacy.

Changing attitudes: flexible approaches

Further along the evolutionary path of public diplomacy are states, both rich and poor, that offer diplomatic training but that have not traditionally regarded strategic outreach as a necessary or appropriate part of the diplomat's task. The Thais, for example, with an ancient and distinctive diplomacy, do not yet include public diplomacy in their training programme, although departments within the Thai Foreign Ministry have responsibility for mobilizing the culture and beauty of Thailand in pursuit of tourism, trade and investment.

Similarly, the Turks have not traditionally placed great emphasis on diplomacy to publics, although now with a new law on transparency and accessibility the Turkish government is encouraging greater openness in all ministries, including the foreign service. The Turkish Diplomatic Academy is actively looking at how to support the strikingly energetic public diplomacy effort launched by the Turkish government in EU member states.

Interestingly, in some states with relatively traditional concepts of diplomacy, training nevertheless includes engaging with *domestic* publics. For example, in the diplomatic academies of Chile, Mexico and Paraguay public diplomacy does not appear in the curriculum at all.

Yet all three academies conduct workshops at *sub*-national levels, in their countries' regions, both to convey government ideas on foreign policy and to receive feedback from the locals on foreign policy issues. (Canadian trainees, too, go out to schools and colleges to explain and to listen.) In the case of Chile, each trainee diplomat also has to take part in a group research project on a domestic issue that has international implications, and to establish links with private-sector and non-governmental organizations in developing a policy strategy.

Similarly, the Indian Foreign Service Institute ostensibly does not teach public diplomacy, but it has a three-pronged programme that effectively equips Indian diplomats with public diplomacy skills:

- The first component of the Indian programme is a module on communication skills, both written and verbal, including presentation and public speaking.
- Second, trainees are given solid grounding in the work of the media and of parliament. This includes short secondments to the External Publicity Department of the Foreign Ministry and to the Bureau of Parliamentary Studies.
- So far, so standard. After all, most states train their diplomats in communication and media skills. But the third element of the programme is the most interesting, in that Indian *culture* is an integral part of the diplomatic curriculum, especially the range and variety of classical Indian dance and music. Trainees are sent to the Indian Council of Cultural Relations for cultural orientation as well as familiarization with the administration of cultural exchanges. They are also taught the history of classical Indian diplomatic thought as contained in the epics and literature so that 'Indian values' are internalized in their diplomacy.

The Indian Foreign Ministry is keenly aware of the transformation of India's global image since the late 1990s with the upswing of the Indian economy, particularly the global success of India's software and financial services industries. This has been further reinforced by the growing economic and political influence of the Indian diaspora. Indian diplomats are thus being equipped to build on this wider affinity for Indian culture and values, consciously connecting with *peoples* as well as governments.

The French place similar emphasis on cultural relations in diplomacy. One month of the ten-month course offered to foreign diplomats by the *Ecole Nationale d'Administration* is given to communication – both government-to-government and government-to-publics.

By contrast, the Germans have maintained a clear distinction between the formal diplomatic work of press and public affairs on the one hand, and cultural relations and education policy on the other.[2] The separation of the two functions is reinforced in Germany in so far as foreign relations is a federal matter, while the *Länder* are responsible for education and culture. Painful recent experiences of state propaganda[3] have channelled the German public diplomacy effort primarily into the cultural and educational sphere, as exemplified by the work of the Goethe Institute. The *Auswärtiges Amt*'s (German Foreign Ministry) own training in this sphere is principally limited to highly advanced one-week language courses in communicating with the public in writing, on the telephone, in speeches and through the media.

Formal public diplomacy training

One branch further up the evolutionary tree are the foreign ministries offering training in public diplomacy as such – although mainly still in the service of the national interest.

The pre-eminent exemplar, with enviable resources, is the US State Department's Foreign Service Institute (FSI). The FSI has a set of 13 public diplomacy courses ranging in length from one day to eight weeks. The core of the programme comprises two eight-week courses, one for Information Officers, the other for Cultural Affairs Officers, which offer comprehensive coverage of the tasks of public diplomacy and training in relevant skills. The course outlines provide a useful quarry for those devising their own (and with more limited resources, perhaps shorter) programmes. Both courses largely comprise presentation, demonstration and discussion. In addition, there are individual research projects, visits to other agencies and hands-on practice with computer-based tasks. The relatively few simulation exercises are short and concerned with the practice of skills rather than modelling in one simulation the whole public diplomacy task from strategic planning to implementation and evaluation. In addition to the two core courses, the FSI offers short courses introducing the concept of public diplomacy, and explaining the respective roles of the four main US government bodies that are responsible for the American programme: the Office of Global Communications; the Office of International Information Programmes; the Bureau of Education and Cultural Affairs; and the Bureau of Public Affairs.

As in most countries, the formal training of America's diplomats concentrates almost exclusively on the transmission of policy, on 'managing the message'. Diplomats are trained to manage and make the most of government programmes of educational and cultural exchange, such as the Fulbright and Humphrey Fellowships. Participants undertake individual research on the countries or regions in which they will serve, but the balance between equipping diplomats to send rather than to receive is reflected in the fact that only one presentation hour in 16 weeks is devoted to cultural sensitivity and only two hours to understanding another culture.

The Canadian Foreign Service Institute (CFSI) offers three types of public diplomacy course. The first is a two-day course in Advocacy (advocacy being defined as the systematic exercise of influence in support of Canadian interests), when some 40 to 50 officers are trained each year. Each course focuses on specific issues in particular socio-economic contexts, and is designed to support a major public diplomacy campaign. It includes drafting a real strategy that can then be implemented. As with much of their diplomatic training (in which Canada leads the world in e-learning for diplomacy), the Canadians have developed an online advocacy course, complete with case studies in different socio-economic contexts.

The second course is a two-week programme in Ottawa for locally engaged staff serving as public affairs officers at post, promoting Canada through information, education, academic relations, media and cultural means. In 2003 this programme of training for public diplomacy tasks was expanded to include locally engaged political-economic officers as well.

The third element comprises two one-day pre-posting courses on how to manage and coordinate public diplomacy programmes abroad. These courses promote the idea that public diplomacy is a 'mission critical' function at post, and that a high degree of cooperation is required among the various programmes to deliver on mission objectives. These courses are also supported by an internet site offering guidance in mobilizing an integrated public diplomacy programme.

Meanwhile, the United Kingdom is perhaps the first state to have adopted a government-wide approach to contemporary public diplomacy (as distinct from the all-embracing totalitarian confections of the Nazi and Soviet eras). A Public Diplomacy Strategy Board was created in 2002 to coordinate government policy and practice. It includes senior representatives from the eight key internationally orientated ministries and agencies, as well as non-governmental specialists in foreign affairs, marketing, design and broadcasting. The Board is chaired by the Permanent Under-Secretary at the Foreign and Commonwealth Office (FCO). The aim is to maximize effectiveness through coherence. A Public Diplomacy Policy Department has also been created, within a new Strategy and Information Directorate, drawing together the work of the formerly separate Cultural Relations and Information Departments. The emphasis has changed from administration from the centre to the provision of programme budgets into which posts bid for project funding – thus facilitating appropriate focus on local priorities and rapid response to change. (Every post has its own Public Diplomacy Committee, responsible for developing its own strategy and project programme.) The primary medium and direction of communications have changed as well – from print to electronic, from push (via publication) to pull (via direct access through continuously updated websites).

Fully one-quarter of the FCO's budget is devoted to public diplomacy, the bulk given to the BBC World Service (£220 million p.a.) and to the British Council (£180 million p.a.), which are independent of the FCO, with their own boards of governors and carefully guarded political neutrality. Their task is to facilitate networks, to 'connect futures' – to use a British Council phrase – especially among the young of all societies. In comparison with the often short-term, specific policy-orientated activities of formal diplomacy, their objectives are long term, building relationships within the UK but also willy-nilly among individuals, groups and peoples across the world.

A good example may be seen in the work of the British Council in Uganda. Some of its activities are traditional – educational exchanges, inward visits, teaching English. But many of its activities are new – facilitating contacts between Ugandans, and between Ugandans and neighbouring countries. Examples include the funding of meetings of female politicians from the states of the Great Lakes region so that they can share experiences and help to empower one another, or funding the conferences of African business managers to build networks of small and medium enterprises in Africa, and to discuss best practices, thus facilitating 'mutual partnerships for change'.

Here, however, two issues are confronted. First, there is a fine but important line between facilitating the creation of worthwhile new organs and linkages within civil society, and establishing what in effect would be 'front' organizations. Trainee diplomats would need to be alerted to the political dangers of straying into the world and covert mindset of the intelligence agencies. The second issue is that long-term network-building is a job already being undertaken, often with real excellence, by governmental international development agencies such as the United States Agency for International Development (USAID), the Canadian International Development Agency (CIDA) and the UK's Department for International Development (DFID), as well as by organizations separate from foreign ministries, such as the British Council and the Goethe Institute. In one respect they are all promoters of the national interest, and hence an arm of state diplomacy, simply through their national identity. But they also extend beyond the state into the realm of transnational networks.

Public diplomacy as a profession

A key question for both overall policy and training policy is whether – as Shaun Riordan and others argue – this work should be part of the core task of the professional diplomat, or whether it is a *parallel* role to be carried out by professional network-builders, a form of para-diplomacy that builds bridges between cultures, acts as a catalyst for reform and development, and promotes peace and prosperity through *interlocking*. Network diplomacy, it is said, addresses the ways in which people are the same, building bridges between those who share the same human goals, while state-centred diplomacy facilitates relations between groups of people who by definition see themselves as being distinct.

There may be something in this differentiation, but for the professional diplomat it is a misleading dichotomy. So much of international interaction is now non-governmental that the diplomat simply has to inhabit both dimensions in order to seek to represent effectively the national interest (however widely that may now be defined) in the complex web of governmental and non-governmental relationships that comprise the contemporary international system.

The British approach reflects the assumption that the British Foreign Ministry is responsible for both elements – even if largely at one remove in respect of the work of the quasi-autonomous network-builders. Diplomats acquire an operational understanding of public diplomacy principally on the job, and specialist training is available both in public diplomacy and in the management and budgetary control of projects funded by the FCO itself.

The British programme is similar to but – constrained by budget pressures – is not as extensive as that offered at the FSI. The core course is a one-week programme entitled Public Diplomacy, which is principally designed for Press and Public Affairs Officers. It is offered eight times a year. Significantly, just over half of the participants on each course are locally engaged staff from posts abroad. In addition, there is a counterpart course conducted in a different region of the world every three months – responsibility for getting the British message out is devolved (as for the Canadians) largely to those who understand the local culture from within.

The course commences with a broad overview of the nature of public diplomacy, and of the government-wide interministerial strategy. It addresses core national messages and key operating principles (research-based, evaluation-based, priority-targeted in regional groupings, engaging the successor generation as well as the 'authority' generation). It also reviews the range, scope and sources of funding available for both long- and short-term activities. The course syllabus combines presentations from all FCO departments offering services to public diplomacy in the field, with study visits to the British Council and BBC World Service. There is as yet, however, little or no cross-fertilization of ideas, experience or organizational culture through the joint training of staff from all of the ministries and agencies engaged in the collective public diplomacy effort.

The FCO's public diplomacy course offers practical training in personal presentation and media skills, principally delivered by outside professionals under contract.[4] There are also simulation exercises in key public diplomacy tasks at post, including project identification, design and management. While comprehensive in scope, this course is short, and is not yet compulsory for all officers taking up appointments abroad. Heads and Deputy Heads of Mission have specific pre-post training in media skills and personal presentation, and the FCO offers two- and three-day courses in political work and project management that address *inter alia* public diplomacy objectives. But these useful elements do not add up to a coherent programme. The all-embracing approach to the public dimension of diplomacy at the strategic level is not quite yet reflected in the training programme of individual British diplomats.

The way forward for training?

At the top of the evolutionary tree in training for public diplomacy – at least of the countries covered in this survey – is the Republic of Korea. Like others, the Korean programme deals in communication and media skills and promoting the national interest. But in addition to these staples, Korea has a programme for mid-career and senior diplomats that seeks to understand how the practice of diplomacy itself is being affected by changes in the international system, how the concept of national interest is changing, and how civil society and international NGOs contribute to transnational relations. The Republic of Korea conducts sociological analysis of the impact on diplomacy of mass democracy and what it terms 'over-communication syndrome'.

This seems an appropriate way forward for training in public diplomacy. At present, despite all the varied and impressive attempts at public diplomacy training, which in their different ways address the national priorities of the states that they serve, what is clearly missing from almost all of them is comprehensive and conscious engagement with the expanding and changing nature of the international environment in which the professional diplomat operates. No one yet has developed a core syllabus that confronts the young diplomat with his or her two universes – the state-centred and the network – and that provides them with the twin toolboxes necessary to engage with both universes at the same time and in coherent synergy. (The middle states are perhaps closest to it: those such as Australia, Canada and South Africa, much of whose international clout is built on the public aspects of diplomacy.) This is not surprising, as there is more than enough for any diplomat to do just to fulfil the state-centred part of the job, the mundane real world of visas, line management, speechwriting and ministerial deadlines. And it will still be necessary to train people rigorously to carry out their traditional tasks well: to observe with alert political antennae, to analyse dispassionately, to advise from a depth of knowledge, to manage efficiently.

But to these traditional tasks it is now essential to add – and to train for – thinking flexibly, imaginatively and strategically about public diplomacy, pulling together all of the tools and resources of formal diplomacy to get key national messages *out* and *understood* – a comprehensive approach to 'winning people over'. And beyond this essentially national perspective, it is now equally important for training departments to help raise the eyes of the trainee from the email inbox to the horizon, preparing them to operate effectively in the parallel diplomatic world of transnational civil society, without the skills for which they and their ministries will be progressively left behind.

Designing the perfect course

What might such a course look like? It might comprise some of the elements that are there in embryo already: starting with the analytic approach of the South Koreans to the changing playing field; encouraging trainees to grapple with the evolving roles of state and non-state entities and to assess the extent to which their own profession (and ministry) is adapting successfully to the changes. In addressing the nature of contemporary diplomacy, the course would offer insights into the interpenetration of formal diplomacy and public diplomacy.

The course might then focus on the nature of public diplomacy itself – objectives, targets, tools, strategies and operating principles – giving trainees a comprehensive grasp of the concept and the several roles that public diplomacy plays both in promoting national interest and in connecting people.

The extent to which it will be possible to include some or all of the practical training offered in the long American courses will for each government largely be dependent on staff time, training time and funding available. But the relevant categories are fairly well recognized: personal presentation, media skills, computer and software skills, website management, marketing, project management and budget, research and evaluation. Most of these might be offered most effectively (and cost-effectively) by consultant professionals rather than by foreign service officials, although course design and content need to be focused on the realities of diplomacy rather than drawn from often-irrelevant commercial business experience.

However, as diplomacy is no longer the sole province of a foreign ministry or even of government, the course might usefully embrace participants from as wide as possible a cross-section of the constituencies engaged in the country's international life: foreign ministry and line ministries, civil society organizations, business and banking, minority groups, and locally engaged staff from posts abroad, bringing other cultural perspectives to bear. For obvious practical reasons, not all might be represented in every course, but an attempt could be made to maximize the mix across the training programme as a whole.

Given such a cross-cutting approach, the course might focus specifically on training for *facilitation* (in the sense used by Shaun Riordan in his thoughtful chapter on the network model of diplomacy.) This would entail training young diplomats (by simulation and case study) to work with civil society organizations and manage the foreign ministry's or embassy's relations with them; to manage also the interaction with international aid and development agencies, and with the field operations of other ministries in one's own and other governments.

Beyond the mechanics of linkage and management, the course would include a module on cross-cultural communication, supported by studies of country, region, religion and culture, as appropriate to each individual or group. This should not be a modest bolt-on, but an essential organizing principle and core theme of each course: focusing on the target, thinking about needs, priorities and perceptions in order to understand better, then to be able to communicate more effectively both in transmitting and in receiving messages. Different courses might be offered at intervals, each focussing on a particular region or culture.

As for methodology, individuals clearly learn in different ways and a mixture of learning activities – passive, active and interactive – would be appropriate. That aside, as much course time as possible might be given to active simulation, engaging participants directly in the process for which they are being prepared, through exercises approximating real tasks and addressing current issues. Trainees would thus have the dual benefit of learning in some depth about the substance of a live issue in their field, while practising dealing with it. If the course gives trainees enough time to prepare, case studies of successful strategies and operations might be offered. Effective case methodology ideally entails drawing perceptions and conclusions from students, on the basis of their own prior study, rather than simply relating success stories. But any example of best practice would be better than none.

The course should embrace the practice in Latin America and Canada of taking trainees out to talk to the locals, if possible away from the capital city and up country, offering practice both in explaining national policy and in listening to the ideas and concerns of citizens, including importantly those of minority groups. These conversations should include school and university students, ensuring that trainees have experience of connecting with young people and their generational perspective.

In the end, the overall course design will hinge on whether the foreign ministry decides to prepare its diplomats for essentially traditional diplomacy, for 'tradition plus' incorporating strategic outreach to win minds in the wider public, or for 'wider diplomacy', including both traditional and network diplomacy. Conservative diplomats, especially those in administrative cultures in which authority and the right to speak for the government are still the prerogative of only a few, might welcome cutting public diplomacy loose from the foreign ministry: leave the image-making to the admen and the tourist board; leave the network-building to the cultural and development gurus; and let the pros in the green eye-shades get on with the hard-nosed, still vital business of managing state-to-state relations in a still state-centred, even if increasingly multilateral, system.

Yet all three specialisms are clearly integral components of contemporary diplomacy. And all three need to be drawn together within the embrace of the foreign ministry, whose task it is to coordinate a government's activities abroad – including that of helping to facilitate non-governmental activities by non-government bodies.[5] Consequently all three functions – and the way in which they mutually support each other – need to be fully understood by any young diplomat.

Conclusions

This chapter has concentrated only on the public diplomacy of nation states. There is another study to be made on preparing officials for the public diplomacy of multilateral institutions, as complex bodies such as the European Union think through what it is that they represent and how they should be represented. As networks in themselves they might be expected to embrace – and to train for – network diplomacy, while continuing to provide their officials with the essential tools for operating effectively in the Westphalian system.

However, as in the case of governments, while multilateral institutions devote considerable resources to self-promotion, specialist training for strategic outreach lags behind. The United Nations, for example, has highly sophisticated and well-funded programmes to influence public attitudes, but has no training in public diplomacy for its international officers. The European Commission, similarly, has 128 delegations worldwide and significant resources given to making known the EU's work, but has no programme of training in public diplomacy.[6]

It may simply be a matter of time. The concept of public diplomacy is for many – even for enthusiasts – still a trifle blurred. State diplomacy and network diplomacy coexist, but as yet in uneasy harness. It is perhaps for these reasons that most programmes of training for public diplomacy, where they exist at all, are packages of disparate skills development without much of a central core. It is difficult to generate a training programme of any intellectual coherence without clearly defined parameters.

The trainers may thus have a substantive contribution to make to the profession that they serve: in the process of course design they simply have to clarify what it is that they are preparing young diplomats to do. In so doing they will be forced to make choices about what to include, and why. And in answering the 'why' they may help to bring into sharper focus the elusive double helix of contemporary diplomacy: the relationships between states and the inchoate networks that public diplomacy has emerged to address.

Notes

1. The author is grateful to the foreign ministries of Australia, Botswana, Canada, Chile, France, Germany, India, Israel, the Republic of Korea, Malaysia, Mexico, the Netherlands, Nigeria, Norway, Paraguay, South Africa, Thailand, Tunisia, Turkey, the United Kingdom and the United States, and to UNITAR and the European Commission, for their assistance to the research underpinning this chapter.
2. Dr Albert Spiegel, Head of the German Federal Foreign Office Directorate for Cultural and Educational Policy,'Public Diplomacy: The German View', British Council Staff Conference, 18–19 March 2002.
3. '...the disastrous hijacking of German culture for political purposes...', in Spiegel, 'Public Diplomacy'.
4. The FCO has created its own Film Unit, which produces training films as well as productions in six languages for exhibitions and for general release on topical issues. It is staffed by former media professionals.
5. Foreign ministries face a double challenge: of ensuring coherence in the public diplomacy effort of government as a whole, including that of quasi-autonomous bodies; and of securing the agreement of other parent ministries involved that it is the foreign ministry's proper role to serve as coordinator-in-chief, forging a functional link between state-centred and network diplomacy.
6. A new training programme in European diplomacy is being developed for the nascent European External Action Service, which will incorporate a specialist course in public diplomacy. The European Diplomatic Training Initiative comprises contributions from leading providers of diplomatic training in (thus far) 12 European countries.

Index

Note: 'n' following a page number indicates a reference from the notes.

Printed in Great Britain
by Amazon